W9-ABP-058

Daughters of Joy, Sisters of Misery

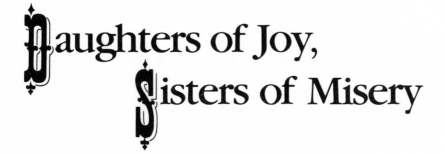

Daughters of Joy, Sisters of Misery

Prostitutes
in the American West,
1865–90

Anne M. Butler

University of Illinois Press

Urbana and Chicago

This book is printed on acid-free paper.

Library of Congress Cataloging in Publication Data

Butler, Anne M., 1938–
    Daughters of joy, sisters of misery.

    Bibliography: p.
    Includes index.
    1. Prostitutes—West (U.S.)—History—19th century.
2. Prostitution—West (U.S.)—History—19th century.
I. Title.
HQ145.A17B88   1984   306.7'42'0978   84-195
ISBN 0-252-01139-2

In memory of
Walter Rundell, Jr.

Contents

Preface

Nineteenth-century prostitutes blended into the American frontier with an easy agreeability. The environment and the women—both bawdy and rollicking—complemented each other perfectly. So natural was their association that these "soiled doves" of the American West have become standard fixtures in the imagery of the frontier. The mere mention of the western saloon elicits a cast of glittering "painted ladies" who move about a noisy, crowded bar dispensing earthy fun to a boisterous clientele. Variations on this high-spirited scenario imbue the prostitutes with personal qualities that range from the most endearing to the most repelling. Clearly, a lively corps of prostitutes, with or without integrity, is woven into the fabric of the frontier era in the American mind.

Yet, in looking back to the frontier, Americans have often mistaken hardship for nobility, deprivation for courage, brutality for glamor. Of course grand adventures and joyful moments can be found in the frontier experience, but the everyday existence taxed one's physical, mental, and emotional strength. In such a world of instability and dislocation, there is no reason to believe that ordinary people suddenly established new values or elevated societal groups traditionally regarded as outcasts to positions of high esteem. Quite the opposite. I believe that a new and unsteady society felt the need to reaffirm old values, cherish them more dearly, and impose them more stringently. Bawdy and rollicking though the American frontier might have been, it had not totally forgotten the essentially conservative values of its cultural antecedents.

Despite this, Americans have extracted from the frontier mosaic only the most fanciful notions of the prostitutes who lived there. Prostitution, on the American frontier and elsewhere, was always enmeshed in a complex web of human attitudes, defined with scorn and jocularity, and circumscribed by rigid societal responses. It is unsettling that, while curiosity about prostitutes has never been scarce, society's fascination has been marked by a prurient tilt toward sensational erotica and moralistic judgments. As a consequence our historical understanding of this worldwide, long-established institution has remained incomplete for many years.

More recently, research trends have encouraged scholars to turn their attention to the less notable or seemingly unimportant groups in society. Prostitutes fall naturally into this category. Scholars now recognize that in many cultures, across a wide sweep of time, prostitutes represented an important societal ingredient. From a variety of scholarly persuasions, a growing body of literature closes the gap between mythical nonsense and orderly knowledge.

Generally, I concur with the findings of the recent scholarly works on prostitution mentioned in the bibliography of this book. For the women involved, prostitution was a form of employment, but one encumbered with many different kinds of restrictions. Prostitutes were decidedly not helpless victims, but, on the other hand, some scholars stress the acceptance of prostitution as a well-thought-out career decision more than I do. Additionally, I do not find the emphasis that some place upon the friendships among prostitutes. The patterns of society and the structure of the profession did throw prostitutes into intense daily associations with each other. From this, certainly, friendships emerged, but on the frontier the overriding characteristics of many prostitutes' personal relationships were highlighted by largely negative interaction. I also differ with those who argue that prostitutes in the West were warmly received in communities during the earliest frontier days and then shunted aside as society stabilized. I believe that the gaudy visibility of frontier prostitutes has been misconstrued as wide-spread social acceptance that simply is not substantiated by historical evidence.

Misconceptions abound because of the paucity of studies that focus on American frontier prostitution. There is an abundance of popular writings about frontier prostitution, some of which are revered as "classics." I have deliberately excluded them here out of my conviction that frontier history must move beyond the invented, anecdotal tales that celebrate the West as an epic of romantic conquest. Although several good journal articles dealing with prostitution in a particular urban community have appeared recently, no major work on prostitution in the American West was available until Marion Goldman's *Gold Diggers and Silver Miners* (1981). Much of Goldman's analysis is grounded in sociological perspectives, and her rich descriptions of the Comstock Lode society effectively portray the "sporting life" in a mining community.

The Warren Beatty/Julie Christie film, *McCabe and Mrs. Miller*, sparked my interest in the subject of frontier prostitution. Their image of scruffy prostitutes working out of canvas tents amidst great snowdrifts struck me as markedly different from the usual beautifully costumed dance hall girls of other films. Given the vast expanses of the American frontier, I wondered how prostitution functioned from locale to locale. Additionally, one of the most fascinating aspects of the American frontier is its dynamic of change, wherein it perpetually evolved away from its own essence until its former definition became lost. It is this quality of evaporation that gives the frontier its elusive attractiveness, and makes prostitution there a special epic within the general history of the institution.

The culmination of my interest in frontier prostitution came in an 8,000-mile research trip through the trans-Mississippi West. My goal was to use as many different types of sources—especially from a variety of public records—in as many unculled collections as possible. I returned with a varied and rich assortment of materials gathered in twenty repositories in twelve western states. The result is this essentially narrative history of frontier prostitution. While no historian can legitimately claim to have examined "every primary document," the bountiful yield I found convinced me that there is ample documentary evidence to support a reevaluation of the lives of frontier prostitutes.

Throughout the long research process my major professor, Walter Rundell, Jr., set the scholarly tone that permeated my work with him. He consistently supported my efforts with vigor and impeccable guidance. He directed me through every stage of the project, which without his advice and interest would never have been completed. Shortly before this book went to press, Professor Rundell died in his sleep at age fifty-three. His death robbed the historical profession of a distinguished and prolific scholar; I lost a mentor and friend for whom I had boundless respect and affection.

Other friends and colleagues assisted along the way. Douglas Martin has counseled and guided me since my undergraduate days at Towson State University. At the University of Maryland I owe thanks to Ira Berlin, David Grimsted, and Alison Olson—all of whom shaped my thinking. Richard Farrell contributed in so many different ways to my historical training and to this work that words of thanks are simply inadequate.

Jeanne Miller repeatedly set aside her own work to help refine concepts. Richard A. Baker not only edited and reviewed the manuscript but supplied confidence when mine weakened. His perceptions and assistance sustained me through the difficult process of revisions.

A great number of archivists and librarians, both in the East and the West, gave much needed aid. Thanks go to the staff of the National Archives, Arizona Historical Society, Austin Public Library, Colorado Historical Society, Denver Public Library, and the Kansas State Historical Society. To my good friends in Texas—David Murrah and the staff of the Southwest Collection at Texas Tech University, and Byron Price and the staff of the Panhandle-Plains Historical Museum at West Texas State University—I am particularly grateful. A warm nod goes to an anonymous police officer in Wyoming. His personal love for history led me to a long-forgotten, invaluable set of Laramie municipal records stored in the back of the police vault in the Albany County Courthouse.

My typists, Jane Martin and Martha List, deserve more thanks than I can express. Both worked on this manuscript with unfaltering good humor and efficiency, despite the impossible deadlines that I always imposed.

A special family is given special thanks. My mother contributed both intellectual and financial support through the many years of my schooling. My children, Dan and Kate Porterfield, have grown up with this topic and are probably relieved to see it achieve "respectability." My husband, Jay, not only assumed most of my family responsibilities, but was a good spirited worker, companion, and chauffeur for the research trip we made through the trans-Mississippi West. I can never thank him sufficiently.

Abbreviations

AC	Arrott Collection, New Mexico Highlands University, Las Vegas, New Mexico
ACCH	Albany County Court House, Laramie, Wyoming
ADL	Arizona Department of Library, Archives, and Public Records, Tucson, Arizona
AHS	Arizona Historical Society, Tucson, Arizona
ASA	Arizona State Archives, Phoenix, Arizona
ATCC	Austin-Travis County Collection, Austin Public Library, Austin, Texas
CSA	Colorado State Archives, Denver, Colorado
CHS	Colorado Historical Society, Denver, Colorado
EPFL	Enoch Pratt Free Library, Baltimore, Maryland
FTU	Fort Union, New Mexico
GPO	Government Printing Office, Washington, D.C.
IHS	Idaho Historical Society, Boise, Idaho
KSHS	Kansas State Historical Society, Topeka, Kansas
NA	National Archives, Washington, D.C.
NMSRA	New Mexico State Records and Archives, Santa Fe, New Mexico
PPHM	Panhandle-Plains Historical Museum, Canyon, Texas

RG   Record Group

SC   Southwest Collection, Texas Tech University, Lubbock, Texas

UNML   University of New Mexico Library, Albuquerque, New
          Mexico

UW   University of Wyoming, Laramie, Wyoming

WHC   Western History Collection, Denver Public Library, Denver,
          Colorado

WSAHD   Wyoming State Archives and Historical Department,
          Cheyenne, Wyoming

Introduction

> I think there are somewhere near four thousand people here—
> the wickedness is unimaginable and appalling. This is the great
> center for gamblers of all shades, and roughs, and troops of
> lewd women, and bullwhackers. Almost every other house is a
> drinking saloon, gambling house, or bawdy. . . .[1]

These words, penned in 1868 by Episcopalian missionary Joseph
Cook, captured the flavor and intensity of the nineteenth-century frontier. Lurid descriptions of wanton behavior, detailed with an air of horrified respectability, became special characteristics of western accounts.[2]
Few questions needed to be asked about the general locus of Cook's
reports, for the unmitigated social chaos and rampant lewdness fit not
the staid eastern city, but only the "Wild West." The shocked cleric's
letter, notorious crime districts sprinkled about the Atlantic seaboard
notwithstanding, clearly addressed the madcap conditions on the western frontier, booming with post–Civil War expansion.

Reverend Cook, fired with missionary zeal, naturally focused on the
chaotic and unstable scenes he encountered in western society, yet his
account hardly proved singular. The startled reverend's non-clerical
frontier contemporaries also wrote of excitement, adventure, corruption, opportunity, and greed cast upon a stage of mountains, deserts,
rivers, and plains. Their accounts detail with stark simplicity the struggles
of newcomers who vied for physical and societal control in an alien region. The tenor of frontier life, so closely bound to the striking geographic features of the West, reflects a distinctive era within the history
of the United States.[3]

The clarity with which the region west of the Mississippi River to the Sierra Nevadas can be identified makes this a particularly useful arena for research. Within this setting of plains and desert circumscribed by mountains can be found the tumultuous experiences so vividly described by Reverend Cook.[4]

Additionally, within this region, a clear cast of characters came to inhabit the land. It seems almost too simple to identify the types associated with the frontier. No one confuses a cowboy with a miner, an Indian with a farmer, or a pioneer wife with a dance hall girl. These apparently one-dimensional characters seem easy to understand, and that they played any role of importance in the emergence of frontier institutions is hardly worth serious reflection. Nevertheless, these stereotypical figures afford a unique opportunity to examine some of the shaded complexities in the story of frontier institutional development.

Certainly, several different groups of frontier characters lend themselves to such a historical analysis. Any of the popular figures—cowboy, trapper, miner, Indian—might provide material unusual and enlightening, but in the context of institutional processes in the West, the subject for study may be especially useful if drawn from among those who appear to have been the unimportant, the smallest contributors to the building of society. If the least significant can be seen to have participated in the growth of society, then perhaps some better understanding of the community as a whole can be realized. Accordingly, this work focuses upon women employed as prostitutes in the American West, for, at first glance, no group suggests less involvement in the institutional development of frontier society.

After the Civil War the boom years on the frontier created an atmosphere in which prostitutes flourished in a highly conspicuous manner. Despite this, prostitutes, who added to this visibility by the garishness of their lives and the sensationalism of their conduct, achieved only a peripheral status in frontier society. Nonetheless, along the route to their ultimate historical obscurity, these women made unmistakable contributions to the development of frontier institutions.

Conflicting social concepts, moral disagreements, and ambiguity of terminology have served to keep the definition of a prostitute in dispute. This confusion is further compounded by the habit, especially in America, of stressing the criminal aspects of prostitution almost to the exclusion of all other concerns. Definitions also tend to emphasize that prostitution involves the offering by a female of her body for lewd purposes and with the expectation of economic gain.[5] Because of its directness, concern for economics, and absence of moral or criminal indictments, the definition of prostitute given by Abraham Flexner in his work on prostitution in Europe will be used in this study. Flexner defined a prostitute as any person "who habitually or intermittently has sexual relations more or less promiscuously for money or other mercenary considerations. Neither notoriety, arrest, nor lack of occupation is an essential criterion. A woman may be a prostitute, even though not notorious, even though simultaneously otherwise employed in a paid occupation."[6]

Identification of those who comprised the prostitute population in the American West is central to the question of how these women interacted with the rest of society. Historian Robert Schick suggests that in the second half of the nineteenth century there were perhaps 50,000 such women in the trans-Mississippi West.[7] The search for these prostitutes showed that "demi-monde," the fanciful European phrase, captured the essence of the institution. Shrouded in their own grey world, hidden by false names and make-believe pasts, and alienated from the main body of society, frontier prostitutes succeeded in blurring their historical identity. Few left any written documents for the historian to peruse.

The identification process, hindered by fragmented records and a snarl of folklore, required caution. Further, status divisions within the profession were often vague, making it difficult to ascertain how a prostitute rated among her peers. Generally, prostitutes worked in one of four styles: brothel dweller, saloon and dance hall worker, crib woman, or streetwalker. Women in brothels enjoyed the best status, both in and out of the profession, with the order descending to the women who plied their trade on the streets; however, the divisions among these levels were not as rigid as their classifications suggest. Prostitutes arranged variations of these groupings and thereby confused attempts to assign them to simple categories.

It was not uncommon for a woman to work the saloons of a town, as well as maintain a rented house where she entertained customers. Sometimes a second prostitute moved in briefly, then moved on to another location. It was equally vexing to try to label the category of the brothel prostitute who established a domestic situation with a customer, abandoned the arrangement, and then returned to rent a room from a madam. Some left brothels in urban areas, traveled to frontier regions, worked the saloons for a time, and moved back to the brothel. The least desirable situations existed among the crib women and streetwalkers, regarded as the lowest groups of prostitutes. Cribs, common through-out frontier communities, were small structures, usually clustered to-gether in an alley or along a roadway. Some were flimsy shacks with only space for a cot and a chair, while others built of brick or adobe remain as tourist attractions today. The accessibility, lack of protection, and bleak locations of the cribs made this category of work just a step above the lowly streetwalker. When women slipped into these catego-ries, it meant almost surely a permanent demotion. Brothel owners or madams were no longer willing, perhaps because of a woman's age, un-stable conduct, race, or simply the excessive competition, to provide the comforts and advantages of working in the house.

Because of these various murky conditions associated with prostitu-tion, and because the people who did keep the records seem to have had little appreciation for the internal structure of the profession, in-formation about the participants was best extracted from a combination of sources. Census lists, police dockets, jail registers, military corre-spondence, trial testimony, inquests, courts-martial, newspapers, post returns, and cemetery records brought forth the society of the demi-monde. These sources rolled back the veil of euphemisms that blan-keted this aspect of frontier life for so many years. The records yielded not only the names of individual women but, more important, general information about the world of the frontier prostitutes.

The purpose of this study is to describe the quality of life for prosti-tutes who lived in various locations on the post–Civil War frontier. It considers how a profession, structured with its own traditions, adapted and functioned in a region where major societal institutions struggled for survival. It is concerned with the contributions prostitutes made to frontier institutional development, and the final rewards for prostitutes who participated in the experience. An understanding of the material experience of the prostitutes, their relationships with the surrounding institutions, and their relationships with each other can sharpen our current perceptions of frontier society. The life of the frontier prostitute has been but slightly recognized in historical literature. Disregarded as social, economic, or political entities, prostitutes are included only for a

dash of spice in frontier accounts. It is appropriate that these long ne-
glected women take a more meaningful place in the saga of frontier
history.

Notes

1. Reverend Joseph Cook, *Diary and Letters* (Laramie, Wyo.: Laramie
Republican, 1919), p. 12.

2. For examples see Frances C. Carrington, *My Army Life and the Fort
Phil Kearney Massacre* (Philadelphia: J. B. Lippincott, 1910); Elizabeth B.
Custer, *Boots and Saddles: or Life in Dakota with General Custer* (Wil-
liamstown, Mass.: Corner House, 1977); John J. Finnerty, *War-Path and
Bivouac: or the Conquest of the Sioux* (Norman: University of Oklahoma
Press, 1961); Francis Parkman, *The Oregon Trail* (New York: New Ameri-
can Library, Signet Classics, 1950); Sarah Royce, *A Frontier Lady* (Lin-
coln: University of Nebraska Press, Bison Books, 1977); Patricia Stallard,
Glittering Misery: Dependents of the Indian Fighting Army (San Rafael,
Calif., and Fort Collins, Colo.: Presidio and Old Army, 1978).

3. A wide-ranging body of literature, much of it stimulated by Frederick Jackson Turner's frontier thesis, deals with the regional significance
of the American West. See the works of Ray Allen Billington, especially
America's Frontier Heritage (Hinsdale, Ill.: Dryden Press, 1966). Other
useful writings include Richard A. Bartlett, *The New Country: A Social
History of the American Frontier* (New York: Oxford University Press,
1974); chapters 1 and 26 in Allan Bogue, Thomas D. Phillips, and
James E. Wright, eds., *The West of the American People* (Itasca, Ill.: F. E.
Peacock, 1970); Jerome O. Steffen, *Comparative Frontiers: A Proposal
for Studying the American West* (Norman: University of Oklahoma Press,
1980).

4. The Pacific frontier represents an interesting area for study unto
itself. John W. Caughey maintains that the Pacific Slope has its own geographic and historical unity. See his *History of the Pacific Coast of North
America* (New York: Prentice-Hall, 1938), p. vii. See also Dorothy Johan-
sen and Charles M. Gates, *Empire of the Columbia: A History of the
Pacific Northwest* (New York: Harper and Brothers, 1957), and Roderick
Peattie, *The Pacific Coast Ranges* (New York: Vanguard Press, 1946). The
conceptualization of a region within a region first came from Douglas D.
Martin, Towson State University, Towson, Maryland, Oct.–Dec., 1978.

5. The difficulties of definition are especially well handled by Vern
and Bonnie Bullough in the introduction to *An Illustrated Social His-*

tory: Prostitution (New York: Crown, 1978), pp. vii–xvii. The Bulloughs explain that definitions must not only include all the possible forms of prostitution, but also the legal and social determinations that each society makes about prostitution. Fernando Henriques in *Prostitution and Society: Primitive, Classical, and Oriental* (New York: Grove Press, 1962; first Zebra edition, 1966) also objects to the vagueness of many definitions and the broad sexual categories that are included. Henriques contends that too many definitions focus only on the actions of the women, or that only economic reasons are cited as the cause of prostitution. This, he says, does not provide for the nymphomanic prostitute, nor for any other sexual factors that bring women to prostitution (pp. 13–18). The Bulloughs point out that a stumbling point is the difficulty in ascertaining when sexual promiscuity becomes professional prostitution (p. ix). The universal element seems to focus on some form of economic gain for the prostitute. In this study only female prostitution is considered.

6. Abraham Flexner, *Prostitution in Europe* (New York: Century, 1920), p. 11.

7. Robert Schick, "Prostitution," in *The Reader's Encyclopedia of the American West*, Howard R. Lamar, ed. (New York: Thomas Y. Crowell, 1977), p. 973.

Daughters of Joy, Sisters of Misery

1

The Prostitutes

Some women worked at various and intriguing jobs in the trans-Mississippi West. Martha Maxwell supported herself and her twelve-year-old daughter from her earnings as a taxidermist. When most of her neighbors listed property holdings worth zero dollars, Mrs. Maxwell claimed real estate valued at $500 in the 1870 Wyoming census. In Denver, Hannah S. Hutchinson earned her living as a seller of hygienic undergarments. This income she supplemented as an enumerator for the 1880 federal census. In Arizona, Francisca Corta pursued a career as an unlicensed physician. Undaunted by such a minor detail, she sued a patient, Isabella Carillo, for $18 in back fees. The court dismissed the suit. Several hundred miles away, Corta's legitimate counterpart, Dr. B. A. Adair, pitted herself against environment, local prejudice, and primitive medical conditions to bring health care to the northern frontier. These women represented the singular and unusual in work experiences for frontier females.[1]

The essence of enterprise in the American West burst from the land and the physical resources. The West built its industries in the outdoors and reveled in the vastness, the richness, and the beauty of that world. One frontier venture after another sought to extract the wealth held by nature, and the processes used were not gentle.[2] As industry wrestled to harness the frontier, the occupations that evolved called for menial laborers to perform heavy, dirty, backbreaking work. The world of the western industries—lumbering, mining, freighting, cattle-driving—produced a masculine labor group. The very nature of the work, as well as the limited capabilities of women untrained in physical accomplishments, excluded females from direct employment in most frontier in-

1

dustries. A masculine ambiance and a masculine work force permeated the American frontier.[3]

With frontier work largely closed to females, most women found western employment possibilities limited.[4] Occupations for skilled or semiskilled female workers failed to materialize. Even employment as clerks, secretaries, or office help fell to males. Some women got a chance to clerk in a store, but often such ventures were owned and staffed by members of one family. Some women managed boarding houses, but unless a widow found she could convert a family home into a commercial dwelling, such operations required generally prohibitive initial capital investment.

Schools employed some female teachers. In this profession vacancies were few, salaries low, and local restrictions so severe that teaching seemed closer to bondage than employment. The first two school teachers to arrive in Laramie, Wyoming, received a salary offer of $50 a month from the school board. The two women agreed to that wage for a term of three months but then insisted it be raised to the princely sum of $75 a month.[5]

Outside urban areas, teachers and other women could find work on Indian reservations. Here females, both whites and Indians, worked as laundresses, matrons, and cooks. In general though, women found little to entice them to isolated reservations, characterized by poor housing and meager salaries. In these areas, teachers averaged an annual wage of $450 to $650, while domestic help earned between $250 and $350 a year.[6] These women, like most, faced a frontier world where a short supply of jobs, paltry wages, and inflated prices blended into a dismal economic picture.[7]

The severe restrictions on employment failed to halt the migration of females into the trans-Mississippi West. Motivated by a variety of personal circumstances, women—single, married, widowed, and divorced—gravitated toward the American West. Among those who made the trek, the domestic pioneer women and military brides have been exalted to the exclusion of the larger force of employed women.[8]

As a diversified group, working women shared one universal trait on the frontier: the need for employment. With few choices women turned quickly to those jobs they could capture, often working as laundresses, waitresses, theater girls, milliners, dressmakers, and actresses. These careers, which failed to meet the requirements of nineteenth-century respectability, attracted large numbers of the poor and ignorant.[9] Communities did not hesitate to use the needed services of these women, while simultaneously castigating them for their poverty and ignorance. Unequipped to respond constructively, the women caught in these grey-zone occupations hovered about the edges of the frontier social structure, saddled with an ambivalent identity and, predictably, burdened with minimal wages.

No group typified these problems more than that which included dressmakers, milliners, and seamstresses. Unlimited competition, the absence of distinguishing skills, and social patronization combined to rob these jobs of promise. Generally, prospects were dim for these women who found the demand for their sewing erratic. In urban areas usually one or two dressmakers established a sufficient business to invest in a regular newspaper advertisement. The *Butte Miner*'s weekly promise from Mrs. Stephen Benjamin and Miss LaCaille to provide expert workmanship at reasonable prices was duplicated in other frontier journals by other semisolvent milliners.[10] Such an ad might appear for as long as a year and a half, then without comment disappear.

By chance some other employment might be secured, but it was rarely much of an opportunity. Regin Constant, a visitor in Denver from Illinois, commented in his journal, "Fannie has taken in a young lady from Kansas to stay a while and work for her board until she can get employment as a dressmaker."[11] His added notation that Denver, filled with pleasure-seekers and fortune hunters, could not possibly employ all the newcomers, left small hope for the career of the Kansas dressmaker.

Migrant frontier women, in the style of the Kansas dressmaker, surely were no less driven by economic expectations than men. Excluded from extensive direct employment within the frontier industries, working women had to recognize the limited scope of their own economic possibilities. For some frontier women work in prostitution best suited their economic chances and interests. The configurations of western society and the distribution of population permitted women to pursue this professional opportunity in either an urban or rural setting.

Prostitutes lived in all the urban areas in the years 1865–90. The larger the urban community, the greater the potential for disparity in the standard of living for prostitutes.[12] Accordingly, a very small number of women secured sufficient funds to purchase real estate. The experiences of a few notorious, but prosperous, madams have clouded the realities of urban prostitution and prompted some cities to exalt their infamous and wealthy locals as scintillating examples of the fun-filled life of the prostitute.[13] In consequence, some of the more substantial information about urban prostitution has been overlooked.

Urban prostitution drew its employees from various racial groups. White women contributed the greatest numbers to prostitution in the western cities. Blacks, long invisible in American frontier history, also participated. Oriental women made up some part of the occupation in the Rocky Mountain states, but their involvement was less than a rabid anti-Chinese public thought. In parts of Texas, Arizona, and New Mexico, Mexican women worked at this trade. Among all these groups racial divisions in the houses varied from locale to locale. Much of the composition of the profession depended upon the urban location, each of which produced varied experiences. A comparative look at the Texas cities of San Antonio and Austin revealed such variety.

San Antonio hosted three distinct groups of prostitutes. The Spanish-speaking prostitutes native to the city came from the peasant slums across the river. Wealthy Mexicans and the Anglos who poured into San Antonio after 1845 looked upon them with almost equal loathing. In addition to enmity, the Anglos brought competition with prostitutes from their own culture. By 1865 both groups of prostitutes were entrenched. Their numbers increased after the Civil War when newly emancipated black women became a third prostitute contingent. The presence of a large military establishment kept the demand for prostitutes high in San Antonio, but the importance of social status in this community kept all prostitutes destitute. A despised group, the Mexican women occupied the lowest rung on the ladder of social acceptance, with blacks only slightly ahead, and white women at the top of a scorned heap.[14]

In Austin, Texas, in contrast, the division between prostitutes was almost exclusively between blacks and whites. Registered arrests for 1876 included fifty-five black and thirty-seven white women arrested and charged with prostitution. These figures remained fairly consistent for the years 1877 and 1878. In 1877 fifty-one black prostitutes were arrested as compared to thirty-six whites. A year later forty-nine blacks and forty-one whites were arrested. The number of arrests for any one female varied from one to nine times for a single year. The majority of the Austin prostitutes, white or black, were arrested three or four times a year. By June 1885 arrest figures in Austin altered. Between June and December of that year only thirty-two white prostitutes faced arrest, whereas sixty-five of their black colleagues were arrested and convicted. Names of Mexican prostitutes simply did not appear in Austin's records for these years. The three-year-period of 1876 to 1878 contained only two names of Mexican prostitutes, and during the six-month period in 1885, only three.[15]

The very complexity of the racial structure of San Antonio, coupled with the conservative tone of that city, may have served to stabilize the approaches directed toward the prostitute population there. No appreciable shifts emerged in public attitudes or arrests there from 1865 to 1890. Secure in a local system of discrimination with Mexicans in the lowest stratum and committed to toleration of all prostitution for the gratification of the military, San Antonio had little interest in changing the mechanics of vice control. As a result, a stabilized prostitute structure remained unaltered throughout the frontier era.

On the contrary, different circumstances existed in Austin. Austin catered not to a highly visible military, but to a more sedate, reputation-oriented group of politicians who came to town to run the affairs of state. Within the city, authorities had only two major groups of prostitutes with whom to contend. From among them the more discreet plied their trade in political circles, protected by their contacts. Miss Sallie Daggett, best known of the local madams, operated in this fashion. Arrested only once in 1876 and once in 1877, Miss Daggett did not hesitate to call for the police when property was stolen from one of her rooms.[16] Miss Daggett and her employees may have escaped prosecution because of their "status," but on the streets of Austin police were not so benevolent. In Austin the authorities, charged with the day-to-day management of the state capital, were quick to scoop up those prostitutes, black or white, who acted as a public nuisance. Police attention later shifted to the black prostitutes of Austin. The differences in the arrest figures for the 1885 period demonstrated that the erosion of black freedom after Reconstruction touched even into those areas of life thought unseemly. Black prostitutes in Austin, as well as in other frontier communities, were subjected to a double dose of discrimination. Not only did they violate the moral code of society, but they bore the added burden of being the "wrong" color.

Urban frontier cities further north also contained prostitute populations of mixed background, and these women endured varying kinds of local discrimination. The absence of large numbers of Mexicans turned local prejudice toward another group. In the urban areas of the Rocky Mountain states that prejudice was directed at the Chinese prostitute or, more correctly, at all Chinese. In this atmosphere the Chinese prostitute suffered much the same treatment as her countrymen. The Chinese began their move out of California after 1850; more than fifteen years passed before they had settled through the Nevada Territory, Montana, and Idaho, and had finally arrived in Denver around 1870.[17]

By the early 1870s, J. P. C. Poulton, lecturer, writer, adventurer, and a future editor of the *Cheyenne Daily Leader*, complained about the prevalence of Chinese prostitutes in Denver.[18] He claimed that a local Chinese agent contracted for groups of women brought from their homeland for purposes of prostitution. Poulton charged that these women, processed through San Francisco, were forced to earn a $400 freedom fee before the agent released them. This practice, he continued, explained the proliferation of Chinese prostitutes throughout Colorado, Wyoming, Utah, and Nevada.[19] Poulton, though a journalist and a western figure of some reputation, concluded his remarks with the subjective and questionable observation, "The Chinese are an unprincipled, bigoted and superstitious people. They are self-conceited beyond description and are not of any possible benefit to the county."[20] Poulton's remarks reflected a general American sentiment that "Chinese filth and disease" threatened the safety and welfare of American society. In 1875 these notions were reinforced by a study of the American Medical Association that declared Chinese diseases "beastly," and "Chinese syphilis" more deadly than any other form.[21] Under such circumstances, the Chinese prostitute could only be regarded as the filthiest and most threatening of the Oriental immigrants. Oddly, local newspapers and U.S. census records for 1870 and 1880 failed to reveal the widespread Chinese prostitution in the Rocky Mountain states that Poulton had alleged.[22] Although some Chinese prostitutes could be found in these areas, the exaggerated claims of prevalence reflected but one element in a pervasive anti-Chinese sentiment in America.

The intense nature of the anti-Chinese campaign misdirected information about the prostitute population of the Rocky Mountain urban areas, for black and white women remained the dominant groups. Of 360 identified Denver prostitutes, 204 were white, 44 were black, 2 were Mexican, and 3 were Oriental. The remaining 107 women could not be assigned ethnic identification.[23] The failure to record ethnicity in newspapers or personal accounts usually indicated that the prostitute was white, but some exceptions must be allowed among the 107. The direct importation of large groups of French prostitutes to Denver in the 1880s swelled the ranks of the white houses.[24] Although Denver houses tended to maintain color separation, all prostitutes congregated in the Market Street area.[25]

Racial segregation was not absolute and sometimes even disappeared. In Laramie, Wyoming, the content of jail registers made ethnic identification very difficult. Consequently, of the 203 Laramie prostitutes it could only be ascertained that 40 were white and 9 were black.[26] Although the remaining 154 racial identities were not indicated, the jail registers suggested that racial divisions in houses of prostitution blurred in Laramie.

Octavia Reeves, a black madam from Cheyenne, migrated to Laramie after the unfortunate murder of one of her prostitutes. Driven from town by a spate of bad press, Mrs. Reeves settled in Laramie with at least one of her Cheyenne co-workers, Hattie Turner.[27] Between January and April 1883 Octavia Reeves and her inmates were arrested three times by the Laramie police. Of the seven women arrested with Mrs. Reeves, the racial identity of five was not recorded, but the docket listed Hattie Turner as black and Sophie Rickard as a white seamstress.[28]

Other group arrests in Laramie might have contained racially mixed houses of prostitutes. From 1877 to 1886 names of white and black prostitutes appeared mixed on the jail register. Although those names could indicate merely the arrests for a certain day, identical groups of names appeared together repeatedly with the first charged with running a bawdy house and the others as inmates.[29] Sallie Thixton, a white prostitute, died in Laramie in 1881 in the care of a black prostitute, Lizzie Palmer.[30] While white prostitutes outnumbered blacks in Laramie, as well as in Cheyenne, rigid racial divisions within the profession seemed uncommon.

In rural areas ethnic divisions among prostitutes intensified as the composition of the local population became more homogenized. A rural house operated either for soldiers at an outpost or for drivers along freight routes. These brothels often were incorporated into a ranching operation, managed by a husband-wife team, staffed with white prostitutes, and rarely acquired a favorable reputation. Nearby military garrisons regarded them as cesspools of vice.

John G. Bourke, whose military diary covered twenty-four years of his frontier career, despised these ranches. In 1877 he complained about a cluster of dwellings located only three miles from Fort Laramie. Incensed as he rode each day past the ranches of the Cooney, Coffey, and Wright families, Bourke wrote: "Each of these establishments was equipped with a rum-mill of the worst kind and each contained from three to half a dozen *Cyprians* [*sic*], virgins whose lamps were always burning brightly in expectancy of the coming bridegroom, and who lured to destruction the soldiers of the garrison. In all my experience, I have never seen a lower, more beastly set of people of both sexes."[31]

Bourke did not acknowledge how he came to know the number of prostitutes who lived at these ranches. His numerical estimates, though, were about right, and he would also have found the women to be white. Other Wyoming ranches patterned those that Bourke encountered. Where the owners were white, the prostitutes who lived in their homes were also. William and Ella Brown managed this sort of rural brothel near La Porchelle Creek, Wyoming, in 1880. White, young, and migrant, the Browns boarded four prostitutes of the same description. John Curtis and J. A. Gordon ran a similar business near Rawlins, Wyoming, while Sarah Petite had a small rural operation outside Chugwater, Wyoming.[32] White prostitutes worked in these little businesses.

Just north of Laramie, along the rail line of the Union Pacific, Mary and Ed Brady conducted a ranch/brothel business in the 1870s. This property belonged to Mary Brady and was assessed for $62.72 in taxes during 1875.[33] No names of resident prostitutes could be linked to Mary Brady, but as early as 1872 she was charged with "keeping a common, ill-governed and disorderly house to the encouragement of idleness, drinking and fornication."[34] Between 1872 and 1875 Mary Brady ran afoul of the local authorities on various occasions until she faced the district court on the charge of threatening the life of one Thomas Dillon.[35] The Brady ranch, like those around Fort Laramie, typified one type of rural prostitution operated by whites.

Such farm brothels were distinct from another kind of rural prostitution. This was the hog ranch, a building built and staffed by saloon owners for the service of the nearby military forts. Hog ranches, a slang term popularized by the military, represented a professional urban operation adapted to rural circumstances. Located one to three miles beyond a post's fortifications, hog ranches catered to enlisted personnel. Saloon owners imported both white and black prostitutes. By focusing on the institution of the hog ranch, the military has insisted that prostitution remained an off limits, undesirable by-product of military life. In truth, the hog ranch was only one aspect of the military association with prostitution.

Life around the military establishments helped to promote other aspects of rural prostitution. Removed from families and other social contacts, military personnel and civilians attached to the military quickly established prostitute relationships with local women in all areas of the West. Regardless of how isolated the location of a fort, military people did encounter a local population. These situations specifically gave rise to the employment of Indian women as prostitutes.

In 1865 James H. Carleton of the Department of New Mexico submitted a report on the condition of the Southwest Indians to U.S. Senator James R. Doolittle (R-Wis.), chairman of that body's Committee on Indian Affairs. When asked by Senator Doolittle to comment upon the prevalence of prostitution among these Indians, Carleton wrote: "Prostitution prevails to a great extent amongst the Navajos, the Maricopas, and the Yuma Indians, and its attendant diseases . . . have more or less tainted the blood of the adults, and by inheritance the blood of the children, who from diseased parents become possessed of but feeble energies, feeble vitality; in short become emasculated in body and mind. . . ."[36]

Carleton hoped that his report would inspire the national government to extend military control over Indian matters to eliminate the introduction of corruption from traders. He maintained that lack of cooperation between the War Department and the Indian Department encouraged the demoralization of Indians. He argued that under the existing structure ". . . the interference in their social relations by the not infrequent taking and prostitution of their squaws forcibly or with their own consent and the introduction of illicit trade . . . prove . . . that the present system for their government is not a just, honest, or consistent one."[37]

Despite Carleton's appraisal of the desperate conditions among the Indians, his proposal for military supervision to eliminate vice lacked perception. The traders alone could not bear the responsibility for the introduction of prostitution among Indian women, for the army joined in as well. As early as 1859 Lieutenant John V. D. DeBois noted that Pueblo women could be bought as long as secrecy was maintained.[38] Although Carleton may have blinded himself to the contributions of the military in this social disorder, he painted a grisly and prophetic picture. The continued mismanagement of the reservation system encouraged the increase of Indian prostitution.

The U.S. policy toward Indians of confinement on reservations and supervision by nearby garrisons proved the catalyst for the spread of prostitution among all the tribes. Ignored by officials, Indian women slipped in and out of garrisons to earn a few dollars or to secure a little extra ration. Only as the frontier era moved to its maturity did officials begin to admit to the ravages among Indian women and families. In 1875 the post surgeon at Fort Randall in the Dakota Territory bragged that the garrison reported only one case of gonorrhea in ten months. This unfortunate event he attributed to the presence of two white prostitutes stranded at the fort by inclement weather. The episode reinforced his conviction that the Sioux women who daily crossed the river to visit in the fort were remarkably free of venereal disease.[39] Only six years later widespread venereal disease among the the soldiers at Fort Randall was blamed on contagion from the reservation across the river.[40]

Few army officers or Indian agents dared to denounce the reservation circumstances as openly as W. L. Lincoln, an agent in Montana. With candor and passion unusual for a governmental report, Lincoln wrote: "There is but little said in their favor regarding their moral standing, and for this there is no doubt but that the Government is largely to blame. . . . [When I first came here] . . . the soldier had also come to stay. The Indian maiden's favor had a money value, and what wonder is it that, half clad and half starved, they bartered their honor . . . for something to cover their limbs and for food for themselves and their kin."[41]

Elsewhere, other Indian agents began to raise voices of protest about escalating situations. From Arizona came an Indian agent's letter to report that Indian mothers came to him to beg that he stop the spread of prostitution among their daughters.[42] In 1887 the annual report of the commissioner of Indian Affairs showed 1,704 cases of venereal disease among Indians on all reservations.[43] A year later, agents of the Kiowa, Comanche, Wichita, and the Ponca and Pawnee agencies complained about drunkenness and increased venereal problems. A colleague at the

Omaha and Winnebago Agency in Nebraska hinted that these difficulties stemmed from increasing prostitution among Indians on his reservation.[44] At the Union Agency in Indian Territory the agent actually charged "tramps, vagrants, whiskey peddlers, prostitutes, and lunatics" with the disruption of Indian morals. His solution included deportation of such intruders to Kansas and Texas.[45] By 1889 the familiar refrain appeared in almost every agency report. The agents regretted to report that venereal disease, alcoholism, and moral disorders prevailed at their reservations.

Clearly, prostitution adapted to both the rural and urban frontier and did not confine itself to any one type of community. Part of the adaptation process involved the employment of available ethnic groups as prostitute women. Among those represented, white and black women figured most prominently. Mexican, Oriental, and Indian participation depended in large measure upon the locale. Yet all five groups, whether in urban or rural settings, whether integrated or segregated, shared common cultural elements that made prostitution a reasonable outgrowth of their experiences.

Four of the five prostitute groups drew directly from cultures where the pre-industrial experience produced women generally accustomed to hard work, few comforts, and a life from birth to death that remained exactly the same. Such women came from essentially marginal agricultural societies where domination by a wealthy class or invader molded the patterns of life from generation to generation. Experience deadened the notions of economic relief, administrative justice, or an alternate way of life. For many of these women the transition from manual to sexual labor involved little or no adjustment in their societal concepts.[46] They brought with them the baggage of the past and became part of the frontier sexual marketplace.

Mexican women typified this profile. The arrival of the Spanish in the sixteenth century unleashed forces in the Southwest designed to produce an unparalleled racial tangle. The conflict between the Spanish and the Indians, the domination by the Spanish, the emergence of a North American Spanish population, the expulsion of the Spanish, and the ascension of Mexican authority all contributed to the unending cycle of victory and defeat, oppression and submission that comprise the history of the Southwest. The growth of a Mexican peasant population served the power interests within both the Spanish and Mexican hierarchies, while it also helped to structure class relationships defined by the aristocracy. Despised by the wealthy, these peasants eked out their existence. Some pursued a little farming or herding, some clustered about the cities and garrisons. For the women in these little communities the arrival of Anglos in the cities and at the forts provided an opportunity to secure food, blankets, or a little money by prostitution. Few changes in life style or expectations were required, and few developed.[47]

Some of these social forces in the Southwest spilled over into the Indian society as well, but Indian prostitution was not peculiar to any one frontier location. All Indians came from pre-industrial societies built upon agricultural and hunting economies. The arrival of the Spanish in the Southwest in the 1500s and the Anglos on the Plains about 1800 marked the introduction of factors designed to reverse the direction of Indian peoples and lead them into economic dependency, warfare, and social disorder. Totally excluded from peer participation in the economic transformation of the West, Indians perceived that the fortunes of victory no longer swung from tribe to tribe but now rested entirely in the hands of the dominant white society. The barest essentials of life depended upon the largesse of an ungenerous government. Small wonder that the women turned more and more to prostitution as the reservations systematically curtailed an Indian economy whether based on either the old order or the new. For Indian women prostitution did reflect the destruction of the Indian social order.[48]

Oriental women carried with them to North America the societal hierarchy that they had lived with in China. The Chinese called upon the system of controls as they knew it in their own country to create an American Chinese society based on rigid institutions. In America the Chinese merchants gained a status they had never possessed at home and parlayed that into a network of control. Based on an indentured servant concept, the merchants and their agents encouraged Chinese laborers to abandon the poverty of China for the promised wealth of North America. The emigrants generally complied for they came from a life of control and rigidity, similar to the structure the Chinese merchants established. Clearly it was repressive, but American society, motivated by hatred and ignorance, chose to ignore the maze of control maintained by the Chinese merchants. The Chinese overlords used this repugnance to their own advantage and carved out a society within a society as they continued to dominate the Chinese emigrants; among them were Oriental women imported for prostitution.[49] These women simply moved from one controlling hierarchy to another without a transformation in their own societal roles. Brought from a pre-industrial society and closeted in a minority subculture, Oriental prostitutes had little opportunity to develop changed self-concepts in their new environment.

Black women entered the ranks of prostitution after the close of the Civil War. Their previous experiences in American society exposed them to unskilled or agricultural labors. Some few escaped this destiny during slavery, but most black women remained uneducated and untrained. Thrust into a society that did not want them, left with no means of support, some black women turned to prostitution in the West. The appearance of the black brothel represented an extension of the cultural interaction that generations of black women had been taught in slavery. Sexual availability without matrimonial protection permeated the experiences of female slaves. Long eliminated from the inner circles of profit, advancement, and status, black women did nonetheless understand the art of survival. For some the transformation from slave to prostitute flowed from the debilitating social and economic effects of bondage.[50]

White prostitution followed the pre-industrial social mold in much the same manner. Although drawn from a variety of geographic and national backgrounds, these prostitutes were cast in the same sexual/economic mold as their colleagues. White prostitutes, like the white frontier population at large, migrated to the West from eastern and midwestern states. First generation, native-born Americans, these children of immigrants drifted toward the West as eastern urban areas offered less and less economic opportunity.[51] The meandering routes they chose brought them to the frontier only after brief stops in other locations. European immigrants who joined them in the West also followed erratic patterns of migration. The problems of transportation, weather, and available cash influenced the movement of whites to the frontier. Once there, the native-born population consistently outnumbered the immigrants.[52]

White prostitution in Wyoming reflected this fact. Of 724 prostitutes identified in the territory between 1865 and 1885, the ethnic origins and birthplaces of 506 remained obscure, a comment upon the invisibility of prostitute populations. From among the 218 whose birth locations could be given, 153 were born in the United States. Of these, 107, or slightly more than 64 percent of the prostitutes of known origins in Wyoming, were native-born white Americans. The largest volume of immigrants arrived, respectively, from Ireland, Prussia, England, and France. Canada, Scotland, Switzerland, and Denmark sent an insignificant number of representatives.[53]

Through direct and indirect contributions, the most significant European pre-industrial influences upon frontier prostitution evolved from the Irish experience. Although the tide of Irish immigration began in the 1820s, the greatest numbers crossed the ocean after the famine of the 1840s. Between 1845 and 1855 death or migration claimed 2 million Irish inhabitants.[54] Of those who sailed for America, little relief from the grinding poverty existed in the tenements of eastern cities. Not only poverty pursued the Irish, but the rancor and prejudice that haunted them in Ireland flourished in America. The United States continued to heap abuse upon the Irish. Undaunted by these responses and faced with few alternatives, the Irish continued to fill the eastern urban areas. Between 1845 and 1855 the Irish population increased from one in fifty to one in five in Boston. New York recorded similar changes.[55]

Prefamine days in Ireland centered upon a marginal agricultural society dominated by English landlords whose blatant lack of justice fostered hatreds among the Irish peasants. Difficulties escalated during the famine, and those who escaped arrived in America scarred, bitter, and submissive. Battered and broken, the Irish immigrants did not look to education to secure trades and professions and careers;[56] rather, they huddled in tenements until the ghettos were bursting at the seams. Then, surrounded by unemployment, starvation, and scorn, as their parents before them had migrated from village to city, first generation offspring often migrated from city to frontier. The same forces that drove the parents drove the children, and those children carried the entrenched concepts of societal management by the unpredictable and often unjust wealthy. It remained for those Irish who stayed in the eastern cities to alter the Irish perception of life, politics, and revolutionary action.[57]

With generations of social malaise to condition them, the women among the Irish group made excellent candidates for prostitution. They fit perfectly into the schema of sexual/economic experiences of pre-industrial personalities thrown into the frontier industrial complex.

As for other white prostitutes, whether immigrant or native-born, the frontier absorbed them easily. A receptive frontier atmosphere welcomed them, and prostitutes of all persuasions clearly understood the mechanics of the profession.

Not only did prostitutes share the background of pre-industrial cultural experiences, but they commonly shared another trait: age. Age was a particularly sensitive matter in a profession where physical appeal supposedly counted for everything. If a prostitute did not intend to mislead through deceit when asked her age, she might through ignorance. Details of family history, birth locations, or parental information simply did not assume importance among prostitutes, if their sketchy responses to census enumerators are an indication. If they knew their personal data, they often did not record it among their effects. Prostitutes died or disappeared with such details left to speculation.

Nonetheless, the general profile of the frontier prostitute is one that is notable for its youthful element.[58] In one brothel in Atchison, Kansas, of the twelve working prostitutes, six were between fifteen and nineteen. Five ranged in age from twenty to twenty-nine, and one gave her age as fifty-nine.[59] A survey of eleven brothels located in Denver in 1880 revealed that of the seventy-seven women in these houses, fifty-one gave ages between fifteen and twenty-four. Of the remaining twenty-six, only five reported ages over thirty-five.[60] The same year showed similar figures for the Wyoming Territory. Of seventy-one prostitutes listed in the census, twenty-six fell in the age group of fifteen to twenty-four. Twenty-three women listed ages between twenty-five and thirty, and only seven gave ages of thirty-five or older.[61] From among the known prostitutes buried in Cheyenne between 1875 and 1890, eight were fifteen to thirty years old, four were thirty to forty, two were over forty, and the ages of two were unknown.[62]

Prostitution employed young women. The prime years came between the ages of fifteen and thirty. After thirty, although some prostitutes lingered on, many looked for employment in related fields; manager for one or two younger women, saloon operator, or abortionist figured among the most common choices.[63]

Harder to establish was the age at which young women entered prostitution. This obviously occurred at some moment earlier than when a woman's actions first caught the attention of the authorities. In April 1876 Belle Vernon died in Cheyenne at the age of seventeen. For more than a year before that she made regular appearances in the court dockets of Laramie, charged with drunkenness and prostitution. Belle Vernon worked and traveled with an older colleague, Nellie Wright, who ultimately arranged the young girl's funeral.[64] This practice of guiding the young into prostitution reached its zenith in the grotesque actions of Mary "Adobe Moll" Gallagan in Denver. The local press discovered that Mary Gallagan kept two little girls in her house for purposes of prostitution. One, a white child, was eleven years of age. Civic horror heightened at the news that the other, a thirteen-year-old black girl, had lost both arms and one leg in an accident with the rail cars.[65] Although the bizarre qualities overshadow the story, the youthfulness of the girls reflected soliciting techniques in this profession.

Numerous factors contributed to the development of a female labor force on the frontier. American society championed the notions of the protected, virtuous woman as the guardian of morals and values.[66] Despite these ideals, many American women faced a life that necessitated they find employment. Within the working world, women found that few jobs awaited them, and the existing ones offered less than lucrative pay. These problems enlarged in a frontier environment that catered to masculine workers. Here women desired not only employment but some of the boom profits attached to the burgeoning frontier enterprises. From this combination of elements, a substantial prostitute population emerged on the American frontier.[67]

Prostitution permeated both the urban and the rural frontiers. It was not confined to one type of community or one aspect of frontier life. At bustling cow towns or isolated military posts, prostitutes became part of the population. Accordingly, prostitution reached out and touched upon all groups of women in all areas of the West. For its employees, prostitution drew from among Mexican, Oriental, Indian, black, and white women. Each of these groups traced some cultural experiences to a pre-industrial agricultural economy mixed with control by other cultures or a ruling hierarchy. For many of these women the sexual and economic patterns of the frontier world required little adjustment in their concepts of life, survival, or femininity. Who worked in the brothels, the saloons, and the cribs of the frontier? The poor and the young.

Notes

1. U.S. Bureau of the Census from the Ninth Census (1870), Wyoming Territory, Roll 1748, RG 29, NA; U.S. Bureau of the Census from the Tenth Census (1880), Colorado, Roll 88, RG 29, NA; Pima County Justice Docket: Criminal-Civil Cases, Feb. 9, 1886, ASA; Dr. B. A. Owens-Adair, *Gleanings from a Pioneer Woman Physician's Life* (Portland, Ore.: Mann and Beach, n.d.).

2. Robert V. Hine, *The American West: An Interpretive History* (Boston: Little Brown, 1973). Hine's entire volume is essential for understanding the frontier experience. The interaction between people and environment is expressively presented, and pp. 300–34 are especially important.

3. Ibid., pp. 125–38, 268–82.

4. Whether a woman lived in the East or the West, nineteenth-century work opportunities were not particularly attractive. For example, in 1870 women in Baltimore, Maryland, listed the following among their occupations: ironer and washer, wet nurse, school teacher, vest maker, cigar factory worker, huckster, domestic servant, saleslady, and oyster house worker. Income from such employment remained insignificant, if the number of women listing personal property or real estate holdings can be relied upon. In Baltimore's Third Ward of 135 women between the ages of fifteen and forty-five who listed these occupations, only two cited any personal monetary worth. U.S. Bureau of the Census from the Ninth Census (1870), Maryland, Roll 572, EPFL.

5. "Reminiscences of Early Laramie by Miss Stewart," C. C. Coutant Collection, Folder #91, WSAD. A comparison of the cost of living in the East and the West is carefully presented by Duane Smith in *Rocky Mountain Mining Camps: The Urban Frontier* (Bloomington: Indiana University Press, 1967), pp. 199–205. Smith concludes that higher prices and inflation plagued the West. The teachers certainly had need of their raise, for prices stayed high in Laramie during this period, and citizens complained of thread at five cents a spool and eggs laid by sick hens for ninety cents a dozen.

6. For samples of wages see the *Annual Report of the Commissioner of Indian Affairs to the Secretary of the Interior* (Washington: GPO, 1885–89). Names and wages paid for all employees at Indian reservations are given for these years.

7. Wages for men in frontier areas varied according to the stage of the boom era. As communities stablilized, wages dropped, according to

Smith, *Rocky Mountain Mining Camps*, pp. 199–205. In the beginning of a boom period when laborers were in high demand, workers earned from $4 to $7 per day. The annual wage for men ranged from $1200 to $2100. Numerous economic fluctuations and regional variations prevent these figures from being absolute, but even a quick glance reveals the disparity between the wages of men and women.

8. Although women have not figured in the bulk of frontier literature, when they have appeared it is respectable women who have been written about. The journals and memoirs of pioneer women receive considerable press. The publications of Elizabeth B. Custer typify this. See *Boots and Saddles: or Life in Dakota with General Custer* (Williamstown, Mass.: Corner House, 1969; also in paperback edition by the same publisher, 1977), and *Following the Guidon* (Norman: University of Oklahoma Press, new ed., 1966). A scholarly treatment of this subject is found in Glenda Riley, "Images of the Frontierswomen: Iowa as a Case Study," *Western Historical Quarterly* 8 (April 1977): 189–202. For examples of notions of feminine respectability in the West, see Dee Brown, *The Gentle Tamers: Women of the Old Wild West* (Lincoln: University of Nebraska Press, 1958); Agnes Morley Cleaveland, *No Life for a Lady* (Boston: Houghton-Mifflin, 1941); Everett Dick, *The Sodhouse Frontier: 1854–1890* (New York: D. Appleton-Century, 1937).

9. Poverty as a restrictive element that led women to prostitution and then encompassed all aspects of the women's lives is fully explored in Frances Finnegan, *Poverty and Prostitution* (Cambridge: Cambridge University Press, 1979).

10. *Butte Miner,* passim 1881.

11. Regin H. Constant Journal, July 24, 1880, WHC.

12. The development of the urban frontier remains a valid research topic, although several good studies discuss the growth of western towns from an economic perspective. See Robert Dkystra, *The Cattle Towns: A Social History of the Kansas Cattle Trading Centers* (New York: Atheneum, 1968); Joan Bishop, "A Season of Trial: Helena's Entrepreneurs Nurture A City," *Montana, the Magazine of Western History* 28 (July 1978): 62–71; Smith, *Rocky Mountain Mining Camps*. For a discussion of shift in emphasis, see David C. Hammack, "Problems in the Historical Study of Power in the Cities and Towns of the United States, 1800–1960," *American Historical Review* 83 (April 1978): 323–49.

13. Perhaps no city has done this more than Denver. Local citizens, including retired madams, contributed a host of information and misinformation about the prostitutes' activities in late nineteenth-century

Denver. This vast array of materials is found in the Caroline Bancroft Papers, WHC. Although some of these papers remain closed at the request of Miss Bancroft, others reveal that citizens of Denver have flamboyant, but often contradictory, memories of the past. Nonetheless, the result has been that the names of Mattie Silks, Jennie Rogers, Verona Baldwin, and Lil Powers are prominent in Denver folk history.

14. Anne M. Butler, "The Frontier Press and Prostitution: A Study of San Antonio, Tombstone, and Cheyenne, 1865–1890" (Master's thesis, University of Maryland, 1975), pp. 14–40. For an interesting account of how several cities in the United States divided their red-light districts according to race, see Richard Symanski, *The Immoral Landscape: Female Prostitution in Western Societies* (Toronto: Butterworth, 1981), pp. 135–38.

15. Record of Arrests, City of Austin, vol. 1, Jan. 1, 1876-Jan. 1, 1879; Record of Prisoners, vol. 1, Sept. 1, 1884-Feb. 1, 1886, ATCC. For an excellent analysis of prostitution in Austin and the public's response throughout the community, see David C. Humphrey, "Prostitution and Public Policy in Austin, Texas, 1870–1915," *Southwestern Historical Quarterly* 86 (April 1983): 473–516.

16. *Daily Democratic Statesman*, July 22, 1880, Apr. 18, 1882; Austin Register of Police Calls, 1879–80, Aug. 5, 1880, ATCC. Sallie Daggett, also known as Sallie Nichols, appeared in the Austin city directories throughout the 1870s and 1880s. See any Austin city directory for these years, ATCC.

17. Rose Hum Lee, *The Chinese in the United States of America* (Hong Kong: Cathay Press, 1960), pp. 33–39. An informative description of the structure and functions of Chinese prostitution in San Francisco is found in Lucie Cheng Hirata's "Free, Indentured, Enslaved: Chinese Prostitutes in Nineteenth–Century America," *Signs* 5 (Autumn 1979): 3–29. Although it does not entirely accommodate the geographic regions of this work, the article's detailed content must be considered in understanding the experience of Chinese prostitutes throughout the West. See also Richard Symanski, *The Immoral Landscape*, pp. 129–31.

18. According to some reports, Japanese prostitutes were in Denver as early as 1860. Travel restrictions on Orientals suggest that the women had to have been imported secretly. Americans were so uninformed about Orientals, it would have been an easy matter for them to confuse Chinese and Japanese women. For an excellent treatment of this subject

see Yuji Ichioka, "Ameyuki-san: Japanese Prostitutes in Nineteenth Century America," *Amerasia Journal* 4 (1977): 1–21.

19. J. P. C. Poulton Papers, Lecture Journal, pp. 35–39, WHC.

20. Ibid., p. 39.

21. Stuart Creighton Miller, *The Unwelcome Immigrant: The American Image of the Chinese, 1785–1882* (Berkeley: University of California Press, 1969), pp. 163–65.

22. Chinese names in the census for the Wyoming Territory and the city of Denver for 1870 and 1880 are absolutely minimal; at most three or four Chinese males lived together and ran a laundry. Newspapers made little complaint about Chinese prostitution, although some towns were rabid on the subject of opium dens, Chinese labor competition, or any increase in the local Chinese population. See *Laramie Daily Sentinel*, May 24, 1870; *Black Hills Daily Times*, Sept. 29, 1877; *Butte Miner*, Nov. 23, 1879, Dec. 3, 1879, Feb. 25, 1880, Feb. 27, 1880, Nov. 24, 1881. The absence of Chinese in census records could reflect the refusal of an enumerator to enter the Chinese quarter of a town.

23. Identification of prostitutes came from combined sources. The *Daily Rocky Mountain News* name index at the Denver Public Library contained identification materials for every individual mentioned in the paper. *The Description Record: City and County of Denver, 1862–1921 Murder Book of Detective Sam Howe* was especially valuable. Held by the Colorado Historical Society, this unusual scrapbook contains personal data, case histories, and mug shots of Denver prostitutes. The U.S. censuses for 1870 and 1880 at the National Archives added further information.

24. *Denver Republican*, May 5, 1889. This article reported a raid on one hundred French women of Denver, several of whom spoke no English. Included among those arraigned were several black women and some long-time Denver prostitutes who were not immigrants.

25. *Denver Republican* and *Daily Rocky Mountain News*, passim. Designation of prostitutes often referred to "a woman of the Market Street area." By 1880 the name of this roadway had been changed to Holladay Street. The blocks most inhabited by prostitutes intersected with 15th, 16th, 17th and 18th streets.

26. The same combined techniques were used for prostitutes in Wyoming. The *Laramie Daily Sentinel* and the *Cheyenne Daily Sun* contained some information. Jail registers for Laramie and Cheyenne, in-

quests, and cemetery records, along with the U.S. censuses for 1870 and 1880 added data.

27. *Cheyenne Daily Sun*, Feb. 3, 1882, June 6, 1882; Justice of the Peace Dockets: Albany County, City of Laramie, Jan. 27, 1883, Feb. 27, 1883, and Mar. 27, 1883, ACCH.

28. Justice of the Peace Dockets: Albany County, City of Laramie, 1883, ACCH; Wyoming census for 1880, WSAHD.

29. Justice of the Peace Dockets: Albany County, City of Laramie, 1883, passim, ACCH.

30. Inquest, July 21, 1881, Office of the Clerk of the Court, ACCH.

31. John G. Bourke, Diary, vol. 22 (Feb. 11–Apr. 23, 1877), p. 1848, UNML.

32. Wyoming census for 1880, WSAHD.

33. Albany County Tax List 1875, ACCH.

34. Albany County Criminal Files, Sept. 11, 1872, ACCH.

35. Ibid., Case 208, July 21, 1875.

36. James H. Carleton, Superintendent of the Department of New Mexico at Sante Fe, to Hon. J. R. Doolittle, U.S. Senate, July 25, 1865, pp. 2, 3, AC.

37. Ibid., p. 8.

38. Journal of Lieutenant John V. D. DeBois, Aug. 10, 1859, p. 117, AC.

39. Medical History of the Post, Fort Randall, Dakota Territory, Feb. 24, 1875, and Mar. 6, 1875, RG 94, NA.

40. Ibid., Sept. 5, 1881.

41. W. L. Lincoln, Report of the U.S. Indian Agent, Montana, in the *Annual Report of the Commissioner of Indian Affairs to the Secretary of the Interior* (Washington: GPO, 1885), p. 130.

42. Letters Received by the Office of Indian Affairs, 1863–80, Microcopy 234, Roll 26, Arizona Superintendency, 1863–80, RG 75, NA.

43. *Annual Report of the Commissioner of Indian Affairs to the Secretary of the Interior* (Washington: GPO, 1887), p. 408.

44. Ibid., 1888, p. 98, 105, 170.

45. Ibid., p. 132.

46. Helen Campbell, *Woman Wager-Earners: Their Past, Their Present and Their Future* (Boston: Roberts Bros., 1893), pp. 22–27. Mrs. Campbell specifically noted that women were reduced to an unskilled use of the needle and that this produced a system of blind competition among women. She saw the progression as one from sexual to manual service

as women entered industry as unskilled workers. A glance at the agricultural societies suggested that the reverse was true: prostitutes switched from manual to sexual service.

47. See Anne M. Butler, "The Frontier Press and Prostitution," pp. 14–40; Robert V. Hine, *The American West*, pp. 210–11.

48. The transformation of Indian economics has not been thoroughly researched. The most direct presentation can be found in the *Annual Reports of the Commissioners of Indian Affairs*. Any one of these volumes for the years 1885–89 demonstrates how completely the old order of Indian life faded away or was transformed on the reservation. These reports can be contrasted with the historical presentation of early Indian life for any number of tribes. For example, see John C. Ewers, *The Blackfeet: Raiders on the Northwestern Plains* (Norman: University of Oklahoma Press, 1937), and Frank Waters, *Book of the Hopi* (New York: Viking Press, 1963).

49. Gunther Barth, *Bitter Strength: A History of the Chinese in the United States: 1850–1870* (Cambridge, Mass.: Harvard University Press, 1964). Barth's book deals primarily with the Chinese experience in California, but it is essential for an understanding of the structure and function of Chinese society in American society. Rose Hum Lee, *The Chinese in the United States of America,* presents a scholarly discussion of the stages of Chinese assimilation in which it is clear that physical and cultural differences kept the Chinese in a condition of perpetual abuse. The result was massive ignorance about the Chinese on the part of white society. Stuart C. Miller's *The Unwelcome Immigrant: The American Image of the Chinese, 1875–1882* is an excellent explanation of the emergence of anti–Chinese sentiment in the United States.

50. The literature concerned with the processes of slavery is extensive. Two studies which are particularly relevant for black women are David B. Davis, *The Problem of Slavery in Western Culture* (New York: Cornell University Press, 1966), and Gary B. Nash, *Red, White, and Black: The Peoples of Early America*, Prentice Hall History of the American People Series (Englewood Cliffs, N. J.: Prentice-Hall, 1974).

51. Prostitution as an eastern institution remains to be thoroughly researched, yet there seem to have been certain characteristics common to both regions. For example, the 1870 Baltimore census showed that of thirty-six prostitutes from the Third Ward, four were foreign born and nine others were born in Maryland or Pennsylvania of foreign-born par-

ents. Native-born prostitutes also recorded New Jersey, Ohio, New York, and Virginia as birthplaces. Some may have listed Maryland simply because they were living there at the time of the census and did not know the correct answer. Some amount of transiency appears to have been common to prostitutes in both the East and the West, but to a lesser degree east of the Mississippi River. U.S. Bureau of the Census from the Ninth Census (1870), Maryland, Roll 572, EPFL.

52. Ray A. Billington, *America's Frontier Heritage,* Histories of the American Frontier (New York: Holt, Rinehart and Winston, 1966). This entire study is critical to an understanding of the patterns of frontier society; see especially pages 23–46 and 184–97. Billington cites the tendency among frontier people to drift around from community to community as a unique American trait. Smith, *Rocky Mountain Mining Camps*, pp. 24–28, reinforces Billington's observations with an analysis of census data from several communities, especially Custer, Idaho, and Pinal, Arizona. American-born migrants dominated in numbers. An excellent analysis of the numbers and contributions of immigrant groups to the rural Great Plains area is found in Frederick C. Luebke, "Ethnic Group Settlement on the Great Plains," *Western Historical Quarterly* 8 (Oct. 1977): 405–30.

53. See n. 26.

54. Joseph O'Grady, *How the Irish Became Americans* (New York: Twayne Publications, 1973), p. 27.

55. Several studies deal with the immigration of the Irish. See William Shannon, *The American Irish* (New York: Macmillan, 1963), p. 28; James B. Walsh, ed., *The Irish: America's Political Class* (New York: Arno Press, 1976), p. 358; Joseph O'Grady, *How the Irish Became Americans*.

56. William Shannon, *The American Irish*, pp. 16–34.

57. Thomas N. Brown, *Irish-American Nationalism: 1870–1890* (Philadelphia: J.B. Lippincott, 1966).

58. Eastern prostitutes undoubtedly shared this characteristic, at least in Baltimore's Third Ward. Of thirty-three reported ages, thirteen prostitutes listed themselves between the ages of fifteen and nineteen, sixteen gave ages of twenty to twenty-nine, and four gave ages of over thirty. U.S. Census, Maryland, 1870, Roll 572, EPFL.

59. Kansas State Census, 1875, KSHS.

60. U.S. Census for Denver, Colo., 1880, Reel 88, RG 29, NA.

61. Wyoming Territorial Census for 1880, WSAHD.

62. Register of Burials for Cheyenne Cemetery: 1875–1932, WSAHD.

63. *Arizona Weekly Citizen*, May 1, 1881; *Tombstone Epitaph*, Apr. 27, 1882; Cochise County Court Records, Civil Case 442, Apr. 12, 1882, ASA. These cases are examples of women who ran small operations. The Tombstone case involved an older women who supervised a younger colleague and probably killed the younger girl with an illegal abortion. The Cochise County case concerned the suit against Lulu Robbins of Tombstone for rent and damages to a saloon she operated. The *Black Hills Daily Times*, Jan. 19, 1884, gave lurid details of a murder trial of Mrs. Elizabeth Orr, charged with homicide by abortion. Mrs. Orr was accompanied by her daughter Mrs. Ireland, a saloon operator. Later the same month Mrs. Ireland was involved in a saloon murder.

64. Justice Docket, July 16, 1874-May 16, 1876, ACCH; Register of Burials for Cheyenne Cemetery, 1875–1932, WSAHD.

65. *Daily Rocky Mountain News*, July 7, 1876, Sept. 21, 1876.

66. It may have been that in the East the professional prostitute was indeed somewhat "protected." It appears that in Baltimore's Third Ward several family residences also included openly declared prostitutes or six or seven seamstresses. The males in such dwellings listed occupations that included shoemaker, carpenter, coachmaker, retired merchant, and bookkeeper. All listed wives and, in some cases, children younger than the age of fifteen. As will be demonstrated, the living arrangements of prostitutes in the West evolved along slightly different lines and appeared to be connected with family operations only in rural areas where ranchers also maintained a small brothel. U.S. Census, Maryland, 1870, Roll 572, EPFL.

67. The selection of prostitution as a career opportunity that could be temporary or offer some measure of upward mobility is stressed more and more in the literature. For examples see Judith Walkowitz, *Prostitution and Victorian Society* (Cambridge: Cambridge University Press, 1980); Ruth Rosen, *The Lost Sisterhood* (Baltimore: Johns Hopkins University Press, 1982); Marion Goldman, *Gold Diggers and Silver Miners* (Ann Arbor: University of Michigan Press, 1981); Joel Best, "Careers in Brothel Prostitution: St. Paul, 1865–1883," *Journal of Interdisciplinary History* 12 (Spring 1982): 597–619.

"Squirrel Tooth" Alice, Dodge City prostitute of the cow town era captures all the haunting, romantic beauty that is traditionally believed of prostitutes. (Kansas State Historical Society, Topeka)

Less romanticized is this photograph of a woman thought to be a Wichita prostitute. (Kansas State Historical Society, Topeka)

This woman is also believed to be a prostitute, but like so many in the profession, her identity is obscure. (Kansas State Historical Society, Topeka)

A man and woman stand at the entrance to a tent saloon, the "Riverside." Next door other Leadville, Colorado, residents gather outside the combination bank and saloon. (Courtesy Amon Carter Museum, Fort Worth, Texas)

This festive illustration of the Abilene Dance Hall from Joseph McCoy's *History of the Cattle Trade* helps to explain how hurdy-gurdy girls came to be thought of as demure dancing partners. (Kansas State Historical Society, Topeka)

This photograph taken about 1878 in Dodge City, Kansas, depicts carefully posed patrons inside the "Varieties" Dance Hall owned by H. B. Bell. (Kansas State Historical Society, Topeka)

Although this photograph is from the Yukon Territory in 1899, it is a good example of the cribs common throughout the West. (Courtesy Amon Carter Museum, Fort Worth, Texas)

Prostitutes gaze at the camera from Bell Birdard's Denver parlor house in 1885. (Courtesy Amon Carter Museum, Fort Worth, Texas)

2

Companions and Colleagues

Prostitute Kitty LeRoy met her death in a Deadwood, South Dakota, saloon when shot by her husband, Samuel Curley. Curley's act, prompted by a jealous rage, ended the checkered career of the twenty-eight-year-old jig dancer. Kitty LeRoy deserted one husband in Michigan to pursue the life of a saloon performer. Her travels took her to the dance halls of Texas and California. While in Texas she acquired a male companion and abandoned the young son of her Michigan marriage. From California Kitty LeRoy made her way to Deadwood where she and the Texas gentleman quarreled and parted company. A marriage of questionable legality to Curley followed. Kitty chose as her new mate a man of solid reputation, well known and well liked in the territory. The Deadwood community apparently regarded them as husband and wife, although Kitty continued her employment as a dancer-prostitute at the Lone Star Saloon. Evidently Curley did not interfere with Kitty's work, but only with some of her conduct. While on a trip to Denver, word reached him of a reconciliation between his wife and the Texas traveling companion. Incensed, Curley returned to Deadwood, slipped into town, and attempted to arrange a showdown with his rival. When the object of his wrath declined the invitation, the irate Curley announced to a black saloon employee that the time had come for Kitty to die. Curley crashed up the steps to Kitty's second floor, saloon-top room, engaged her in brief conversation, murdered her, and committed suicide. The next day the folk at the Lone Star Saloon, in a gesture of less than good taste, laid out the bodies together in the death room. Washed and dressed, husband and wife lay side by side amidst the gore and blood of the previous evening.[1]

More than just a melodramatic frontier tale, the story of Samuel and Kitty Curley underscored the personal turmoil in the lives of prostitutes. The usual image of the prostitute depicted a single woman, far from home and family, who pursued her sordid life in singular guilty misery. Although many single women resided in houses of prostitution, such a description did not apply to every prostitute, nor did brothel residence preclude all family contacts.

Complexity, rather than simple isolation, characterized the personal associations of prostitutes. Despite variations in their housing accommodations or status in the profession, most prostitutes found themselves subjected to crude, uncouth associates. The unpolished, even coarse, conduct of their social existence placed one more wedge between prostitutes and the mainstream of society. Their personal conduct rarely alleviated the debasement of their lives or altered the prejudices with which society viewed them. If anything, the colleagues and companions of prostitutes only added to the undesirable milieu of their lives and enlarged the social hostilities they encountered.

In death, Kitty LeRoy revealed that she had been more than simply an anonymous dance hall girl. Her chaotic life touched the lives of others, for she maintained relationships of some duration with three men and mothered at least one child. Her own erratic and irresponsible behavior brought all these contacts to a shambles as she bounced from one part of the frontier to another, yet the circumstances of Kitty LeRoy's life matched closely the lives of her frontier colleagues, and she did not walk alone as the only wife and mother among the frontier prostitutes. Slick images of the powdered saloon dancer, the obese madam, and the lonely streetwalker obscured the number of Kitty LeRoys who, while wives and mothers, engaged in prostitution.

Marriage did not automatically mean residence with the husband, nor did it mean retirement from the profession. What matrimony did mean, whether through legal ceremonies or common law arrangements, was that prostitutes, like their sisters in respectability, attempted to find security and stability through permanent relationships. That they so seldom succeeded stemmed from both the kinds of men they married and the economic and social inertia attached to prostitution. The introduction of children to these domestic scenes compounded the confusion for parents already weighed down with personal and economic struggles. Predictably, marriage and family life often did not break the dismal patterns found in the lives of prostitutes.

When asked, prostitutes did not hesitate to convey an assortment of garbled domestic information to census recorders, police officers, and newspaper reporters. Some respondents certainly lied or answered in ignorance. Some replied with as much honesty as they could. Some, even though married, much in the style of modern day entertainers, retained the professional title "Miss" and clouded the understanding of their family arrangements. In general, direct interrogation of prostitutes did not set aside all the vagaries of their identities. Of seventy-one prostitutes identified in the 1880 Wyoming census, thirty-seven listed themselves as single. Some probably had spouses somewhere. Thirty-four women, or almost 48 percent of those identified, answered that they were either married, divorced, or widowed at the time of the census.[2] The census of the same year in Denver showed that single women appeared to dominate among prostitutes in that urban center. From eleven dwellings, a total of fifty-five prostitutes were identified. Of these, the records showed thirty-three as single, while only five registered themselves as married and seven as divorced. Four married women lived with husbands, and one had a small child. Two single women had small children.[3]

These simple figures hinted at the involvement of prostitutes with family situations but did not begin to show the human forces entwined in those impersonal statistics. Several episodes in the lives of prostitutes added the human dimension to the record. From these stories the atmosphere of disorder, central to the daily existence of prostitutes, can be partially reconstructed. An unending stream of violence and grief brought an aura of physical and psychological misery to the world of prostitution. Immersed in a routine of unmitigated chaos and social rejection, prostitutes had few opportunities to develop into balanced, stable persons. These unpleasant realities, however, did not keep them from marriage and motherhood.

Whether prostitutes married before or after they entered the profession had little bearing on the lives they shared with their spouses. The marriages of prostitutes failed miserably in the area of domestic tranquility. The most disreputable frontier males became the husbands of prostitutes and filled their lives with crime and mayhem. Marriage only increased the disruption in prostitutes' lives and pushed the women further from respectability, stability, or monetary security. Rather than encouraging a woman to resign from prostitution, marriage further tied her to the institution in the West.

Frequently, through marriage, the prostitute formalized a liaison with her pimp or saloon owner. In these arrangements husbands not only tolerated but expected their wives to solicit sex as a means of augmenting the family income. Brothel operators Oscar Lee and Tom Cooley of Hemphill County, Texas, both married prostitutes in their establishments. Both women numbered among the regulars scooped up once a month by the authorities. Tenie Shelton, wife of Oscar Lee, was arrested and convicted at least four different times between July and October 1887.[4] She fared better than her colleague, Ebb Cooley, wife of Tom Cooley. Ebb Cooley was arrested on charges related to prostitution no less than thirteen times between 1887 and 1889.[5] A final entry for Ebb Cooley listed her as charged with common prostitution and noted "left town." With her in jail at that time was prostitute Cora Cooley, charged with assault to murder.[6] The jail record offered no clues as to the identity of the new Cooley. If she were the daughter of Tom and Ebb Cooley, she began her career in the shadow of illustrious parents, both of whom were among the most frequently arrested of the local vice crowd.

In May 1888 one of the jail regulars, Mollie Jackson, was dismissed from court, her vagrancy charges dropped. A court notation next to her name stated, "Married and living a better life."[7] Mollie Jackson's name did not appear again in the docket, and perhaps she did improve her situation. If so, she differed from other married prostitutes in Hemphill County. The two women married to Oscar Lee and Tom Cooley could not claim that matrimony took them out of prostitution or altered their cycle of court appearances.

Other marriages appeared to be on-again, off-again associations. They involved husbands of the same unfortunate caliber and promoted the same two constant elements: a continuation of external disorder and a lack of inner balance. Thrown into the frenzied atmosphere of the frontier, couples embarked on matrimony that had neither economic nor social substance. The circumstances surrounding these marriages point to stormy relationships destined to end abruptly.

These ingredients abound in the story of Mrs. Lottie "Sorrel Mike" Ables Picket of Montana. Her own instability foreshadowed the doom of her marriage. A prostitute who followed the mining fortunes of Helena and Butte, she won fame based on her frequent suicide attempts over a period of several years. In Butte only a short time, she followed her usual pattern and tried to do away with herself with an overdose of laudanum. The *Butte Miner* used the occasion as an exercise in humor and reported with glee that only two weeks before this episode Miss Lottie had married a local bartender, Picket by name.[8] The paper feigned ignorance about the true identity of Lottie Picket and enjoyed making "innocent" sport of her. The newspaper attributed the attempted suicide to the fact that the "felicity of the married state was found by experience to fall short of her girlish imagination concerning the same. . . ."[9] When the hour arrived for Lottie to appear for work at the saloon "where her husband earns an honest living by looking on while his wife dances,"[10] it became apparent to her companions that Lottie, heavily drugged, hovered near death. The efforts of her friends to revive her proved successful, and Lottie recovered. Since this had not been her first attempt, it appeared likely that it would not be her last. The press was not to be disappointed, for less than one year later the paper announced that only prompt medical attention saved the life of "Miss Lottie," who had taken an overdose of morphine. No mention appeared in this brief account of the bartender husband or his whereabouts.[11]

A year and a half later the events in the life of Lottie "Sorrel Mike" Pickett came to a climax. Now referred to as Lottie Ables, the press again took up her story.[12] The paper recounted, with mock seriousness, that matters at Lottie's small frame house had gotten out of hand. A young woman named Dolly, who lived with Lottie and claimed to be her younger sister, came home one afternoon to find Lottie seriously wounded from a gunshot to the abdomen. When the press and police arrived, the dying Lottie insisted that a man shot her as he tried to leave her house without paying for his wine. The "sister" stoutly rejected this story and declared she had no doubt that Lottie shot herself, the second attempt upon herself in less than a week. This time Lottie Pickett succeeded. She died two days later and the town paper laconically stated, "Miss Ables was only thirty years old, had a living husband, and had come to Butte from Helena where she made repeated suicide attempts."[13]

During her life in Butte, Lottie Ables Pickett managed to demonstrate most of the problems of the prostitute. Young, Lottie Ables could only have been about twenty-seven when she arrived in Butte. At that time she had already established a reputation among the prostitutes of Montana. At best she could be described as an unstable, suicidal person who may have tried a geographic cure as the solution to her miseries. She tried matrimony and chose a man whose profession encouraged her to remain a saloon dancer-prostitute. Regardless of whether they ever lived together in her brothel-district residence, the community recognized them as husband and wife. Those details of the marriage were less important than the characteristics of Lottie's life that the match reflected. Poor personal judgments, a hasty marriage, a partner from within the profession, continuation in a life of prostitution—all made ridiculous by a scornful press—these ingredients highlighted the domestic life of Lottie Pickett. The grim end for "Sorrel Mike" only concluded the scattered, disorganized saga of a woman who ricocheted about the frontier devoid of internal balance or personal direction.

Desertion and the demands of seasonal migrant work may have influenced the conduct of some of these unconventional marriages. The strain of long separations did not add ballast to marriages grounded in shaky foundations. Indeed, prostitutes, accustomed to these conditions in marriage, did not seem to even consider contacting the absentee husband in hours of crisis. Other than in the role of pimp, husbands did not often assume the role of guardian and protector for prostitutes.

The tortured sequence of events in the life of Denver prostitute Emma Moore placed her squarely among the married prostitutes whose disjointed domestic life instilled in her no sense of expectation that her husband would function as her protecting champion. Her choice of mate, C. C. McDonald, worked as a manager of variety shows with which he toured the frontier. The fall of 1889 saw McDonald headed for Helena, while Emma stayed behind in the Denver brothel of Ella Wellington. Here, during the fall, the young woman fell sick and turned to an aging gambler, Abe Byers, for assistance. Byers moved Emma to his house where he both cared for her during her illness and began to abuse her physically when she recovered. At last able to work again, Emma Moore returned to her employment at Ella Wellington's and continued to spurn the efforts of Byers to win her back. A confrontation between the two occurred in a parlor at Wellington's, and police had to be summoned to protect Emma Moore from the death threats of Abe Byers.

These tangled events made their way to the pages of the Denver press where they were presented as little more than silly antics of a hot-tempered gambler in pursuit of a prostitute half his age.[14] Like most anecdotes in the lives of prostitutes, this one carried more weight than the humor-filled press account suggested. Beneath the superficial events, Emma Moore's life seesawed back and forth in an atmosphere of unpleasantness. Matrimony to McDonald had not induced Emma Moore to retire from Wellington's bordello, for her employment there appeared to continue uninterrupted. Separation from her husband, either by choice or desertion, made him inaccessible when she needed assistance. Too sick to remain in her brothel, Emma Moore turned to a customer for help. Byers offered that, but at the same time did not hesitate to pummel the young woman when she wanted to leave him. Unwilling to stay in Byers' house, this prostitute did not set out to join the touring husband in Montana but returned to Wellington's. Neither her behavior, nor that of the two men in her domestic environment, indicated that Emma Moore looked for a release from prostitution through these relationships. Domestic life did not represent Emma Moore's ticket out of prostitution and into respectability.

Lost in the story were the circumstances surrounding Emma Moore's marriage to McDonald. Perhaps only a matter of convenience, or a spur-of-the-moment decision made without time to know the man's character, the marriage failed to offer her a chance to escape from prostitution. A short acquaintance with McDonald perhaps convinced her that the wrath of Byers or employment at Wellington's was a better choice.

Not every prostitute married after an impromptu courtship; some legalized their relationships only after a lengthy period. Unfortunately, the courtship often forewarned that a rocky road lay ahead. Charles George Masterson of Wyoming cut a wide swath through the territory before his marriage to prostitute Georgie Lightheart. Masterson first came to widespread public attention when charged, along with two co-workers, in the theft of several tons of coal from the Union Pacific Railroad. The purpose of the theft was to supply a couple of local brothels with heating materials. Masterson testified that he hauled a ton of coal to the infamous Ida Hamilton house and another ton to the Golden Gate brothel, both in Cheyenne.[15] Other charges included that the men used shop materials and time to repair a buggy and a sewing machine for prostitutes. A great furor was raised over these revelations, but the *Laramie Daily Sentinel* dismissed the whole trial as an exercise in pettiness. The trial cost the county about $2000 and the outcome resolved nothing. Some small rivalry among railroad workers had started the investigation, and all seemed willing to forget it.[16]

Masterson's next skirmish with the law came when he received a one-year prison sentence for charges of assault with intent to kill. Incarcerated at Laramie, his prison records described him as an unappealing sort with "short built[*sic*], stoop[ed] shoulders, walk[s] slovenly, always talks and nothing original."[17] Masterson managed to serve his time and won release in 1875. His occupation, common laborer, did not prepare him for better employment; he lingered on in Laramie.

His next court appearance in Laramie concerned charges of forgery, and the authorities held him over for the district county court.[18] Sometime during the following three months, Masterson posted bail because in August of 1877 he and prostitute Georgie Lightheart were charged with open fornication.[19] Later that same month Masterson again entered prison, this time following conviction for the forgery charges. Masterson's new prison record now listed him as married and the father of one child. His nearest relative was given as "Georgie Masterson, Cheyenne."[20]

Between the time of Masterson's first release from the Laramie prison and his second entry, he formed a union with Georgie Lightheart. Whether they actually were married in a civil ceremony may be questionable in view of the charges of fornication. Regardless of the legality of their relationship, they did have a child by 1877, and despite the expectation of the officials that Mrs. Masterson could be reached in Cheyenne, she stayed on, at least temporarily, in Laramie. On August 30, only six days after Masterson entered prison, his wife pleaded guilty to charges of prostitution in Laramie.[21] Again, on October 1, Georgie Masterson was arrested along with a group of Laramie regulars, Nellie Davis, Cora Cooper, Annie Hamilton, and Lizzie Stevens.[22] During the next year Georgie Masterson's name was not recorded in the Laramie arrest register, but she may have worked Cheyenne during these months. By September 26, 1878, she had returned to Laramie, and on that date Georgie and her newly released husband were arrested and charged with disorderly conduct. The Mastersons paid their fines of $7.50 each and disappeared from the Laramie court dockets.[23] That they then moved away and established a home based on domestic security and participation among the socially acceptable elements of frontier society seemed improbable. Masterson's recidivism and Georgie's continued presence in the Laramie brothels while both a wife and a mother did not bode well for the future of this family. The very circumstances of their reunion that brought them wrangling into the Laramie courts set the tone of their relationship. Marriage and parenthood did not appear to divert them from the haunts and the associates of their earlier lives.

Even in those marriages where a bond of sentiment joined husband and wife, the underlying implications of involvement in a profession marked by personal degradation cast a shadow on the quality of the union. In Montana prostitute Fannie Matthews tangled with a neighbor over a property boundary. Over several days the quarrel escalated until a man named Hammond came forward to defend Fannie Matthews. Tempers flared and Hammond died in a shoot-out. The *Butte Miner* publicized this tale when it learned that a town official turned Fannie Matthews away from the room where the corpse lay. The paper knew Matthews and Hammond to be husband and wife, and the paper castigated the heartlessness that refused the request of a grieving widow to dress her husband's body for burial.[24] For the moment the press, infamous throughout the frontier for the mockery with which it treated prostitutes, allowed a surge of human sympathy for the recent widow.

Insensitive though he appeared, the official who turned Fannie Matthews away showed less hypocrisy than the newspaper. In his eyes the death of a prostitute's husband made the woman no less socially offensive. Even if the man demonstrated an unnecessary degree of coldness and the paper sounded a sincere note of compassion for the woman, maudlin sentiment blinded the reporter. He failed to recognize that, while alive, Hammond stood with those men who knowingly supported a wife's participation in an exacting, demoralizing, illegal profession. No amount of tears changed the reality that Fannie Matthews's husband participated in her life of prostitution. Widowhood hardly promised to bring changes in her career.

Physical and emotional violence colored more prostitutes' marriages than romance and gentleness. Caught in a limiting economic structure, prostitutes, corrupted by their profession, could not have looked for much but an extension of the corrosiveness of their work experiences. Unfortunately, they probably did. Unable to break the social and economic vise around them, and poorly equipped to understand how to change their own erratic behavior, many prostitutes continued their unrealistic pursuit of permanent alliances.

The full implications of both the economic stranglehold and the disastrous futility of these marriages seemed only an occasional concern for prostitutes. The tragic encounters of associates brought the tenuous position of all prostitutes into sharp focus. The misfortunes of a Molly Forrest became the unspoken threat to every woman.

Mollie Forrest married Joe Scott of the Black Hills region when she was not more than twenty.[25] Scott had acquired an unsavory reputation all about the Black Hills, and his name preceded him to Helena. In 1880 the husband and wife arrived in Helena where both were arrested after Scott assaulted a night clerk who intimated that the two were not married when they registered at the hotel. The authorities released the couple only after Scott produced evidence that they were legally wed. This unpleasant episode behind them, the husband and wife moved on to Butte. The Scotts arrived in Butte on a Friday evening, and Mollie immediately started to work in a dance hall. On Tuesday evening she and Scott fell into a quarrel at the saloon, and Scott dragged his wife to her prostitute's room directly off the dance floor. There he shot and killed the beautiful young woman, blowing away the side of her face and the back of her head. "Attired in the cheap finery of the dancing saloon," Mollie Scott breathed her last as her stunned dancer colleagues watched the blood pour from her mutilated face.[26]

A horrified reporter from the *Butte Miner* who witnessed the scene felt moved to write a long passionate description of the death in that little room. His prose underscored a major flaw in the marriages of prostitutes when he wrote, ". . . the poor fallen woman made the last sacrifice it was in her power to make—the sacrifice of her life through her love for the man whom she had cheerfully supported from the gains of her arduous calling."[27] Even allowing for the dramatic sense of overstatement and romanticization, the reporter, nonetheless, touched on the central difficulty in the personal attachments that prostitutes attempted to make. Shocked by the bloody sight before him, the reporter stepped aside from the hectic life in the mining town of Butte and saw the dreadful lives the camp prostitutes were living and the parasitic nature of their intimate attachments. This insight deepened when, upon paying his respects to the deceased, he found a collection of other prostitutes gathered about the body. Their mood at the wake stirred him to write, ". . . it is only then that they appear to realize their true position and to understand the constant danger to which they are exposed in the brutal and uncontrollable passions of the men whom they make at once their masters and companions." [28]

Eloquently the writer summed up the entire spectrum of the relationships that prostitutes endured with the men in their lives. Prostitutes lived off male customers, and husbands leeched off prostitutes. Few of these men—unskilled laborers, migrant workers, and criminals—had much opportunity to elevate themselves or the women from the economic and social morass in which they all wallowed. Little in their background, training, or social status provided them with the skills to throw off the burdens they faced as frontier workers. Men with a thin appreciation for the women of their own class and unimpressed with nineteenth-century values about gentility and protection for women, they readily expected the females of their own social background to hawk for them the one commodity the women possessed.

The women responded to this without much challenge and accepted husbands from this sorry assortment; they had few other choices from among the frontier males. The unfortunate eruptions that burst from these associations brought additional decadence and corruption to their lives, yet among these men and women the desires for human companionship and comfort surely ran as high as for any other people. So, despite the gloomy outlook for domestic bliss, couples continued to pair off. The resulting marriages reflected one more unhappy consequence of the pandemonium sweeping the frontier.

If matrimony seemed an unusual venture for a prostitute, the concept of the prostitute as mother was even more startling. The disparate concepts of mother and whore jarred as an incongruous coupling, yet the presence of children, often fully involved in the mother's occupation, manifested itself as a common frontier occurrence. The conditions under which children lived varied only slightly from those of their mothers and suggested that such a childhood did not lead to a serene adulthood or desirable career opportunities.

Census records showed the frequency with which prostitutes lived with young children. Laundresses, dressmakers, milliners, prostitutes, single women, married, divorced, widowed—all listed children with the enumerators. Spread across the frontier these fragmented families displayed some common characteristics. Almost universally the mothers had migrated to the West from some eastern location, but the children had been born in frontier regions. Laundresses who traveled with the military often listed four or five youngsters, each born in a different frontier territory. Often these laundresses registered no husband in the dwelling. The absentee husband and father repeated itself as a pattern among prostitutes who did not follow the military. In addition, prostitutes expressed ignorance about the birthplace of the father or fathers of the children. Surprisingly, not all the prostitute mothers fell into the very youthful category, some apparently giving birth for the first time after the age of thirty.

Most of these characteristics of motherhood existed among the Cheyenne prostitutes. Lizzie Hart, dressmaker/prostitute, appeared in the Cheyenne police courts most frequently between 1868 and 1870. Her daughter, Laura Sherman, was born in 1868. Hart was far from alone among the prostitutes of that town as others with similar situations surrounded her. Miss Mary Dougals, also one of the Laramie-Cheyenne crowd, gave birth to a daughter, Louella, when the washerwoman/prostitute was thirty-four years old. Constance Berstrow arrived in Cheyenne with her son, William Lynch, born in Illinois when this prostitute was thirty-three years old. Josephine Davis migrated from Kentucky to Colorado to Wyoming, pausing long enough to give birth to a son in Nebraska.[29] Dressmaker/prostitute Belle Connors made her way from Ireland to Wyoming where she lived with her son, Willie Piper, born in the territory. Delia DeWitt brought her sons with her from New York when she came to follow the fortunes of the Cheyenne dressmaker clique. Prostitute Belle Barnard claimed that the child Grace, born when Belle was twenty-nine years old, was actually her niece. Only Bridget Gallager, a member of the Laramie-Cheyenne circuit, listed a minor child away at school in the East.[30] Bridget Gallager's record of poverty, drunkenness, and arrest made questionable the resources she might have had to provide for this ten-year-old daughter. The same observation applied to her neighbors, for all these women struggled without husbands and fathers to assist in the family maintenance. The quality of life among prostitutes could only mean the support of children represented a tremendous hardship.

The daily difficulties intensified when illness struck among prostitutes and their children. With few resources and fewer means of assistance, an illness turned the living conditions of prostitutes with children from bad to desperate. Only if some individual saw the need and chose to help could complete disaster be averted. When Georgetown Ella, an

Austin prostitute of local fame, lay ill in the brothel of Charley Cooney, an Austin policeman happened to notice her dire condition. His action consisted of making a notation in the police report book that Ella lay incapacitated. Her four children, he noted, had neither food nor supervision.[31] The officer offered no explanation as to the whereabouts of Cooney, commonly known as the owner of a disorderly house. Cooney's usual conduct did not suggest that he would act kindly toward the children or take care to see their destitution alleviated. Citizens outside the world of prostitution traditionally stayed away from such wretched scenes. Ella and her children had only the brief notation of a police officer to bring them aid, which in all likelihood never arrived.

Other prostitutes found themselves similarly cut off from assistance when illness struck. In Butte an outbreak of typhoid caused some panic in that community in 1881. Newspaper reports kept the town informed about the location of quarantined houses and provided medical bulletins on those children diagnosed as dangerously ill.[32] Only with the danger passed did the paper admit that the quarantine had been in the brothel district. The paper reminded the community that the part of town reserved for prostitutes and Orientals was notable for its filth and all should avoid it.[33] All three of the afflicted children survived, but the squalor of their environment still surrounded them. The social ostracism of their families in Butte had not lessened; the taxing stresses their struggling mothers faced each day did not evaporate.

In Cheyenne the cemetery register pointed to the ultimate conclusion these harsh conditions produced. Death, rampant among children in the nineteenth century, claimed its share from the children of prostitutes. Prostitute Nellie Fischer buried her four-month-old infant when the child succumbed to pneumonia. Lillie White and Mary Brown buried stillborn infants. Kate Bowers, Jane Bloom, and Mollie Jones all buried children whose ages they could not give and whose cause of death they did not know. The child of Mollie Jones went to potter's field. Mattie Milsak lost her son, Walter, at the age of one, and Susie Devrick buried Graham at seven. These represented only some of the children's deaths.[34] Others never were recorded in the register, or mothers disposed of their infants without ceremony.[35]

These scenes of motherhood were repeated in Denver where seamstresses, milliners, and laundresses without husbands earned a meager existence. Some, like Ella Cree, age thirty-three, boarded a younger prostitute and tried to support her two children through a small-scale brothel operation. Ill from the effects of typhoid fever, her children but four and two months, Ella Cree depended upon the assistance she could secure from another prostitute. A similar arrangement worked for Annabella McElhany and Hellen McElhany from Ohio. These two lived in the center of the brothel district with Hellen's five-year-old son. Then there was the earthy Miss Doebler from Germany. This straightforward woman listed herself as single with no occupation. Her three children, ages seven, five, and three, had all been born in different locations: Illinois, Wisconsin, and Minnesota. The mother acknowledged that she had no information about the birthplace of the fathers of the first two children but did know that the father of child number three came from Illinois.[36]

Miss Doebler's frontier wanderings pointed to the essential elements present in the conduct of prostitutes as mothers. The influence of constant moves, the casual acquisition of new mates, the fragmented sense of family identity and background had to impress youngsters. Had the mothers themselves demonstrated a sense of internal order or stability, perhaps the calamitous impact of these external disorders might have been lessened. Such did not prove to be the case. The harshness and brutality of the lives of the mothers descended upon the children in full measure.

Only tales of frontier misery emerged as the heritage of the children of prostitutes. These children appeared but briefly in the accounts of the mothers' lives, but as they passed from the attention of society, where did they go and what became of them? What proved to be the fate of the daughter of Texas prostitute Bridget Holland, who was arrested in 1868 for physically abusing the child?[37] What misfortunes befell the child of prostitute Mary Weisenger after her mother went to the Wyoming prison for eighteen months on a charge of grand larceny?[38] What became of the tiny daughters of Sarah Petite, who supported her children by running a brothel near Chugwater, Wyoming?[39] Where did life lead the daughter of Catherine Thompson after that youngster discovered the body of another prostitute who committed suicide?[40]

It did not matter that no specific answers to these particular cases existed. Other stories suggested the fate of these unfortunates. Like other miserable children raised among the most dissipated of the frontier society, life held little promise for these youths. They, like their mothers

before them, found their lives constricted by poverty, lack of opportunity and social castigation. Daughters carried the heaviest burden and
most, following the only path readily available, trod the unhappy road of
prostitution. Born of illiterate and unskilled parentage, moved from
town to town, uneducated, assigned to the most unattractive residential
sections in every community, these children could hardly avoid a repeti-
tion of the social and economic misery of their mothers.

In fact, the daughters did repeat the lives of the mothers. For some,
prostitution became a family affair, as with the Stottses of Austin, Texas.
During the fall of 1884 Lottie Stotts and her daughters, Ida, age twenty,
and Flora, age eighteen, ran up a series of arrest charges.[41] Austin's court
procedures, less flexible than those of some communities, required that
the women work off the full fine in jail if they were unable to pay the
costs at the time of arrest. Consequently, Austin prostitutes often paid
a portion of the fine and worked out the remainder by scrubbing or
cooking in jail. The Austin regulars languished in jail for up to three
weeks, earning a fine credit of seventy-five cents a day. When they
reached the full amount due, they were off to the streets, and back in jail
within three or four days.

Flora Stotts compiled a lengthy record with the Austin authorities. Arrested on September 8, 1884, the young woman paid $2 on a fine of
$10.60, and then retired to the jail until the debt was cleared. Some days
she got to scour the prison, but on others her record noted, "Work:
nothing. Why: nothing to do."[42] "Turned out at 8:00 P.M." on October 4,
Flora Stotts was back on the usual complaint on November 1; this time
she got to stay with her mother who also entered prison that same day.[43]
Discharged on November 5 the mother, Lottie Stotts, enjoyed her freedom only briefly; the next day she returned to jail charged with assault
with intent to murder.[44] Convicted and sent away to prison, Lottie Stotts
left behind on the streets of Austin two daughters, Flora and Ida, who
continued to be arrested for prostitution.

The circumstances which led these young women to follow their
mother's career shaped them before they ever reached the police court.
Nothing in their court records gave clues to these earlier experiences,
but the childhood of Ida and Flora probably resembled that of their
counterpart, Hattie Severe of Cheyenne. Mollie Severe, a black illiterate
prostitute from Virginia, lived in Cheyenne in 1880. With her resided
her nine-year-old daughter, Hattie, who had been born in Nebraska.[45]

Mollie ended her wanderings and settled in Cheyenne, where eight years later she and the daughter still resided. Now seventeen, the daughter began to appear in the police docket arrested for prostitution and disturbing the peace.[46] Like the Stottses, mother and daughter went to jail together. The family background, coupled with the limited economic opportunities for blacks in Cheyenne, set the course for young Hattie. If she began her career in prostitution at seventeen, then she rated among the unusual for a prostitute's daughter, for early introduction to the life typified the experience of most of these girls.

Exposure to the environs of prostitution and neglect by the mother accounted for some daughters entering prostitution. Prostitute Ella Harvelle brought both these deficits to her motherhood. Mother of three daughters, she floated about the frontier pursuing prostitution and a series of men. Her oldest daughter took up residence in a seedy Cheyenne brothel at about age fifteen. The two younger children were abandoned by the mother when she took off for the Black Hills with a miner friend. The deserted children had been left in the brothel of Frankie Lester, who found herself in an awkward spot. She did not want the girls, who had begged her for shelter, nor did she want the public to know they were living in her back room. When the press learned of the situation and interviewed Frankie Lester, she reluctantly explained her dilemma.[47] The girls had no place to go except to join their older sister in a dive that Frankie Lester rated far below her own establishment. Forced into the role of surrogate mother, Frankie insisted she kept the children removed from her business operation. Despite her honorable declarations, these girls had few prospects of escaping from the Cheyenne brothels. Prostitution had always been part of their existence. Mother and sister before them worked the trade. When the mother returned a year later from the Black Hills, her conduct continued as erratic and disordered as before.[48] If the girls did return to her, slim were the chances their mother checked the family upheaval. For the Harvelle daughters, motherly neglect pointed the way to the future.

Ella Harvelle typified those prostitute/mothers who, unable to grapple with their own misfortunes, lacked the skills, abilities, and initiative to channel the lives of their daughters away from prostitution. But some young women came to prostitution, not as the products of parental negligence, but as the result of deliberate actions by the mother. These episodes may have occurred with much greater frequency than the press and public permitted themselves to realize. When such a case caught the attention of the public, the community response indicated great shock. In 1877 a Denver paper indignantly reported, "A Mrs. Whatley, who keeps a cigar store . . . has a daughter only 15 years old, who has been a prostitute . . . for nearly 3 years, and the most shocking feature . . . is that her own mother deliberately led her into evil courses. . . ."[49] Not content with employing her daughter, Mrs. Whatley further offended the community by soliciting a twelve-year-old who told police she had often stayed with men at Mrs. Whatley's.[50] The shock of the Denver citizenry lacked conviction. Cigar girls, a favorite arrest group for the Denver police, had a notorious reputation in that city. If the population there did not know that young girls engaged in prostitution in cigar stores, they chose to remain ignorant. Only when some episode forced attention to these situations did citizens respond, but only with a brief flurry of indignation and then the furor died away. No report appeared that Mrs. Whatley's daughter and her friend had been removed from that brothel. Shocked as the citizens might be, the circumstances would not prompt their involvement. The unpleasantness of admitting that such a young girl had three years' experience as a prostitute proved more than society wanted to endure.

Prostitution hardly encouraged the most admirable traits of motherhood. Only the strongest personality could have worked as a prostitute and still risen above the corruption, dissipation, and poverty of the profession to rear children in a balanced, stable home atmosphere. This did not happen, for prostitutes had neither the energy nor skills to overcome the social and economic stagnation that encompassed them and their children. The instability and insecurity of frontier life added increased strain to already troubled homes. The relationships that prostitutes maintained with their children, like those with their husbands, soured or warped all the participants.

Husbands and children did not constitute the entire personal circle of prostitutes. Others also touched upon their lives on a day-to-day basis. Prohibited by society's censure from establishing a wide range of friendships, prostitutes circulated freely among their own colleagues. Cast in the framework of a vague, uneasy truce, these friendships took on a strange hue.

Unspoken fears and daily realities limited the development of deepseated friendships. Friction and open hostility often dominated social

contacts. Friendship could not always overcome the climate of unre-
stricted competition. If the conviviality of a common experience underscored relationships, so did spiteful ill-will. An atmosphere based on
competition and human frailities did not lend itself to harmonious
friendships.

Perhaps the major contribution of madams in established houses
came from their ability to regulate the economy and reduce the competition for the women within the house. Because of the short career span
for prostitutes, madams could only ease tensions temporarily; they
could not eliminate them. Houses, although imperfect devices for sta-
bilizing the income of prostitutes and harmonizing relationships with
co-workers, introduced slight control to an industry that lacked a means
to harness the economic rivalries of the employees. Even here, the occupation itself undermined the possibilities for sound, lasting friendships among the women. Outside the brothel few controls existed, and
social chaos reigned among prostitutes. Although some women lived
and traveled together for a few years, the best friendships limped along
constantly threatened by professional insecurities and the terminal
nature of career opportunities. When associations with other prostitutes
broke down, the ensuing encounters increased the personal disorder of
the women, added to their poor public image, and intensified their
alienation from the surrounding society.

Verbal abuse and fights permeated the relationships that prostitutes
had with each other. Explosive and unpredictable, often well lubricated
with generous amounts of alcohol, prostitutes unleashed their furies on
each other. Court appearances concerned disputes among prostitutes
almost as often as charges of violation of anti-prostitution laws. In Denver, between February 1865 and July 1867, one justice book recorded
sixty-six different arrests for forty-three prostitutes. Thirteen arrests
brought charges of fighting or disturbing the peace, nine came from the
use of offensive language in public, and twenty arrests were for drunk
and disorderly charges.[51] Slightly more than 65 percent of the arrests for
that period concerned charges separate from prostitution offenses.

In Austin, Texas, the years between 1876 and 1879 gave even clearer
illustration of the violence that flowed among prostitutes in the daily
conduct of their lives. Police detained 240 different prostitutes in Austin
for that period. Of 405 arrests, 317 concerned charges other than violation of prostitution laws. There were 57 arrests for drunkenness; 69 ar-

rests for fighting and disturbing the peace—5 of which the dockets tied directly to fights with other prostitutes; 129 arrests for the use of offensive language—11 of which the docket indicated involved 2 or more prostitutes; and 65 arrests for assault and battery charges—nine of which were identified as assaults against other prostitutes.[52] Arrests for charges of mayhem represented almost 80 percent of the court appearances for prostitutes over a three-year period in Austin.

The turbulence in the personal lives of prostitutes showed itself in these figures. Much of their violent behavior focused upon each other. Fighting and vulgar language formed the ground rules for the way prostitutes treated colleagues. They conveyed in their verbal and physical attacks their frustrations, anger, and distaste for each other, as well as for themselves. The prevalence of these attitudes surfaced in the pervasiveness of assault charges in every docket.[53]

Prostitutes and society calmly regarded these fights as routine to the lives of the women. In Arizona, when prostitute Fermina Gonzales faced charges of assault upon the person of Carmen Calles, Gonzales argued the attack was justified because the victim took her man away. The court noted in registering the guilty plea of the defendant, "The affair is quarrell[*sic*], such as these women frequently have."[54] Other prostitutes around them had done their share to inspire that feeling in Justice of the Peace Charles Meyers. In the six months preceding the appearance of Gonzales and Calles, Justice Meyers tried at least six cases of brawls among prostitutes.[55] In less than a year after she was the victim of attack, Carmen Calles came before Justice Meyers on two separate occasions for charges of assault upon other prostitutes.[56]

Even when prostitutes managed to suppress the open warfare, their resentments and hostilities showed in the thievery they inflicted upon one another. Humble, poor possessions became the center of huge arguments and often resulted in more court appearances as charges and countercharges flew back and forth. The charges never reached the trial stage in many episodes as the thief might disappear, or a police officer simply confiscated the stolen goods and returned them to the injured party. When the matter did reach a courtroom confrontation, it became an occasion of glee for the local press, quick to seize the opportunity for some colorful reporting about the local brothels.[57] Most incidents, trivial in a monetary sense, revealed more about the quality of life among prostitutes than the press wanted to recognize. As in Annie Ferguson's theft of Emma Halbring's scarf and towels, the thieveries showed how little the women owned, how much they coveted the cheap belongings of others, how easily they lifted things from each other, and how quickly these encounters prompted a move to another location.

Emma Halbring's towels did all that for Annie Ferguson. "One-Arm Annie" left Laramie after this theft and tried life in Cheyenne. There, three years later, the brutality of prostitution caught up with Annie Ferguson. The victim of a vicious beating at the hands of prostitute Fanny Brown, Annie Ferguson lay almost senseless when another prostitute found her. Her face covered with blood, the battered woman told her colleague, "Fanny Brown gave me the beating; I am hurt inside and think I will die soon."[58] The next morning the prostitute lay dead in bed next to a customer who did not know the woman had expired. Fanny Brown's beating and Emma Halbring's towels were merely different aspects of violence in the saga of Annie Ferguson. Distrust and brutality played major roles in her life, and ultimately an explosion of these same elements ended it.

Suspicion and cruelty tempered the shaky bonds of friendship while prostitutes lived, but their common misery transcended the violence of life in the face of death. Pity and sorrow, some of it self-directed, exuded from those who survived. When the beautiful Mollie Scott died from the bullet of her husband, the hour was well past midnight. By nine o'clock the next morning the body of the dead woman who had been in Butte no more than four days was "properly arrayed for the grave, being neatly robed in a white dress, while the kid-gloved hands were peacefully crossed on the breast."[59] Preparation of the body had to have been directed by the several prostitutes gathered at the coffin side. The murderer husband who dashed off in the night certainly did not pause to arrange for her clothing, coffin, and services; that gesture came from her co-workers.

Taking charge of the burial service for a dead associate proved to be one responsibility prostitutes willingly assumed. The prevalent violence brought many unexpected deaths, and burials had to be arranged quickly. With no time to bicker or to contact families, prostitutes stepped in and managed the proceedings. Prostitute Jennie Conway buried her companion, Adelle Sanchez, when that victim died from the bullet of Juan Duran.[60] When a customer accidentally shot and killed Maggie Howard, age twenty-three, in the Cheyenne brothel of Julia McGuinn, prostitute Nellie Wright made the arrangements with the undertaker and the cemetery. She collected about $100 from others in the profession, $15 of which went for cemetery expenses.[61] Experience taught Nellie Wright how to handle these chores efficiently, for only three years earlier she buried her seventeen-year-old drinking and traveling companion, Belle Vernon.[62] At least Belle Vernon's death did not come about from a vicious personal attack. She, like her colleague Mollie Egbert, died of natural causes. Prostitute Helen Jenkins performed the mournful task of laying to rest the twenty-six-year-old Mollie Egbert, who died of consumption.[63] But even if no last moment of bloody assault marked their demise, both Vernon and Egbert surely died from the violent effects of their profession. At seventeen and twenty-six both lost out to the self-destructive abuse they had inflicted on themselves.

Some had no acquaintances who put aside the stresses of life to show them compassion in death. Isabella Williams, an object of public fun in Cheyenne for several years, finally succumbed to the ravages of her life and consumption. When she died at forty-eight, she went to a pauper's grave.[64] Even Ida Snow, resident of Ida Hamilton's widely known brothel, was buried by order of the county when she died of apoplexy at the age of twenty-eight.[65] For some women the rejections of life followed them to the grave, and no feeling friend softened the final departure. These harsh deaths reflected the realities of prostitution more accurately than the surges of sentiment extended to a few.

The dynamics of prostitution encouraged women to indulge in dishonesty, suspicion, fighting, and attack. Friendships appeared out of necessity in their common experience but failed to assume stable qualities because of the nature of prostitution. Workers in an industry that capitalized on their ignorance, prostitutes failed to grasp the benefits of unity. Instead, each woman focused only on her own interests in a career with a limited future. Caught in the economic fever of the frontier, prostitutes fought for a chance to snare a few of the profits. This competitive setting inhibited the development of sound friendships with other workers. Pitted against one another in life, only in death did these women seem to catch a glimmer of their universal plight. These funereal occasions did not exert enough influence to inspire women to break the mold that enclosed them; rather, afterward, they reverted to their original feelings of hatred for each other and continued exchanges of frenzied insults and cruelties.

Laden with a host of social difficulties, prostitutes staggered under the added weight of frontier isolation. In this one area they shared the misery and anxiety of all frontier people. The suffering extracted in terms of human emotion touched all. The daily existence on the frontier—demanding, boring, and brutal—drained the physical and emotional resources of its inhabitants. Only those who possessed balance and strength had any chance of surmounting the traumas attached to frontier life. Prostitutes had neither. In any setting their lives promised little. In a western society that lacked structure and community order, their problems inevitably intensified.

Prostitutes had personal lives and family ties, although the usual image of the prostitute did not depict that. Husbands, children, and co-workers influenced the daily lives of prostitutes. All these relationships floundered in a torrent of destructive qualities and experiences. Personal associations did not enhance the status of prostitutes in society. In fact, the sensational publicity attached to the exploits of prostitutes with any family ties only heightened the antagonism that society felt. The personal relationships of prostitutes added to their social segregation, making them unlikely candidates for civic concern. Their behavior, guided by constant personal upheaval and an overt hatred for their fellow workers, retarded the emergence of a community awareness sympathetic to the desperate economic and social plight they endured. Prostitutes generally acted as if they themselves felt society correctly assigned them to the fringe world where they lived. Their lives regimented by social and economic standards they lacked the skills to alter, prostitutes further solidified these same social and economic problems by their own conduct. Dreary and bleak, the daily life of the frontier prostitute.

Notes

1. *Black Hills Daily Times*, Dec. 9, 1877.

2. Wyoming Census for 1880, cities of Laramie, LaPorcelle Creek, Rawlings, and Cheyenne, WSAHD.

3. U.S. Bureau of the Census from the Tenth Census (1880), Colorado, Rolls 87 and 88, Districts 5, 6, 9, 10, RG 29, NA.

4. Criminal Docket, Hemphill County, Tex., July 25, 1887–Mar. 26, 1891, PPHM; see July 25, Aug. 23, Sept. 23, Oct. 22, 1887.

5. Ibid., July 26, 1887–May 6, 1889.

6. Ibid. Cora Cooley joined the regulars in Hemphill County in 1890; see charges throughout that year, especially Jan.–June, 1890.

7. Ibid., May 2, 1888.

8. *Butte Miner*, Aug. 28, 1879.

9. Ibid.

10. Ibid.

11. Ibid., July 31, 1880.

12. Ibid., Dec. 15, 1881.

13. Ibid., Dec. 15, 17, 1881.

14. This item may be from the *Denver Times*. The clipping is found in the George Watrous Scrapbook, p. 21, WHC.

15. *Laramie Daily Sentinel*, Feb. 24, 1871.

16. Ibid., Feb. 23, 24, 28, 1872.

17. United States Penitentiary Book for Description of Convicts Held at Laramie City, Wyoming Territory, 1873–78, Register Number 25, WSAHD.

18. Criminal Files, City of Laramie, Feb. 8, 1877-Feb. 8, 1878, Apr. 11, 1877, ACCH. The episodes here may not have been Masterson's only clashes with the law. Only after his connection with a prostitute in Laramie became evident did he become a research focus.

19. Ibid., Aug. 6, 1877.

20. United States Penitentiary Book for Description of Convicts Held at Laramie City, Wyoming Territory, 1873–78, Register Number 147, WSAHD.

21. Justice of the Peace Dockets, City of Laramie, Albany County, Aug. 2, 1877–Aug. 2, 1886, Aug. 30, 1877, ACCH.

22. Ibid., Oct. 1, 1877.

23. Ibid., Sept. 26, 1878.

24. *Butte Miner*, Mar. 30, 1880; see also Mar. 27, 1880.

25. Ibid., Aug. 5, 1880.

26. Ibid.

27. Ibid.

28. Ibid.

29. U.S. Bureau of the Census from the Ninth Census (1870), Wyoming Territory, City of Cheyenne, Roll 1748, RG 29, NA.

30. Wyoming Census for 1880, City of Cheyenne, WSAHD.

31. Austin Police Calls, 1879–80, July 9, 1879, ATCC. Cooney's public record included such items as charges of malicious mischief, offensive language, and keeping a disorderly house. Austin Record of Arrest, Jan. 1, 1876–Jan. 1, 1879; see Jan. 24, 1876, and Mar. 24, 1877, ATCC.

32. *Butte Miner*, Dec. 1–13, 1881.

33. Ibid., Dec. 8, 12, 1881.

34. Register of Burials, Cheyenne Cemetery, 1875–1932, WSAHD; see Mar. 4, 1884, Oct. 11, 1887, July 1, 1880, Oct. 20, 1875, June 25, 1876, Apr. 3, 1879, Dec. 25, 1883, Mar. 14, 1886.

35. Every death was not listed in the cemetery register. Annie Ferguson, who died in Cheyenne in 1877, did not appear in the burial list. Sometimes infants' bodies were simply discarded or buried secretly. In Laramie in 1877 prostitute Mary Kean and Mr. and Mrs. Thomas Wicks were charged with not providing a decent burial for a fetus. Inquest, City of Laramie, Feb. 22, 1877, ACCH.

36. U.S. Bureau of the Census from the Tenth Census (1880) Colorado, Roll 87, Districts 2, 3, RG 29, NA.

37. *San Antonio Daily Express*, Mar. 25, 1868.

38. Record of Convicts and Penitentiaries of Wyoming Territory, 1876–92, Sept. 19, 1891, WSAHD.

39. Wyoming Census for 1880, District between Muddy Creek and Chugwater, WSAHD.

40. Inquest, City of Cheyenne, Mar. 20, 1889, WSAHD.

41. Record of Prisoners, City of Austin, 1884, ATCC; see entries Sept. 8–Nov. 16, 1884. Lottie Stotts's repeated arrests can be traced as far back as 1880 and 1881 in the Record of Prisoners registers for those years; references to her daughters Flora and Ida can be found in the 1885 register.

42. Ibid., Sept. 15, 1884.

43. Ibid., Nov. 1, 1884.

44. Ibid., Nov. 6, 1884.

45. Wyoming Census for 1880, City of Cheyenne, WSAHD.

46. Police records for the Severes were very confusing. Their names were recorded in two different registers. Although the arrest dates matched, the first names of the women differed. This was a common difficulty with all records where various officials listed prostitutes by conflicting names. Some of this was caused by the prostitutes' habit of changing names frequently, and some was caused by carelessness in the recording process. The Severes appeared as Hattie, Mattie, and Sadie. It is probable that Mollie, Mattie, and Sadie were one person, the mother. See the Jail Register for the City of Cheyenne, Mar. 2, 1887–Jan., 1890, Feb. 5, Apr. 21, 1888; Police Register, Apr. 22, Dec. 3, 1888, WSAHD.

47. *Cheyenne Daily Sun*, Feb. 14, 1878.

48. Ibid., Feb. 26, 1879.

49. *Daily Rocky Mountain News*, Apr. 28, 1877.

50. Ibid.

51. Justice Docket, City of Denver, Mar. 21, 1864–Aug. 15, 1867, WHC.

52. Records of Arrest, City of Austin, Jan. 1, 1876–Jan. 1, 1879, ATCC.

53. For other examples of widespread violence between prostitutes consult the following dockets: Docket Book of Justice S. F. Yates, County of Clear Creek, Col., Aug. 1, 1867–June 24, 1871, WHC; Court Criminal Docket for Grant County, N. Mex., 1874–76, NMSRA; Police Court Docket, Central City, Aug. 23, 1884–June 29, 1896, CSA; Dodge City Police Dockets, June 3, 1866–Oct. 18, 1886, MS Box 377, KSHS; Justice Docket for Pima County, City of Tucson, 1889–90, ADL.

54. Records of Justice of the Peace Charles H. Meyers, Jan. 1, 1871–July 25, 1873, Aug. 12, 1872, ADL.

55. Ibid., Jan. 24, Feb. 22, May 11, 17, June 6, 24, 1872.

56. Ibid., Dec. 9, 1872, June 12, 1873.

57. For example, see *Cheyenne Daily News*, Feb. 28, 1874, and *Cheyenne Daily Sun*, Feb. 15, 1882.

58. *Cheyenne Daily Sun*, Apr. 10, 1877.

59. *Butte Miner*, Aug. 5, 1889.

60. Register of Burials, Cheyenne Cemetery, 1875–1932, Dec. 18, 1884, WSAHD.

61. Ibid., Mar. 2, 1879; *Cheyenne Daily Sun*, Feb. 25, 1879.

62. Register of Burials, Cheyenne Cemetery, 1875–1932, Apr. 24, 1876, WSAHD.

63. Ibid., Aug. 25, 1880.

64. Ibid., Sept. 20, 1878.

65. Ibid., Aug. 14, 1880.

3

Lives Without Comfort

Prostitutes will ruin any young man, and their aim in life is first
to "mask," then steal, beg, or blackmail him out of his money.[1]

Harshly stated, that comment accurately defined the commerical
nature of prostitution. In the business of selling companionship and
sex, prostitutes gravitated toward those communities with employment
opportunities. They hunted out the mining towns, the construction
sites, the military outposts, the cattle terminals, the supply stations, as
well as the larger urban centers of the frontier. The pursuit of business
turned them in any direction where groups of males gathered. The
women swarmed to the dance halls and gambling joints; they joined established brothels; they set up single shacks, "cribs," in the streets; they
traveled in "cat" wagons from town to hamlet and back again; they
camped beside garrisons. Whether immigrant to the West or native
born, prostitutes declared with boldness their sexual availability. Few
work chances came to the timid, so they plied their trade aggressively
everywhere on the American frontier. In the frantic quest for employment, many succeeded, at least part of the time, for the men of the frontier came to the little rooms behind the saloons, the "female boarding
houses," the shacks, the cribs.[2]

These encounters with customers who exchanged money for sexual
favors defined the essence of prostitution. That women willingly allowed sexual intimacies in return for cash captured the most distasteful
and tawdry aspects of this life for observers, yet the union of the marketplace and sex represented the very basis of the prostitute's existence.

50

Trade with customers constituted the income prostitutes could expect to earn. Some few in the profession worked that trade into a substantial income, but the general economic conditions of prostitutes remained marginal.

Their personal lives afflicted with domestic ills, the professional lives of prostitutes continued the same depressing routine. Their occupational circumstances rested on such a shallow economic base that the general inflation and uneven cash flow prevalent on the frontier only added further instability to the lives of prostitutes. Mired in personal and professional disorder, prostitutes seemed unable to use their pitiful wages as a means to extricate themselves from prostitution; rather, prostitutes simply latched onto customers and tried to drain off monies wherever possible.

Based on this flawed concept, the relationships of prostitutes with customers reinforced the social and economic difficulties of the women. In an atmosphere that encouraged violence, dissipation, and the corruption of character, prostitutes could not construct professional lives of long-range, steady employment with the promise of economic improvement. Despite all this, women might have opted for a continued life in prostitution if they could count the monetary rewards as satisfactory. The difficulties, the deprivations, and the spotty nature of the employment might have been worth the effort if the financial gain to prostitutes merited staying in the profession.

Such, generally, did not prove to be the case. The almost universal poverty of prostitutes showed profits were sparse or nonexistent, and, unlike many occupations, prostitution did not promote employees for experience and longevity. The opposite occurred. Age and long years in the profession counted against women and lowered their economic prospects. For most prostitutes the spare monies earned made their short-lived careers only a limited source of income.

Prostitutes' destitution became markedly apparent in a variety of areas. The kinds of men who frequented brothels, their economic status, and the actual monetary return from these customers helped to explain the poverty of prostitutes. Hindered by low wages, prostitutes found themselves staggered by high costs and overhead expenses within the profession. The final picture of the economic misery of prostitutes was so disastrous that it appeared that some agencies of society had to exist to respond to the utter deprivation of these collections of women in communities. Unfortunately, one searches in vain for relief committees, local welfare services, or humanitarian rescue commissions; such were not part of the nineteenth-century frontier motif. Yet, without some response from society, these women, surrounded by the most grinding poverty, would have perished. The quality of the responses from society showed even more clearly the economic plight of prostitutes. With neither income nor many societal agencies for economic assistance and relief, prostitutes found their own solutions to the miseries of their lives. This cheerless picture began with the customers who came to the prostitutes.

Some men of economic substance and social refinement did contribute to the support of brothels, but primitive frontier communities rarely boasted lush parlor houses designed to cater to opulent politicos and wealthy entrepreneurs. Even where houses of velvet drapes and sparkling chandeliers existed, personal emotional disasters for the employees remained intense. Long-range occupational hazards for prostitutes did not evaporate because the physical surroundings improved.[3] Furthermore, so few prostitutes worked in these situations that the existence of the urbane brothel patronized by courtly gentlemen cannot be regarded as typical of the frontier experience.

In frontier communities men of money used the common bordellos of the town. Here they dallied and moved on. The notion that men of middle- and upper-class backgrounds married prostitutes and removed them from "the life" appear generally unfounded.[4] For these men, blatant prostitution was just one more frenzied aspect of the wild adventure of the frontier.

Examples of these masculine attitudes permeated the memoirs of H. C. Cornwall, mining engineer in Irwin, Colorado. Part of an advance team to map out the town, Cornwall and his partner anticipated that real estate values would jump drastically once the mining rush hit. Within three months town lots that had sold for $10 and $20 apiece soared to the incredible prices of $1000 and $2000. Cornwall and his cabin mate, swept up in the mushrooming economy as miners, merchants, industry personnel, gamblers, and prostitutes poured into Irwin, joined in the festivities of a grand ball for the town. Cornwall commented in his journal that prostitutes Durango Nell and Timberline Kate attended, as well as the few respectable wives in the town.[5] This sort of frivolous atmosphere masked underlying male attitudes toward prostitutes and convinced observers that prostitutes received a cordial welcome among the men during the early stages of frontier development. The frolic of the dance aside, Cornwall revealed a closer picture of the male appreciation for "respectable" women when he wrote, "There were literally scores of young fellows in camp from good families, well educated gentlemen, and there was at that time only one girl from similar circles— sister of Mrs. Reed, wife of the camp doctor . . . forty young fellows calling regularly . . . set up rules . . . only 6 at a time . . . 4 minutes on sofa with girl."[6] The bachelors of Irwin treasured a few moments spent courting the only single non-prostitute female in town.

When the wildness of their frontier days passed behind them, these young men turned away from their bawdy companions of the boom era and married such women as Mrs. Reed's sister.[7] Society looked upon the associations of gentlemen with rough prostitutes as an unfortunate lapse to be overlooked. Community sorrow and regret gushed forth at any indications that an educated or professional man had been debauched by his contacts with prostitutes. In Ouray, Colorado, the newspaper expressed great distress at the news that a young professional gentleman suffered injuries in an accidental fall from a horse. The paper graciously withheld his name for the protection of his mother, but without hesitation identified Florence, his prostitute companion.[8] In Austin in 1880, the *Daily Democratic Statesman* threatened to publish the names of two young men of the town if they continued to appear in public in the company of the "fille de Joie."[9] Such relationships could only bring mental and physical contamination, if not death, to the bright and promising males.

Society need not have feared that the brightest talents among frontier males would be permanently lost to the corruption of brothels. Brothel doors swung open, not so much for the rich and exceptional of the frontier as for the poor and the ordinary. The daily customers who sought and supported the prostitutes on the frontier came from those bachelor collections that the women followed across the frontier. The miners, the laborers, the soldiers—these workers came to the prostitutes. They did not bring with them good salaries or other economic benefits.

Customers simply were unable to improve the prostitutes' standard of living to any large degree. Their own economic prospects fell far short of the bright picture they envisioned when they came to the frontier. As early as 1869 P. A. Spengler, a Colorado miner, wrote, "Times is very dull here . . . since the R road had been finished to California this country has been flooded with men from that line. . . . I had set my pegs this spring for something over a hundred Dollars a month but the rush of men to this section spoilt it. . . . I am now only going . . . to . . . $50 a month."[10] As he further bemoaned his poor prospects for the coming season, Spengler astutely added, ". . . so you see it takes money to get money. . . . The rule in this country is wherever a man hears tell of a extra Dollar is to go for it and many of us don't make much at last. . . ."[11]

He prophetically summed up the situation in frontier economy for the migrant workers who drifted there. The first blush of production turned little towns into wild mobs of money-hungry people. Cash flowed without restraint and then disappeared almost overnight, the productivity dried up, the population evaporated. It happened to Spengler, the miner, and it happened to Cornwall, the engineer. During the weeks of the boom Cornwall could say, "I have never seen a community where money was so plentiful. . . . we averaged about $40 a day a piece, besides several large sums from sale of town lots. We each always had several thousand dollars in bills in our money belts and more hidden in our cabin."[12] For Cornwall and the town of Irwin the high living lasted three months. In the fall of 1880 the bottom dropped out for the Ruby Camp District. The town shriveled to nothing. Cornwall ended the season with less than his grand amount of money. The transients—miners, gamblers, and prostitutes—moved on.

From the financial perspective of prostitutes attached to boom-era coattails, the possibilities of establishing a steady source of income rarely materialized. Even when the women congregated in an area with a high cash flow, they secured only sporadic amounts of money. The occasional windfall filtered through their fingers without changing the basic conditions of life. During the boom years of 1876 to 1879, Texas pioneer and deputy sheriff Henry Heron lived in Fort Griffin. That town capitalized on trade with buffalo hunters and cattle drivers. In the trading season a buffalo hunter could sell his hides for as much as $1500 in the evening and be penniless by breakfast the next morning. Plenty of prostitutes lurked about, ready to skim off as much of that profit for themselves as they could. Heron estimated that more than half the feminine population worked as prostitutes and recalled that "lewd women infested the dance halls and all of them had their shanties sprawled along the river."[13] Jessica Young, another Texas pioneer, had similar memories of the little town of Mobeetie where she claimed "the sporting element" ruled during the boom days. Other customers had to wait for service while Mobeetie merchants catered to prostitutes who had plenty of money to flash about.[14] If they did, they flashed it only briefly. The live-for-the-moment atmosphere encouraged prostitutes to part with their earnings immediately. Money, when they got it, went quickly for material possessions and did not contribute an appreciable improvement in the standard of living. Prostitutes continued to inhabit the shacks and shanties of every frontier town, both during and after the boom period.[15]

The poverty of prostitutes showed itself in areas other than their slum housing. Their indigence affected their encounters with the police, and their jail records showed their unmitigated destitution. In Austin forty-four arrests for vagrancy and prostitution saw four cases dismissed. Among the remaining cases, two women escaped from jail, and five paid their fines outright. Fourteen times women could not pay any portion of the fine and worked out the entire cost in jail. Nineteen times women worked a combination deal where they paid a portion of the fine and worked out the balance in prison. Cash payments ranged from seventy cents to $12.65, although the latter ranked high among ready cash holdings. Most could only ante up between $3 and $5.25 on fines that ranged from $10.20 to $17.80. One woman paid $23.45 on a $30.95 fine.[16] The entire spectrum showed that in only seven of the forty-four cases before the bench did the prostitutes have the cash to pay their fines. For this group of prostitutes almost 85 percent had less than $10 cash at the time of arrest.

Other cities had prostitutes with similar economic problems. For a two and one-half year period between 1867 and 1890 in Cheyenne, eighty-nine female records appeared in the jail register. Of these, only thirteen times did the defendant pay her full fine upon arrest. The amounts of these fines included one for $13.50, two for $10, and ten for $18. The remaining seventy-six cases required some negotiation. Eight women worked out installment payments and were released. Sixty-eight times women either served the full jail sentence, served some time and promised to leave town if released, or paid a portion of the fine and served the remainder. These fines varied from $10 to $116, but the usual

assessment was $18.[17] Almost 86 percent of the cases in Cheyenne for
that period involved prostitutes who were unable to pay a court fine
outright. Of those who could, none had to produce more than $18. This
should hardly have startled Cheyenne authorities, for their police register pointed to the poverty of local prostitutes.

In a two-year period the Cheyenne police register listed 156 women
before the authorities, among them the infamous Ella "Cattle Kate" Watson.[18] The total amount of property taken from the women at the time of
arrest included one satchel, two watches, one pipe, three knives, and
$27.05. The money came from three women: one had $23, one had
$3.95, and one had fifteen cents.[19] Six women surrendered property
when arrested by the Cheyenne police; the remaining 150 had neither
money nor valuables with them. Hardly an affluent group, the Cheyenne
prostitutes could barely keep up with the civil fines. Authorities, faced
with widespread destitution among prostitutes, devised a credit system
so that the jail facilities would not be overburdened with convicted
women who had no option but to sit out a court sentence.

Clearly prostitutes had little or no available cash. Their material goods
could only be described as negligible. Their poverty-stricken condition
at the time of arrest and their inability to pay basic community expenses
attested to their low economic status. Added to that, relegation to the
shanties and shacks at the outskirts of each community completed their
image of squalor.

Based more on situation than on structured rates, the actual income
prostitutes realized from the performance of sexual services varied. The
amount seemed to center on the skill with which a prostitute could separate a customer from as much money as possible. Extra income came
from the sale of beer and wine at inflated prices and from the theft of
customers' money and possessions. The haggling session with a potential customer over expenses needed to be conducted in an atmosphere
of confusion and misunderstanding. In this manner prostitutes claimed
total innocence when confronted with charges of thievery.

These ingredients all influenced an encounter between customer Asa
Williams and prostitute Catarina Gallejo in an 1871 Tucson case.[20] Witnesses testified that Williams had been drinking when Catarina approached him. Williams claimed that he agreed to pay the women $1,
but when he awakened in her room he discovered she had relieved him
of all his funds, a total of $8. When he accused her of the theft, he said,

she quickly admitted it and told him she intended to return his money. The testimony of the prostitute differed from Asa Williams's version. She countered with information that ". . . she asked the Complainant for two dollars and he said he would give it to her if he could lay with her. . . ."[21] Catarina adjourned to her room, and in a few moments Williams joined her there. Now the stories parted, but Catarina Gallejo, obviously experienced in these encounters, anticipated the possible court charges and tried to establish an alibi. She testified, "I then told him if he would pay me seven dollars he could stop with me, he gave me the seven dollars; I then told Gertrude Lagona about he having given me the 7 dollars so that he could not talk about it."[22] The prostitute companion did testify about the episode but pleaded ignorance about the money transactions. Nonetheless, on this occasion the court decision favored the prostitute and dismissed the charges of petit larceny. Catarina Gallejo's techniques typified the manner in which prostitutes schemed to secure the highest possible price from parsimonious customers and to avoid legal prosecution.

Some prostitutes scored more adeptly and walked off with more impressive monetary prizes. In 1879 a prostitute at Sallie Daggett's house in Austin managed to divert a substantial sum from handyman B. F. Young, sent to Austin by his employer for groceries and farm equipment. Dora, the Daggett employee, received about $100 of the cash and another $60 Young had invested in the purchase of beer and wine during a two-day spree.[23] Dora and Sallie hauled in a flurry of cash, but Young wound up in the custody of the marshal. He might have been consoled had he realized that he was only one of many to feel the sting at Sallie's. When a visiting Canadian accused another of Sallie's employees, Duckie Belcher, of taking his $65, the Daggett woman calmly testified that the stranger was drunk, spent the money, and forgot it. The court agreed and dismissed the charges.[24]

These chances proved few for those prostitutes not attached to a slick operation like Sallie Daggett's. With few patrons of wealth, prostitutes resorted to daily petty thievery to improve their income. Sleeping and drunken customers, easy prey for watchful prostitutes, often complained about missing money and jewelry. The police expressed only mild interest in these capers, somewhat convinced that customers got what they deserved in brothels. Most of the police reports listed small amounts of money or trivial articles stolen. One customer told Austin police he thought a "girl at Jessie Mead's" might have taken his watch.[25] Another claimed that Martha Johnson, a black prostitute, stole $25 from his person.[26] Blanch Dumont's Austin house was the scene of a $12 robbery. When police recovered this customer's items, they found $8 of his money, one pocket book, one knife, one necktie, one card case, and one memo book.[27] The three prostitutes involved in that theft had not added much to their income. Once in a while the prostitutes tried for a major theft, but as soon as the authorities confronted them, the goods were returned and the case dismissed. Prostitutes Fannie Kelly and Frankie Howard of Austin succeeded in plying a young customer with drinks and then lifting his wallet with $480. As soon as the police arrived at Fannie Kelly's house, the two women made a search of the premises and found the missing wallet under a bed.[28]

These thieveries helped to inflate poor salaries, or enlarge one's assortment of treasures. Stealing provided the easiest and most direct method for doing that. Customers brought what prostitutes did not have—money—and the women were willing to use any method to get the cash and goods they needed and wanted. Also, thievery within a brothel had a certain vague quality about it that protected prostitutes from prosecution. The Fannie Kellys and Frankie Howards quickly learned how to "find" items that customers "lost."

Beyond this, thievery gave prostitutes a chance to express their unpleasant feelings about customers. The objects of abuse and poor pay at the hands of the customers, prostitutes had in thievery the opportunity to retaliate. For once prostitutes directed the events and found subtle ways to place distasteful customers in a foolish situation. If successful, the laugh was on the customer; if the scam failed, it could be shrugged off as the women waited for the next unobservant male. The absence of respect among those associated with prostitution crystallized in the thefts the women perpetrated against customers. Further, the prevalence of stealing illustrated yet one more destructive dimension within the institution.

The problems of low and sporadic income became more burdensome when prostitutes faced their expenses. Fare for travel and the purchase of shoddy finery, the two most common direct costs, helped to keep savings low. Other professional expenses—exorbitant rents, percentage payments to pimps and landlords, and bribes to police officials, as well as the unending round of civic fines—sapped the limited resources of prostitutes. The systematic recording of expenditures did not comprise one of the elements of prostitution so that personal financial accounts barely existed. On rare occasions society wanted to know about the financial details of the profession, and, when questioned, prostitutes revealed a dismal economic picture.

In Wichita, Kansas, an 1887 grand jury investigation probed the operational procedures of the almost 300 prostitutes in that community. When summoned to testify, Wichita prostitutes explained how a financial web prevented them from accumulating substantial profit. The working arrangements for these women quickly funneled their earnings into the hands of pimps and brothel owners and left the prostitutes only small sums for their living expenses.[29]

The system in Wichita involved a network of hotels and boardinghouses known to rent rooms to prostitutes. Often the women lived in a different location and came to work by hack. In her private residence a prostitute paid $3 to $5 a week for room and board, but rooms rented for prostitution cost her $14 a week. Profits went to the clerks, hotel managers, hack drivers, and madams. The direct testimony of prostitute Millie Wright explained the process of getting established in the Wichita operation: "I told the clerk what I wanted the room for. Told him I wanted it to accommodate men there to make money of. He said that it was all right. . . . Besides the board, I gave them, i.e. the house, one third of what I made. . . ."[30] If the hotel also rented to male guests, they charged the men $6 a week board, $8 less than prostitutes had to pay. If a male guest asked to be accommodated with a woman for the night, then his hotel bill soared to $5 to $7 for a night. In addition, the house made money off the sale of liquor and gaming tables. If a madam succeeded in renting an entire building, she then sublet her rooms to prostitutes at the same rate as the hotels, $14 a week. The madam could expect to pay $75 to $200 a month for her building, although if the same dwelling had been used for legitimate business, the owner could only have commanded a rental of $25 a month.

As for the individual prostitute in this scenario, her pocketbook remained slim. The network of persons to be paid would have discouraged customers from dispensing any regular largesse to the prostitutes. In one transaction prostitute Myrtle Rapp testified, ". . . Was shown to a room by a hack driver, and an old man. Do not know the name of the man who slept with me. When I came into the room he was sitting on the edge of the bed. The old man and the Hack driver went to the room with me. Man paid hack driver $5 for bringing me there."[31]

Out of this sordid scene, the return of a $5 fee would have been remarkable. The customer had already invested at least $10 and perhaps more for his evening with Myrtle Rapp. Add to that the expense of liquor, or a session at the gaming table, and the prostitute could expect only a small gratuity for her services. The testimony of some prostitutes that they handed back fifty cents to $2 to the night clerk indicated they earned only $5 or less. Based on the standard practice of one customer per evening at a fee of $5, all of Wichita's 300 prostitutes would have had to work every night to earn just over $30 a week. Improbable as that was, had it occurred, about $19 of the $30 had to be immediately channeled into living and working accommodations. With over 60 percent of their income poured into housing, Wichita prostitutes routinely turned their wages back into the profession to maintain a place for themselves in the brothel system.[32]

Prostitutes in other towns felt the strain of costly overhead and low income as well. In Boise, Idaho, prostitutes Jean Gorden, Nona Dee, May Bradbury, and Agnes Bush all testified to a grand jury panel about the economics of prostitution in that community. In that city a brothel remained open only upon the payment of a mandatory $30 fee at the police station each month. Rents paid to Boise landlords ranged from $75 to $100 a month. To offset these expenditures, and other contributions to public officials, madams relied on a flourishing liquor business in the brothel, the rent the prostitutes paid for room and board, and probably a percentage of the house earnings. Madams rented rooms in houses for $9 to $15 a week, and kept from four to fourteen prostitutes.[33]

Agnes Bush, the most successful among the madams, ran a business that included both a parlor house and shacks called cribs in her back alley. Prostitutes who resided in the house paid $20 a month for room and board, but those in the cribs paid $48 to $60 a month for rent. Bush controlled twelve cribs, for which she paid a total rent of $275 a month.[34] For the poorest housing for prostitutes Agnes Bush had to pay more than twice the rent on parlor houses. In return for being allowed to live in these squalid shacks, crib women, removed from the protection of the house, paid three and four times the rental of their more prestigious colleagues. As a common progression of a prostitute's career saw her descend from brothel to crib with income appreciably lowered and expenses greatly increased, occupational prospects for prostitutes appeared discouraging.

Regardless of whether a woman worked as a madam, a resident boarder, or a crib prostitute, business expenses depleted earnings. Police authorities, landlords, and pimps all extracted a handsome share from the operational costs of prostitutes. Black market prices inflicted one more societal penalty upon the women. The surrounding social order, while articulate in its opposition to prostitution, did not hesitate to manipulate the system for its own profit. Despite the superficial social, political, and moral objections communities voiced, their economic policies tolerated and supported prostitution, as long as the women workers paid the burdensome price.

Saddled with a gloomy professional existence and subjected to a complex payoff structure, the prostitute's career became one of sordidness and corruption. The combination of so many powerful negative forces served to produce a population of women notable for the coarseness and violence of their lives. Their interaction with customers sank to the lowest levels of depravity. The grasping nature of their economic interests, and the incipient suspicion with which customers and prostitutes viewed one another, reduced the possibilities for ennobling social and sexual relationships. The added anxieties of dislocated frontier people intensified the negative qualities central to prostitute/customer relations and brought forth an unprecedented explosion of disastrous human encounters. As a result, violence and crime dominated the social contacts of prostitutes with customers.

Fighting, drunkenness, and mayhem filled the air of the brothel. Even the most ordinary customer might unexpectedly turn on a prostitute, or some hapless inmate could get caught in the cross fire of feuding customers. The most routine encounters unpredictably erupted into scenes of murder or maiming. A quarrel over a woman caused two men to fire at each other in a dance hall.[35] In Deadwood, the paper complained about the numbers of women appearing bruised and blackened in the dance halls.[36] In Austin between January 24, 1876, and January 21, 1878, eight men came into court on charges of assaulting prostitutes.[37] In Tucson in less than four months, seven cases of physical abuse of prostitutes by customers came to the docket.[38] The women held their own in these attacks, and they too appeared in court on charges of assaulting companions. In Butte, a Park Street woman bashed a customer in the head with a beer glass.[39] In Cheyenne Frankie Lester fired her gun at two Fort Russell soldiers who caused a disturbance in her saloon.[40]

When not the object of a customer's attack, prostitutes frequently participated in the criminal activities of male associates. In Idaho Fannie Clark and Scottie Donnelly got mixed up in a murder committed by three male customers.[41] In Denver seventeen-year-old prostitute Maggie Moss assisted her paramour of three years in an armed robbery.[42] Only a year earlier in Denver, Belle Warden, a black madam, and her employee Mattie Lemmon went to the penitentiary for assisting two men in slitting the throat of a customer.[43]

The social behavior of persons participating in prostitution ranked among the most disruptive and vile on the frontier. A frontier setting and the basic ingredients in prostitution were not conducive to the production of genteel decorum. The corrosive, degrading experiences of the women wore away the most desirable human qualities and often produced hardened, embittered personalities. Only those who could absorb the elements of the institution into their own being could survive. The legions of prostitutes in the West did not march to a gentle drummer; rather, they caroused across the frontier. Their profession did not sanctify them; it robbed them of any opportunities for positive personal development. Cyrus Shores, jack-of-all-trades marshal from Colorado, had seen enough frontier life to be shocked by little, but he expressed his own distate for the rough, uncouth world of prostitution in his description of an 1868 scene outside Laramie. He wrote: "We stopped at Laramie, still camping across the river. The weather was warm and I remember one day dance house women of all kinds came across the river on the bridge, all stripped, and two rough men with them, and they all went in swimming together in front of our camp. Some of the women were big old fat women. I thought at that time it was the worst sight I had ever seen."[44] Shores's life went on to include many wretched scenes, but never any that seemed to repel him as much as this one at the river.

Communities could not be ignorant of the poverty-stricken lives prostitutes lived. As social institutions struggled toward stability, they had to respond to the presence of prostitution in frontier towns. The ways that society responded to the blatant misery of these women contributed to the continued economic and social deprivations of prostitutes. The political, legal, and military establishments developed conventions for prostitution that influenced the direction of frontier society; they found reinforcement for their policies in the public press. The practices these groups devised for the management of prostitution merit separate consideration and will be discussed in other chapters.

Apart from the political, legal, and military establishments, social agencies in frontier towns remained few in number. The unusual circumstances of town-building and the structure of welfare agencies in the nineteenth century did not produce the sophisticated assistance organizations found in more recent times. No unemployment offices, welfare programs, or medical assistance addressed the social ills in frontier communities. Without such agencies, communities needed other institutions for the management of local social and economic problems.

On the frontier that institution with the best opportunity to work for the improvement of prostitutes' lives was the frontier church. Churches, regulated by systematized moral standards, seemed to be the natural agency to respond to the particular needs of prostitutes. The images of comfort and forgiveness that spring from spiritual concepts made local church groups appear to be the likely places for prostitutes to turn for relief. But the churches, influenced by nineteenth-century sexual values and a belief in the basic desirability of family life, failed to provide a practical haven for prostitutes.[45] Reverend Joseph Cook, that first Episcopalian minister to Cheyenne, registered shock at the widespread vice in that community and passed his time with the families of the officers at Fort Russell.[46] He was not singular. Churches tried to bring order and breathed a sigh of relief when they endured the rough frontier days without their spiritual communities weakened by the more rolicking citizens.

When a spirit of charity, misguided or not, did surface among those who professed a desire to act out of Christian motives, cooler heads urged caution. In 1871 a group of women in Denver wished to form a Christian organization to offer the same hand of redemption to prostitutes that men who frequented brothels found extended to them. The women's program included the opportunity for employment and residence with families that would provide loving care for the prostitutes. Flawed though the ideas might appear, they did represent a practical concern for the fate of the Denver prostitutes. A horrified *Daily Rocky*

Mountain News published two lengthy editorials in an effort to squelch the plan. The editor proposed sending repentent prostitutes to asylums because the presence of prostitutes in homes threatened to destroy the virtue of all women.[47] The paper triumphed. Little organized help came to the Denver prostitutes, and by 1877 the respectable ladies of Denver bombarded the city council with petitions to close the houses of prostitution.[48]

In addition to the distaste various religious representatives felt for prostitution, another hindrance to the establishment of effective aid programs was found in the personnel assigned to frontier congregations. In some instances, clergymen themselves got caught up in the frenzy of the frontier and failed to maintain the rigid moral standard expected of them. The Reverend A. R. Mosher wrote of morals in Denver, "I visited a house where a woman made very severe attacks on the Methodist and Presbyterian churches . . . saying she came here a virtuous woman . . . and that the church or churches . . . had made what she was—a fast woman. . . ."[49] Reverend Mosher, himself faced with a morals charge, did not explain how the churches corrupted this woman but only argued that other frontier religious leaders had led some women astray. Other ministers withstood the personal temptations but noted that among the cloth some yielded to the allure of looseness. In 1871 Henry Clay Waltz, itinerant Methodist preacher, recorded in his journal, "Took tea at Mr. Blakes's where are two flashing demoiselles—Mrs. Smith (a Meth.) whose husband is in the penitentiary for shooting through jealousy—and a Miss Collins. Am sorry rumors have fallen on Bro. Fox of undue and criminal intimacy with Mrs. Smith—a vain, fascinating, frizzly little body."[50]

Reverend Waltz appeared to understand some of the forces that captivated Brother Fox, but the unfortunate fact remained that religious agencies simply did not provide well–formed programs to assist prostitutes. Too often predicated on a condescending concern for the moral redemption of the woman, nineteenth-century churches failed to move beyond this concept to the practical problems prostitutes faced if they tried to enter the mainstream of society. A new career as a dressmaker or laundress with prayers and hymns attached did not alter the existing economic and social structure of prostitutes' lives. Success for these redemption programs rested entirely upon their spiritual appeal and did not provide avenues for escaping the stigma attached to identification as an ex-prostitute. Religions geared to the general populace had no adequate provisions for the assimilation of the "morally tainted."

Only a religious program that offered removal from prostitution by the substitution of another environment could hope to succeed. If a religious agency wanted a spiritual transformation of prostitutes, then a total replacement for the existing life had to be offered. Such an agency arrived on the frontier in 1868 when the Sisters of the Good Shepherd came to St. Paul, Minnesota.[51] Unlike other religious missions sent to the frontier for the benefit of far-flung church members, the Sisters of the Good Shepherd, professed nuns of the Roman Catholic Church, devoted themselves exclusively to the needs of homeless, wayward, and criminal girls and women. They did not confine their efforts to Catholic women, nor did it matter how many times a woman returned to them for refuge. Their methods marked the Good Shepherd nuns as an unusual religious group on the frontier.

The Sisters developed a two-part program in St. Paul. One segment they devoted to children from unhappy home situations. This work, entitled the Preservation Program, was kept totally separate from their second endeavor, the Penitent Program for prostitutes. By 1877 one hundred prostitutes lived with the Sisters in the Penitent Program.[52] Many of the prostitutes arrived at the convent by court order, but some young women were committed by family members. When a court sentence ended, the prostitute was free to leave but could, if she desired, return to the House of the Good Shepherd of her own volition.[53]

Inevitably, some women responded to the drastically changed surroundings. At the House of the Good Shepherd a reversal in the daily life of the prostitute came about: order replaced disorder, routine offset bedlam, and civility supplanted abuse. Faced with this more harmonious environment, some prostitutes chose not to return to the mayhem they had experienced in the streets, yet church law did not include a place for prostitutes within religious communities; none accepted women with criminal backgrounds. To circumvent these ecclesiastical restrictions and still accommodate prostitutes who did not wish to reenter brothels, the Good Shepherd Sisters offered two options.

The first of these was an organization of women called the Consecrates. These women did not take solemn religious vows but each year pronounced their dedication to the Mother of Sorrows. They dressed in plain black clothes, recited the Little Office of Our Lady of Dolors each day, and helped with the chores at the House. Assigned a semi-religious status, such a woman was not bound by the strict law of the cloister, and her departure from the House could be easily arranged.[54]

The second choice allowed for a total withdrawal from society and provided for those who desired to profess religious vows. This, the Order of Saint Mary Magdalen, a special church-sanctioned, religious community for criminal women, gave prostitutes the alternative life needed for extrication from the profession. These nuns, a strictly cloistered, contemplative order, lived within the Good Shepherd convent, entirely removed from the outside world. The Sisters of the Good Shepherd managed the secular needs or contacts for the Magdalens. A convent of this branch order opened at St. Paul in January 1878.

To an observer the entire situation appeared inconsistent and impossible. How could a prostitute of coarse, sexual raucousness submit to the life of silent, chaste discipline? If spiritual motivations, which were personal and private, were removed from the equation, more similarities existed than were first evident. A prostitute entered the Magdalens and exchanged an isolated, rigidly circumscribed life among women of unusual dress and demeanor for exactly the same characteristics. The physical deprivation and daily routine found in convent life differed only in kind from that of prostitutes' lives. In a literal manner, prostitutes and nuns lived as the sexual outcasts of society, but one group lived with unmitigated censure and one with general approval. Prostitutes flaunted their sexuality in society, while nuns withdrew theirs. Nonetheless, while they pursued opposing earthly goals, both groups lived at the outermost rim of society.

Obviously many common features, not so divergent as they first appeared, called prostitutes to follow a life of strict contemplation. The tangible changes introduced to their lives, in addition to individual spiritual commitments, came from a stability and security seldom found among prostitutes. Convent life brought an end to physical and sexual mistreatment from customers. In addition, Magdalens found a niche in life where they could live without sanctimonious condescension from associates who had never participated in prostitution. Other Magdalens, retreating from identical experiences, cast no stones; among the Magdalens' protectors, the Good Shepherd Sisters, no apologies were necessary. For prostitutes who understood all too well that the end of the road came quickly, a life of cloistered security presented an option.

Yet the nature of the option itself further indicated the disastrous circumstances of prostitutes. The women faced a choice of one extreme or the other. The ordinary experiences of life and social interaction were denied prostitutes who wanted to leave that occupation. One of the few avenues open demanded the adoption of another extreme form of daily existence. At least some common characteristics between the two institutions—brothels and convents—paved the way for prostitutes who wished to avoid the former life. The number of prostitutes who altered their lives by the adoption of a new system of rules always stayed minimal in the total prostitute population. Over a twenty-year period perhaps fewer than forty of the sixty-seven women receiving the Magdalens' habit at the St. Paul, Minnesota, convent remained until death.[55] Still, the Sisters of the Good Shepherd stood as a singular agency on the frontier for their attempts to provide prostitutes with an alternate life either through education, occupational training, or convent life. That some prostitutes made this transition weakens the notion that these women were all passive victims. The circumstances of their lives made significant change difficult, but possible in some few situations.

In the large picture, most prostitutes never encountered the Good Shepherd nuns, and their lives tumbled forward without any social agencies to assist them. Rejected or ignored by the social and political agencies of society, prostitutes, mired in their own turmoil, followed the predictable road of alcoholism, drug addiction, and suicide. With few supportive institutions in society, many prostitutes, confronted with the jaded realities and grim expectations of their lives, sank rapidly into all forms of dissipation.

Alcoholism and drug addiction went hand in hand in prostitutes' lives. Court dockets and newspaper accounts noted repeatedly the drunken condition of prostitutes.[56] In most towns a prostitute like Belle Williams of Cheyenne appeared with such regularity on charges of drunkenness that her intense alcoholic problem could hardly be ignored.[57] Other prostitutes racked up drunk and disorderly charges along with the usual assault and offensive language charges. Where one stopped and the other began, even the authorities probably did not know.

In death, the extent to which liquor and drugs dominated the lives of prostitutes became clear. The accounts of these ran like a litany of destroyed youth. In Denver Ada Vernon committed suicide by taking morphine, and the paper mourned, "Deceased was 29 years of age and of rather attractive person."[58] In Butte Inez Maybert, after several days of heavy drinking, died from an overdose of morphine. Also in Butte, "Big Lil" made an unsucessful attempt with morphine, while only four months earlier in the same town, Florence Bentley perished from the same drug.[59] In Lewis, Montana, Polly Cunningham "suicided" with strychnine.[60]

From Dennison, Mobeetie, Laramie, Cheyenne, Denver, and San Antonio came the dreary reports.[61] Not once, not twice did the reports circulate, but over and over. Suicide emerged as the most commonly employed means to retire from prostitution. Women fell into comas, breathed their last heavy sighs; town doctors, seldom consulted until any chance of recovery had passed, appeared and jotted down the same sad story: "Sallie Talbot. Age 21 years. About 8:15 P.M. Found, bottle with . . . Laudanum. . . . Failure of respiration about 10 P.M. . . . Died at 12:10."[62] Sallie Talbot's death in 1883 was but one among the prostitutes in Cheyenne. Three years earlier Mrs. E. A. Ingalls, a new prostitute to that community, committed suicide by taking an overdose of chloroform.[63] In 1887 prostitute Kate Scriber, "addicted to the excessive use of alcoholic liquors, as well as opium in its different preparations," died, according to the examining physician, from "chronic alcoholism and dissipation in its various forms. . . ."[64] In Laramie the scenes repeated themselves with at least annual regularity. In 1874 Ada Hart died from a generous dose of laudanum in whiskey and soda.[65] In 1875 Dora Mahr followed Ada Hart to the grave by taking an overdose of morphine.[66] Only a year later Ellen Dougherty succumbed to the effects of the excessive use of alcohol and associated illnesses.[67]

When these accounts of personal destruction were added to the high instances of violence and death as a result of working conditions, the full physical and emotional hazards of the profession took shape. A realistic prostitute anticipated that her life would bring her an erratic income but high professional expenses. Encounters with customers, based on mutual distrust, would enlarge the sphere of personal disorder and physical risk that she experienced. With few amenities in either her personal or professional life, the prostitute who turned to societal agencies for assistance faced disappointment. Frontier communities lacked well-formed institutions for social care. Churches, the frontier organizations with the potential to help prostitutes, did not construct practical programs of help. Instead, the churches tried half-heartedly to mix "rescued" prostitutes with the rest of the congregation. The Sisters of the Good Shepherd established programs that reversed the prostitutes' environment, but their solutions touched only a small number of prostitutes. Most such women stumbled through life without any constructive social or economic aid from the agencies of society. In their desperation, prostitutes depended upon the balm found in alcohol and drug addiction. If all else failed, suicide proved the most effective exit from prostitution. Dreary and taxing, the lives without comfort.

Notes

1. *Ouray* (Colo.) *Solid Muldoon*, Apr. 12, 1889.
2. Some groups of men did not frequent the brothels, or at least not openly. No Oriental males appeared in any of the surveyed dockets. Mexican men appeared only in dockets for New Mexico. Blacks often worked in brothels as cooks and servants. As customers they patronized the black brothels, such as those in San Antonio and Cheyenne. This behavior became prevalent after the formation of the Buffalo Soldiers at the end of the Civil War. Indian males were not welcome. When a prostitute shot and killed a drunken Indian who stumbled into her room, she received an immediate acquittal. C. C. Rister Papers, "Frontier Life and Experiences," Book 1, p. 343, SC.
3. Caroline Bancroft's *Six Racy Madams of Colorado* is a popular history of the most prominent nineteenth-century madams in Denver. The content, told as an engrossing story, cannot disguise the brutality and disorder even in Denver's "nicest" houses (Boulder, Colo.: Johnson, 1965).
4. Marriage records for prostitutes remained one of the most difficult areas to identify as only limited marriage records for civil ceremonies exist. Between 1866 and 1870 fifty-two women appeared before the justice of the peace in Arapaho County, Colo., for marriage ceremonies. As the record only lists the names of the bride and groom, it is impossible to make judgements about which women were prostitutes. Of those listed, one appeared to be a probable case because she came to the ceremony with three female witnesses. This can only be speculation. Justice

of the Peace Dockets, Arapaho County, Civil and Criminal Cases, Aug. 1866-Dec. 1869, CSA.

5. H. C. Cornwall Papers, "The Gunnison County," 1879–86, pp. 17–26, WHC.

6. Ibid., p. 26.

7. A guide to the kinds of women chosen by men of education and wealth can be found in the society columns of frontier newspapers. During the 1870s both the *Butte Miner* and the *Cheyenne Daily Sun* gave ample testimony to the elaborate celebration surrounding the marriages of professional men and military officers. The tone of these marriage items differed markedly from the report of the marriage of two Orientals joined in wedlock at the Ferguson Street brothel of Cheyenne madam Julia McGuinn. Despite the attendance of two police court justices, the article's mocking humor pointedly showed social scorn. *Cheyenne Daily Sun*, Apr. 27, 1876.

8. *Ouray* (Colo.) *Solid Muldoon*, Apr. 12, 1889.

9. *Daily Democractic Statesman*, June 8, 1880.

10. P. A. Spengler, Letter, July 18, 1869, WHC.

11. Ibid.

12. H. C. Cornwall Papers, "The Gunnison Country," 1879–86, p. 25, WHC.

13. C. C. Rister Papers, "Frontier Life and Experiences," Book 1, Recollection and Experiences of Frontier Life As Told by Henry Heron to J. R. Webb, July 17, 1940, p. 1, SC.

14. Jessica Moorehead Young, "Biography of Parents' Pioneer Days," WPA Interviews Collection, PPHM.

15. This subject is treated in Harry Wynne, "Recollections of Fort Worth," Oral History tapes as told to Sandra Myres, June 1969, SC; Harry Ingerton, Memoirs told to J. E. Haley, Apr. 13, 1927, PPHM; *Abilene Chronicle*, Sept. 8, 1870.

16. Record of Prisoners, Sept. 14-Dec. 27, 1884, ATCC.

17. Jail Register, City of Cheyenne, Mar. 2, 1887–Jan. 1890, WSAHD.

18. Police Register, City of Cheyenne, Jan. 1, 1888–Jan. 20, 1890, June 23, 1888, WSAHD. "Cattle Kate" Watson and her partner, Jim Averill, were lynched during the Johnson County War in 1888.

19. Ibid.

20. Details of this case are taken from the records of Justice of the Peace Charles H. Meyers, Jan. 1, 1871–July 25, 1873; see testimony presented Dec. 30, 1871, AHS.

21. Ibid.

22. Ibid.

23. Austin Police Calls, 1879–80, p. 51, ATCC.

24. *Daily Democratic Statesman*, Oct. 5, 1882.

25. Austin Police Calls, 1879–80, Mar. 19, 1879, p. 16, ATCC.

26. Ibid., July 19, 1880.

27. Ibid., Aug. 16, 1879, p. 39.

28. *Daily Democratic Statesman*, Aug. 19, 1880. For a fascinating account of how prostitutes conspired to rob customers in the Denver cribs see Richard Symanski, *The Immoral Landscape* (Toronto: Butterworth, 1981), pp. 56–57.

29. The testimony of this grand jury investigation never became public. The documents were hidden for some years and when found in an attic were deposited with the Kansas State Historical Society. The testimony involved numerous witnesses and the generalizations here are drawn from the testimony given throughout the probe. General Testimony, Wichita Grand Jury Investigation, 1887 (?), 1888, KSHS.

30. Ibid., Testimony of Millie Wright, Jan. 11, 1888.

31. Ibid., Testimony of Myrtle Rapp, Jan. 11, 1888.

32. Ibid.; see the testimony of Ella Jackson, Jan. 9, 1888, and those of Myrtle Rapp, Bessie Jones, Millie Wright, Maud Wilson, Lillie Barnes, and Lou Dawson, Jan. 11, 1888.

33. Minutes of the Grand Jury empaneled Dec. 23, 1908, IHS. This inquiry was conducted in 1908, after the dates of this study, but the scope of the testimony touched on the activities of the vice community in Boise for more than twenty years. For the testimony of these prostitutes, see Jan. 5, 1909, pp. 51–53.

34. Ibid., p. 52.

35. *Butte Miner*, Sept. 10, 1879.

36. *Black Hills Daily Times*, Sept. 5, 1877.

37. Austin Records of Arrest, Jan. 1, 1876–Jan. 1, 1879, passim, ATCC.

38. Justice Docket for Pima County, City of Tucson, 1889–1890; see July 23 and 29, Sept. 6, Oct. 14, 1889, ADL.

39. *Butte Miner*, Sept. 2, 1880.

40. *Cheyenne Daily Sun*, Feb. 21, 1878.

41. *Butte Miner*, Mar. 22, 1888.

42. Sam Howe Scrapbook, Case of Maggie Moss, Apr. 24, 1885, CHS.

43. Ibid., cases of Belle Warden and Mattie Lemmon.

44. Cyrus W. Shores Papers, #42, "Helping Build Union Pacific Railroad," p. 2, WHC.

45. Clergymen, as well as lawyers, physicians, and politicians, emphasized the domestic values found in matrimony and reiterated the dangers lurking outside the sanctity of the home. See Charlotte Perkins

Gilman, *The Home: Its Work and Influence* (n.p.: McClure, Phillips, 1903; reprint ed., Urbana: University of Illinois Press, 1972), pp. 252–71; Aileen S. Kraditor, ed., *Up From the Pedestal: Selected Writings in the History of American Feminism* (Chicago: Quadrangle Books, 1968), pp. 189–203; John S. Haller and Robin M. Haller, *The Physician and Sexuality in Victorian America* (New York: W. W. Norton, 1974), pp. 32–36.

46. Reverend Joseph Cook, *Diary and Letters* (Laramie, Wyo.: Laramie Republican, 1919), pp. 11–15, 45–59.

47. *Daily Rocky Mountain News*, Sept. 10, 17, 1871.

48. Ibid., Mar. 16, 1877.

49. Ibid., Oct. 7, 1867.

50. Journal of Methodist Itinerant Henry Clay Waltz, Aug. 7, 1871, UW.

51. John Edward Forliti, "The First Thirty Years of the Home of the Good Shepherd: 1868–1898," (unpublished Master's thesis: Saint Paul Seminary, 1962), pp. 9–11. See also Sister Mary of the Annunciation Tafelska, "Annals of the Sisters of Our Lady of Charity of the Good Shepherd of Angers" (unpublished and undocumented history of the St. Paul convent). This account was written by one of the Sisters and appears to be drawn both from her own memory and the traditional tales told by the Sisters about the early years. It is not in any way a scholarly document, but it does provide information from the Sisters' point of view. The arrival in St. Paul is treated in pages 1–3 of Chapter 1.

52. Sister Mary of the Annunciation, "Annals," Chapter 3, p. 23.

53. Of the first 1,000 committed to the Sisters' reform program, 40 percent were committed to the House of the Good Shepherd by the courts. In addition, the St. Paul courts sent women from the city workhouse to special quarters in the House for periods of ten to ninety days. Forliti, pp. 54–55.

54. Forliti, pp. 60–62.

55. According to Forliti sixty-seven women received the habit of the Magdalens at St. Paul between the years 1878 and 1898. Of these, thirty-eight professed their vows and remained with the Magdalens until death. Forliti comments on the scant information about these sisters. The very nature of their community has made the publication of information undesirable to them. Once they withdrew from the world, Magdalen Sisters were very carefully protected by the Good Shepherd Sisters. Forliti's information is found on pp. 61–65. According to Sister Rosemary, RGS, in modern times the Magdalens have changed their name to Sisters of the Holy Cross. Today they number fewer than 200 and count among their sisters women who entered without first having

been assisted in one of the Good Shepherd houses. Sister Rosemary, R.G.S., letter to author, Mar. 16, 1979.

56. For figures on arrest for drunk and disorderly charges, see Chapter 2.

57. *Cheyenne Daily Sun*, Dec. 8, 1877, Feb. 6, 1878, Feb. 16, June 3, 1882.

58. George Watrous Scrapbook, p. 23, WHC.

59. *Butte Miner*, Nov. 11, 1881, May 26, Feb. 20, 1880.

60. Ibid., Nov. 5, 1881.

61. *St. Jo Daily Times*, June 9, 1883; Jessica M. Young, "Biography of Parents' Pioneer Days," WPA Interview File, PPHM; *Laramie Daily Sentinel*, May 4, June 17, 1871; *Daily Rocky Mountain News*, Aug. 14, 1880, Apr. 11, June 7, 1882, Aug. 18, 1885; *Wyoming Tribune*, Dec. 25, 1869; Coroners' Reports, Mar. 17, 1880, May 11, May 29, 1889, WSAHD; *San Antonio Daily Express*, Feb. 14, 1882.

62. Dr. W. A. Wyman Collection, Physician's Visiting Lists, May 12, 1883, WSAHD.

63. Coroner's Report, Mar. 17, 18, 1880, WSAHD.

64. Coroner's Report, Laramie County, Apr. 20, 1887, WSAHD.

65. Inquest, June 17, 1874, ACCH.

66. Inquest, July 20, 1875, ACCH.

67. Inquest, Sept. 25, 1876, ACCH.

4

Officers of the Law

... When I was County Attorney, and by reason of being her lawyer in the adjustment of several legal matters in which she was involved, I gained her complete confidence and learned much about her early life which was known to none ... who were acquainted with her as the owner of the biggest dance hall and bagnio in the Panhandle.[1]

These and other reminiscences from the biography of Judge James D. Hamlin of Texas painted a colorful picture of Amarillo madam Ella Hill. Judge Hamlin remembered his client as an admirable and beautiful woman, endowed with "regular features and a heavy suit of raven hair." Hamlin believed that Madam Hill came from a good family but entered a life of prostitution out of necessity. An early attempt to support herself and her two daughters by waitress work ended in failure. Forced to turn to prostitution to maintain the care of her children, the young mother found she could make a handsome living. Her daughters boarded with a family in Fort Worth and accepted the mother's story that she ran a boarding house in Amarillo. She visited the girls regularly until they were grown and had married well, still ignorant of their mother's profession.

In Amarillo Ella Hill built a reputation for impeccable honesty in the management of her brothel and dance hall. High-rolling ranchers for miles around knew that lives, money, and reputations were secure at Ella's. She was reputed to keep exact accounts of customer expenditures, extract that sum, and return the remainder of a bank roll intact. Drunken ranchers expected that at Ella's they would be fed, cared for, sobered up, and sent home with their possessions and remaining money intact.

According to the judge, Ella Hill did not restrict her quality behavior only to matters of the brothel operation. A local rumor persisted that when Amarillo had no building for a church, Ella Hill made the largest contribution to the construction fund. When traveling preachers passed through Amarillo, Ella Hill required her employees to dress in their best and attend a special Sunday afternoon service. Nor did her concern for the well-being of other prostitutes stop at obligatory church attendance. After her retirement, Ella Hill moved to Wichita, where she operated a hand laundry business that employed only former prostitutes. Upon her death her body was returned to Amarillo for burial. Judge Hamlin noted that only a handful attended the graveside services, he among them. He made no mention of the two successful daughters.[2]

Apocryphal stories such as this one about Ella Hill serve to confuse important details about the experiences of prostitutes on the frontier. Although the judge's account, no doubt, contained some fragments of truth, much of his story rested on Amarillo folklore hearsay, or perhaps on information concocted by Ella Hill herself. The final impact of the judge's recollections was the presentation of yet another madam with a "heart of gold," tragically trapped in an immoral life while trying to attain moral goals. Sentimental though such stories may be, they neglect certain information about the lives of prostitutes. For instance, in Hamlin's account, he played almost no role. He glossed over his own participation in her life in an obscure sentence, and cast himself as an objective raconteur. Somewhere beneath Hamlin's superficial tale lay an explanation about his legal encounters with Ella Hill, both as the county attorney and later as her lawyer. What sort of legal business did Hamlin conduct for Madam Hill? Given their initial contact from opposite sides of the law, what factors influenced the establishment of their business relationship?

The answers to these questions are not to be drawn from the nostalgia of Judge Hamlin, for his recollections, intended to recall a folksy frontier era, bowed to the filter of time and memory, both of which sifted away the harsh or unpleasant. Yet Hamlin's chatty, antiseptic story about Ella Hill pointed to one more overlooked element in frontier prostitution.

The relationships between prostitutes and officers of the law gave foundation to the mechanics of frontier prostitution. Mayors, county judges, prosecuting attorneys, sheriffs, marshals, and justices of the peace actively contributed to the support of prostitution through the use and misuse of public office. As the public agents charged with the development of community order, frontier officials operated in an unusual environment. Frontier communities, located in remote areas far from the traditional systems of restraint, thrust institutional responsibilities upon these officials. Public authorities enjoyed an unusual opportunity both to enlarge the social order and improve their own status. These goals they achieved, at least in part, by the conduct of their relationships with prostitutes and other members of the vice community. Without the peculiar involvement of officials, frontier prostitution could not have existed as it did for the bonanza years.

Not all frontier officials reacted in precisely the same manner to the town prostitutes. Conduct ranged from moral rigidity to professional and personal depravity. Although the latter appeared more common to the frontier experience, both approaches created the same result for prostitutes: their condition remained unchanged. The frontier power structure possessed the autonomy to inflict any control it wished over local prostitutes. If, in addition, judges, marshals, or mayors sought to make a personal gain off the women, no agency prevented their actions. On the contrary, communities happily charged officers of the law with the task of dealing with prostitutes if in exchange citizens could be undisturbed by the sordid realities around them. Frontier officials had free rein to set the tone for the manner in which prostitutes would be treated. Prostitutes responded by accepting this power of public officials, and, where possible, adding sexual and social intimacies to reinforce their liaison with authorities. The conduct of frontier officials helped to perpetuate prostitution, maintain the marginal existence of its employees, and further solidify the negative status of prostitutes in the community.

Public officials contributed to the process of negative relationships in several ways. Ostensibly the opponents of prostitution, municipal authorities cultivated divergent standards about local vice communities. Within each community any one or a combination of attitudes influenced official policy toward prostitution. Civic economic considerations, as well as personal sexual interests, accounted for some public posture, but the opportunity for personal gain underscored the prevailing policy in many communities. Possibilities for personal gain included political advancement, civic promotion, and monetary rewards. Since many officials functioned as both public servant and private businessman, it often became difficult to separate personal advantage from civic need. Frequently community officials exhibited little desire to make any distinction between the personal and the public realms. Rather, the astute understood the maneuvers necessary to keep the two spheres united and readily skimmed off the rewards where they could. Tangled standards and goals produced a frontier authority notable for its lack of consistency and integrity in matters of local prostitution.

The authorities in mining communities offered especially suitable examples of these circumstances. Thrown together in a chaotic urban setting, public officials secured their positions more by chance than ability. No less influenced by the economic frenzy than any other camp residents, those in public office had extra chances for personal advancement. The actual monetary returns from the mines came but to a few, so those with a keen eye quickly understood that the profits rested in the services demanded by the community. Those who promoted and controlled the entertainment districts could expect a handsome return. Such ventures fell naturally into the hands of lawmakers and town officials.

The mayor, city council, and sheriff of Tombstone, Arizona, typified such an establishment. Civic authority rested in the hands of a shady crowd that drifted into Tombstone after the city was founded in 1878. Drawn by the lure of a major silver strike, merchants and businessmen began to open saloons, hotels, and stores. Their success hinged upon the success of the strike. Small wonder that these gentlemen willingly served in public office without remuneration, for their personal interests harmonized perfectly with the civic goals of Tombstone.[3]

John Philip Clum dominated the scene as editor of the *Tombstone Epitaph* and mayor of the city. In 1879 Clum arrived in Tombstone after a three-year stint as agent to the Apache Indians. As editor of the Tombstone paper, Clum quickly emerged as a controversial figure, an ardent town booster, and an active champion of the local mining operation.[4]

When Clum captured the mayor's office in 1881, other prominent businessmen joined him in town government as city councilmen. Typical among them was Godfrey Tribolet. Tribolet owned a local brewery and built the popular Crystal Palace Saloon. Not only did the Crystal

Palace host some of the wildest of Tombstone's residents, but the second floor housed the office of the Tombstone chief of police.[5]

A common home for these civic opposites facilitated municipal efforts to protect all local interests. During the administration of John Clum, the Tombstone government aided an amicable merging of civic and private goals. Both as mayor and as private citizen, Clum understood the dynamics of town government, and he never relented in his promotion of Tombstone as an ideal mining district. With little trouble Clum eased himself into a civic policy based on the merger of public and private responsibilities.[6] During his tenure as the editor/mayor he ignored those civic conditions that might have distracted from the favorable municipal picture he wished to paint. In the pages of Clum's *Tombstone Epitaph* the town appeared only as a productive, folksy community. Prostitution, gambling, crimes of violence—these topics Clum studiously ignored.[7] Despite Clum's apparent desire to avoid a public recognition of Tombstone's disorders, opposition newspapers were not so discreet. One editor noted, "Tombstone has been the scene of very many murders, and its reputation in this line seems to be well maintained."[8] But for Clum, the continued prosperity of Tombstone superseded all other considerations. If toleration of a flourishing community of prostitutes added to the entrepreneurial promise of the town, then the editor/mayor showed himself ready to follow that path.[9]

If Clum expected the city councilmen to support his philosophy, they did not disappoint him. In March 1882 the city council voted to remove restrictions on the locations of brothels.[10] Formerly confined to the saloon district along Allen and Fremont streets, houses of prostitution now had permission to spread throughout the residential sections. The *Tombstone Epitaph* expressed mild sympathy for those in neighborhoods who might now find bordellos lining their streets and noted that the town "plague-spot" ought to be confined to a limited area.[11] Here the editor/mayor acknowledged the concerns of his "respectable" community but in no way suggested that prostitution should be eliminated from the commercial life of the town. Some local citizens, as members of both the residential and commercial interest groups, required double-edged diplomacy from the mayor, but he did not introduce programs to eradicate prostitution.

In addition to the mayor and city council, other public figures added to the questionable conduct of city government. Among these was John

H. Behan, the first sheriff of Tombstone. Not as famous as Wyatt Earp, his rival in an affair of the heart, Behan earned his own place among frontier authorities of uncertain reputation.

Behan came to Tombstone by a circuitous route. He arrived in the Arizona Territory in 1869. With him he brought his new bride, Victoria, whom he married only a month earlier in San Francisco. The Behans settled in Prescott, Arizona, and there a son was born to them in 1871. Only two years later the marriage faltered, and in 1875 Victoria Behan filed for divorce. Her complaint charged that in 1873 Behan "at divers times and places openly and notoriously visited houses of ill-fame and prostitution at said town of Prescott." [12] Although Mrs. Behan charged her husband with the carnal knowledge of several "inmates," she singled out Sada Mansfield, "a woman of prostitution and ill-fame," to be named as corespondent. [13] The scandal in the neighborhood and Behan's constant threats of physical violence and unrelenting verbal abuse led Victoria Behan to seek a divorce with child support, alimony, and division of their common property.

The dissolution of his marriage turned Behan away from Prescott and toward Tombstone, where in 1879 he secured the job of sheriff. His administration of that post proved to be a stormy one. The job of sheriff offered almost unlimited opportunity for the collection of bribes and graft. One of the easiest responsibilities to abuse was the monthly collection of gambling, prostitution, liquor, and theater fees. Freed from any system of checks, a sheriff could slip into the habit of double taxation with little or no trouble. A common technique, one fee was recorded for the public accounts book, and the second quietly went into the sheriff's pocket. Rumor and counter-rumor of such shenanigans surrounded Behan's performance as sheriff. [14]

Added intrigue arose out of a rivalry between Behan and Wyatt Earp, both of whom sought the affections of "actress" Josephine Marcus. Earp won in this love duel, but not before enmity flared between the two men. [15] The loss of Josephine Marcus and an escalating scandal about the misappropriations of county funds finally drove Behan from Tombstone.

Despite his questionable civic record, which included rumors of graft and a public quarrel over a "notorious" woman, Behan added to his clouded reputation, first as the assistant warden and then, between 1883 and 1890, as superintendent of the penitentiary. His administration, characterized by prison disorder and mismanagement of public funds, finally brought a storm of protest from the press. In 1890 the *Arizona Republic* complained that more than $50,000 a year inexplicably passed through the hands of prison officials. The editor argued that less than half that sum should have provided adequate care for the 143 prisoners.[16] The newspaper's concerns seemed reasonable since an 1885 prison report not only heaped praise on Superintendent Behan's administration but also raved about the potential profit due the territory from the work activities of the prisoners.[17] In 1890 Behan faced censure for misuse of civic funds as well as for permitting the prison to be run in a "coarse and brutal manner."

This charge included more than the undisciplined disorderly condition of the male prisoners; it focused specifically on the condition of the single female prisoner, twenty-one-year-old Manuela Fimbres. Convicted with her pimp for the murder of a Chinese male, this young woman, already the mother of an eight-year-old child, began her sentence on March 30, 1889. The prison contained no female ward, and Behan failed to construct even makeshift arrangements for the new inmate. Instead he permitted the woman to roam freely through the prison, accessible to all the males—guards and prisoners. The predictable occurred, and the birth of a son was followed by an immediate second pregnancy. The conditions of institutional mayhem, the ribald attitudes, and the atmosphere of depravity that surrounded these events finally caught the attention of the press and the territorial government. John Behan, replaced by a new superintendent, left to assume yet another position of public trust, inspector of customs.[18]

The symbiotic relationship between frontier law officers and frontier vice dominated the professional life of John Behan for more than twenty years. His career moved forward, despite the implications of malfeasance in at least two public positions. Behan typified those public officials whose experiences in local vice situations showed the possibilities for political advancement, civic promotion, and monetary rewards. Between 1879 and 1890 Behan's civic duties, financial interests, and sexual attitudes mixed with the pattern of his public life.[19]

John Behan's saga, though blatantly seamy, differed only in degree from those of other frontier officials. Some Tombstone leaders emerged with reputations less scathed by the frontier era. Their personal conduct perhaps more circumspect, their historical publicity perhaps more mythcoated, the John Clums, Godfrey Tribolets, and Wyatt Earps

seemed no less willing than Behan to reinforce local vice for the promotion of civic and personal gain.[20] The willingness of public officers to
tolerate or encourage prostitution and other vice served as an essential
ingredient in the maintenance of frontier social disorders. Without the
odd partnership between authorities and the social outcasts, prostitution could never have retained its highly visible characteristics throughout the frontier era.

Yet not all public officials participated quite so openly as did the
Tombstone crowd, many of whom numbered among the most boisterous of frontier types. Other town officials, residents of more diversified
communities, bickered about public policy. Their disagreements and
ambivalence contributed another dimension to the peculiar relationships between authorities and prostitutes. Community leaders often
found they could not concur on a direction for local policy. Civic groups
that might have structured programs for constructive, or at least consistent action, allowed themselves to fall into disputes that sapped political
energies, diverted the attention of the public, and left prostitution
unchanged.

Communities caught in such arguments needed a forum where they
aired their differences. In frontier towns where formalized institutions
lagged behind population growth, local newspapers acted as the voice
of the community and helped to define local issues. As the outspoken
champions of local economic and social progress and the sniping critics
of their political opposition, most newspapers reflected a vigorous interest in community events and filled an institutional void throughout
the frontier. Consequently, frontier journals became the instrument
through which communities expressed their confusions, ambivalences,
and disagreements about prostitution and the local policies that dealt
with it.

Faced with the opportunity to forge a progressive and responsible
policy concerning the horrid conditions under which local prostitutes
lived, frontier presses, almost without exception, failed to accept the
challenge.[21] Instead attitudes of ridicule, scorn, humor, or maudlin sen-
timentality permeated newspaper reports. Newspapers, often staffed by
persons ill trained to discuss social issues, seemed unable to resist the
temptation to present prostitutes as objects of mockery. Only when
death struck among prostitutes did papers shift gears and assume a shallow sympathy for the deceased. If the death occurred after a prostitute

moved away from a town, then the obituary played heavily upon the theme of nostalgia. The ex-resident became a paragon of honesty, despite her lost virtue. Her reputation soared to heights it had never enjoyed during her stay in the community.[22] These mawkish obituaries perhaps served to ease the conscience of reporters who had perfected the skills of cruel humor. More important, these articles, like some reminiscences of frontier diarists, created a false impression that burgeoning communities welcomed prostitutes with equanimity.

Nothing could have been further from the truth, yet even when the press tried to address the social problems surrounding prostitution, it fell short of the mark. The perception that economic need produced a population of prostitutes did not rest easy in communities with little place for women workers in industry, but with plenty of men desiring readily available sexual service. As a result, after an editorial or two, the papers quickly gave way to a recitation of the latest scenes in the police courts and the saloons. Any substantial attempts to awaken the social consciousness of communities did not materialize. Newspapers that might have influenced the alteration of local attitudes or helped to change the direction of economic realities for prostitutes did not do so. They continued to express amusement and horror at the conditions in and around brothels and saloons. From time to time, the press castigated the males who frequented brothels and called for punishment for them also. Occasionally, editorials launched vigorous attacks upon city officials for their failure to eliminate the red-light districts. These flurries, only superficial and of short duration, changed nothing.[23] Generally, as a social agency with a responsibility to encourage the well-being of the community, the frontier press bungled a unique opportunity. It possessed neither the personnel nor motivation to become a social champion.

Newspaper reporters promoted the attitudes of society around them. They could not erase from their own thinking a perception of the prostitute as a woman of lost virtue, somehow disgusting yet intriguing. This underlying sexual concept, more powerful than social or political awareness, permeated the frontier press. It exuded from the articles written about prostitutes and expressed itself in a whole vocabulary reserved for prostitutes. Certain designations—"frail sisters," "fille de Joie," "fair cyprians," "nymphe du pave," "lewd women," "queens of the night," "soiled doves," "abandoned women"—kept the mystique of sexuality more prominent than social and economic ideas. The result was that beneath all the reporting, editorializing, and moralizing, the press acted primarily as a publicity agent for prostitutes. The constant and repetitious presentation of names and addresses, coupled with lurid descriptions, served to keep prostitutes in the public spotlight.[24] The resulting attention focused on prostitutes as symbols of forbidden eroticism and not as needy workers on the frontier.

Nonetheless, despite its shortcomings, the frontier press remained the single best barometer of the various local attitudes directed toward prostitutes. The very discrepancies found in newspapers served to show how easily public officials did as they pleased with vice communities. The press, which often used its journalistic attacks as thinly disguised assaults on political rivals, could complain incessantly, and official conduct never swayed. Ultimately, although an excellent gauge of local forces present in a town, the press remained an ineffective apparatus for social reform.

In 1882 the Austin *Daily Democratic Statesman* took issue with a local state's attorney over the trial of prostitute Addie Mercer. Addie Mercer, a well-known woman of the streets, had an arrest record in Austin that dated to 1880.[25] In 1882 her trial on a charge of prostitution ended with a verdict of not guilty, and the defendant paid a fine of one cent. Such proceedings bordered on the farcical. The state's attorney announced publicly that the trial caused more harm than the crime, the commission of which hardly seemed in doubt. The expensive and ludicrous nature of the court episode did not add to the power or dignity of the office of state's attorney. A writer for the *Daily Democratic Statesman* then became indignant that a public official would even dare to make such an observation.[26] Moral outrage and bureaucratic silliness swirled about while the object of this squabble, Addie Mercer, cleared her debt and returned to the streets of Austin. The press bypassed an opportunity to comment intelligently upon the quality of the local courts, the concerns of the state's attorney, or the message such civic conduct conveyed to prostitutes.

Even when newspaper attacks on prostitution displayed deeper, more long-range social concerns, few changes in public conduct came about. In 1871 the *Daily Rocky Mountain News* noted the injustice of prosecuting Denver prostitutes while pimps and saloon owners received immunity. The editors wondered if the mayor feared to indict the men and questioned the merits of harassing the women through continuous arrests and fines. Such a program, the paper charged, served only to raise revenue for street improvements and ignored the sources of prostitution.[27] The *News* advocated the adoption of regulatory procedures similar to those in St. Louis as the best method of improving city morals.[28]

By November 1872 the paper detected no appreciable alteration in local policy. Events of the holiday season sparked the editor's ire on this occasion. The paper denounced the police practice of raiding brothels only when large groups of festive, holiday celebrants could be snared. The paper cited the arrest of at least a dozen young men apprehended on Thanksgiving Eve as proof of the police tactic. These holiday arrests netted the city treasury $18 per person, a sure sign, according to the press, that the authorities only wanted to enlarge city funds without a thought for the problem at hand. Again, they pointed out, brothel inmates and customers bore the legal and financial repercussions inflicted by the authorities;[29] saloon owners and pimps still suffered no inconvenience.

In April 1873 the Central City, Colorado, paper jumped into the argument. Its attack focused on the culpability of Denver officials. First the paper questioned the ease with which the large, wealthier houses— "The Cricket," "The Corn Exchange," "The Occidental Hall"—operated, while small establishments like the "What Cheer House" endured continued raids and paid repeated fines. The paper clearly implicated Mayor Case and Marshal Smith and charged them with official protection of the major saloons and brothels.[30] If the mayor and marshal felt any sting from the charges, they kept it well hidden and prostitution continued as usual in Denver. The winter of 1874 brought fresh grumblings from the *Denver Daily Times*. "The brass band making a discord in our streets, and closely followed by a carriage and four containing several female advertisements of a Blake Street Resort is as glaring and flaring a flaunt from a vile den of iniquity as could have been expected in Denver in 1859."[31] The following day the paper continued its criticism and protested that harlots with their pimps rode in open carriages through the streets of Denver, but still the mayor and the marshal remained silent.[32] By August the complaint had changed slightly and directed its vexations away from the authorities toward the prostitutes. Unhappily, the *News* had to report that Denver prostitutes had adopted the style of their colleagues in the East and operated out of apartments.

Nettie Clark's career ended in 1896 when she was shot and killed in Denver. (Colorado Historical Society)

Abortionist Madam Astle compiled a lengthy Denver arrest record before her death in 1908. (Colorado Historical Society)

Richard DeMady, a Denver resident, was three times a suspect in the murder of prostitutes. (Colorado Historical Society)

Bell Warden, one of Denver's black madams, went to the Colorado penitentiary for her part in the 1884 murder of a customer. (Colorado Historical Society)

Mattie Lemmon, twenty-two years old when given a ten-year prison sentence for murder, died in the Colorado penitentiary three years later. (Colorado Historical Society)

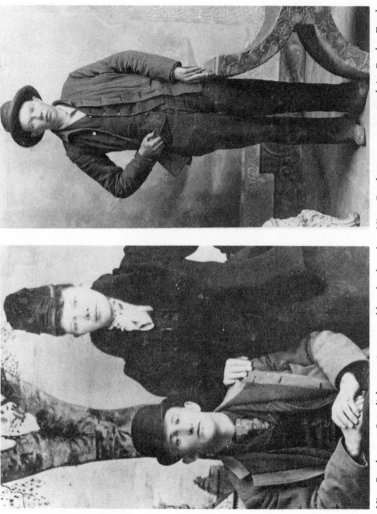

Nina Patchen, a Swedish prostitute, and her husband were charged with murder, but acquitted. (Colorado Historical Society)

Nina Patchen was arrested in Rocky Ford, Colorado, dressed in men's clothing. (Colorado Historical Society)

These women worked in a Creede, Colorado, parlor house in the early 1890s. (Courtesy Amon Carter Museum, Fort Worth, Texas)

This undated photograph, entitled "Intermission," shows the interior of a Denver brothel. (Courtesy Amon Carter Museum, Fort Worth, Texas)

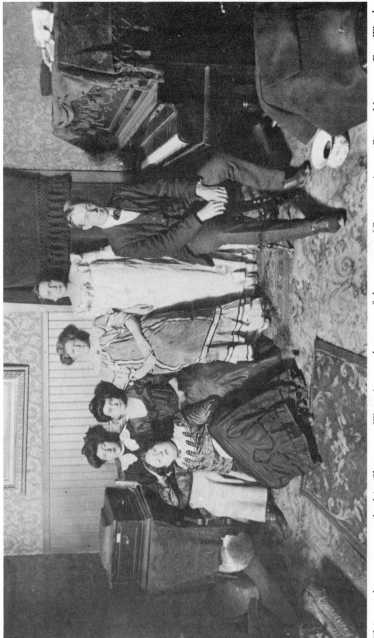

This somber group worked in Cheyenne, Wyoming, at the turn of the century. (Courtesy Amon Carter Museum, Fort Worth, Texas)

These young women staffed the brothel of Madam Sperber in Junction City, Kansas, in the early 1900s. (Joseph J. Pennell Collection, Kansas Collection, University of Kansas Libraries)

The women infiltrated buildings about the city and caused a nuisance to the respectable neighbors. This unfortunate circumstance occurred in Denver because the long inactive authorities had started to raid the regular bordellos over the summer. The paper had not anticipated this undesirable consequence of its editorials against the apathy of the officials.[33] Goaded into action, the authorities succeeded in dispersing the prostitutes throughout the general residential community.

Here was a central chord in the community policies that directed the affairs of prostitutes. When the presence of prostitutes offended the citizens, editorial statements shifted away from criticism of the authorities and focused on the desirability of containment of vice districts.[34] These societal attitudes that advocated the ostracism of prostitutes brought complex ramifications. With society unwilling to confront either the issues or the people involved in prostitution, management of the institution fell to civic authorities whose conduct went unchallenged. Freed from accountability, officials manipulated prostitution as they desired. Prostitutes, beyond the protection of society, entered or participated in alliances with officials as one of the exigencies of survival.

As for the respectable citizens in communities, they displayed little or no interest in the techniques officials employed in their dealings with prostitutes. Communities were satisfied to remain uninformed about the shady negotiations and crooked payoffs that surrounded the red-light districts. When they could not deny the corruption of city officials, they simply ignored it, convinced that judges, mayors, and police officials deserved anything they could get in return for the unsavory job of dealing with the criminal element. Public apathy and distaste permitted public officials almost total license in vice matters. Only on rare occasions was the public forced to confront the nature of official conduct. When these matters came under public scrutiny, those charged with the investigation employed the greatest discretion. The momentum of official public investigation passed quickly without disturbance to community power brokers who settled back into their personal and professional routines without change.

On the unusual occasions when these connections did come under public scrutiny, restraint dominated the investigations. A grand jury hearing in Boise, Idaho, showed that community leaders from all walks of life knew full-well about the area called the "restricted district." For at least twenty years prior to the inquiry, Boise officials managed the red-

light area by a system of containment, fines, and uneven law enforcement. Boise leaders obviously felt the city controlled prostitution effectively by corralling the women into "The Alley." Here about ninety
women lived in both houses and squalid cribs outside the houses. Ministers, businessmen, a doctor, a former mayor, and a judge all insisted
that Boise had an acceptable record in the handling of this civic problem. Most officials thought the cribs excessively offensive and suggested
that they be closed. All witnesses also objected to the illegal sale of liquor by prostitutes and wanted that curtailed.[35]

One clergyman, the Reverend P. Monroe Smock, even advocated the
continuation of the existing system. He argued that vice could never be
eliminated from society, and he thought it unwise to precipitate any action that would lead to the dispersal of "Alley" residents throughout the
city.[36] The "excellent" control that Boise maintained in the red-light district convinced him that no attempt should be made to close the houses
of prostitution.

Other ministers disputed some parts of Reverend Smock's testimony.
For instance, Dr. George Paddock of the Congregational Church insisted
that prostitution in Boise ranked among the worst he had ever seen and
suggested the entire operation be closed.[37] The pastor of the First Presbyterian Church, Charles L. Chamfont, agreed with Paddock and complained that brazen Boise prostitutes dared to hand out signs of advertisement. Chamfont's concluding statements showed his concerns had
little to do with the prostitutes. He said, ". . . the character of the girls
would not be more endangered by closing the houses. . . ."[38] Only the
testimony of L. W. Grub, who may have been among the local ministers,
addressed the topic of the women themselves. Grub hoped that while
enforcing the law, authorities and citizen backers would remember to
show sympathy for the "unfortunates" who lived in "The Alley."[39] Grub's
sentiments stood alone as no other witness expressed interest in the
fate of the prostitutes. Indeed, Mayor John M. Haynes captured the essence of the various testimonies when he called the entire problem
"perplexing" and stated, "I do not want to be conspicuous, but want to
do what is for the best interests of the city."[40]

No sharp disagreements surfaced among civic leaders; they merely
quibbled over procedure and the degree to which the law should be
enforced. The investigation promised to be a tame one, with no public
official threatened by complicity in Boise corruption. A twist in events

erupted when one witness unexpectedly named citizens rumored as recipients of expensive gifts from a local madam, Agnes Bush. This revelation forced the grand jury to make some embarrassing inquiries.

The first person summoned in this matter, newspaper reporter C. Miles, had no difficulty with the questions. Miles readily admitted that he received a diamond ring from Agnes Bush. He told how Agnes Bush invited him to her brothel and presented the gift.[41] Miles accepted it because "I would be a chump if I did not take a $250 diamond."[42] Miles assured the panel that he had not received the ring as a bribe or as payment for any favors. Once Miles had rescued Agnes Bush from a vicious beating, and he thought that might have prompted the gift.[43]

A more delicate civic problem than the chivalry of a newspaper reporter involved the chief of police and Agnes Bush. Witnesses referred vaguely to rumors about a diamond badge that the chief allegedly received from the grateful madam. M. R. Weaver of the Standard Furniture Company testified that he first saw the badge displayed in the window of a friend's store. The friend confided that Agnes Bush wanted him to present this jeweled badge to the chief of police, B. F. Francis. Weaver and several other gentlemen advised their friend not to make the presentation.[44] The matter was skillfully resolved by the clever use of a local organization. When Chief Francis had to explain how he came to own the expensive jewelry, he coolly replied, "I have a very nice diamond Badge which was presented to me in the Elks Hall by John Blake and which he stated came from the members of the Lodge."[45]

The gentle treatment of the chief while under oath, the failure to question Agnes Bush on the origins of the diamond badge, and the refusal to weigh properly the importance of Miles's testimony all combined to make the thoroughness of the grand jury suspect. Their lack of response to other vice topics revealed still further the essential weakness of this investigative body. As the inquiry widened to the topic of gambling in Boise, the full scope of official malfeasance began to emerge.

Cigar store owner Sam S. Drake explained the gambling operation in Boise. Each week proprietors paid $17.50 to another gambler, Harry Leroy. Drake testified that the money had to be placed in an envelope, addressed to "John Brown," and handed to Harry Leroy. In return Leroy promised "protection" for Drake's operation. Other dealers corroborated Drake's experiences, although some negotiated with police officers instead of Leroy.[46]

Oddly, the grand jury did not summon a local notorious clan, the Stewart family, to testify about protection money although gambling witnesses repeatedly identified their residence as a center of both gambling and prostitution. The daughters, Mary and Margaret, age sixteen and seventeen, worked as prostitutes while the rest of the family ran the gambling operation.[47] Yet even without their testimony, other gamblers gave plenty of evidence to implicate the authorities. When John Shanks wanted to open a gambling hall, he testified, he asked Chief Ben Francis for permission, but the chief stalled. Shanks then took his case to Mayor Haynes who told him, "Yes, by God. I believe in an open town."[48] Armed with the necessary permission, Shanks opened and began to pay his $10 a week to Leroy who told him, "Ben Francis wants the money."[49] When the police suddenly closed Shanks's hall, he went directly to Mayor Haynes and complained that it was unfair for him to be arrested when Harry Leroy continued to be open. Shanks's accusations of favoritism included charging the mayor with accepting $100 a month from another open operation, the Hoffman House. The angered mayor suggested that Shanks leave town and take up homesteading. The frustrated Shanks now turned to Jack Wilson, owner of a sheep and wool business, and asked Wilson to carry money to Chief Francis. After this transaction, Shanks approached Francis personally and complained again about the impediments to his gambling business. Chief of Police Francis responded: "Just lay low for a few days and things will be all right. This is a political pull. Haynes is going to run for governor."[50]

Another witness, Mack Gilliam, testified that on one occasion the county commissioners and several citizens asked him to help them gather evidence about illegal gambling at one of the spots with a deputy sheriff named Clawson. As part of his cooperation Gilliam made arrangements to establish his own operation and to pay the $17.50 a week for protection. At this point the "set-up" fell through. Gilliam charged that the trap failed because one member of the citizens' committee warned the police department about the surveillance. Mack Gilliam named attorney Jamee Bogart as the informant.[51]

Bogart's appearance before the grand jury paralleled that of Chief Francis. Bogart gave simple answers to easy questions. The attorney explained that a citizens' committee approached him about the need to investigate gambling that involved the police department. Bogart said he advised the group that they would need firm evidence before charges could be brought. If they secured it, Bogart agreed to take the case.[52] The most obvious question was never asked of Bogart; he left the witness stand without being asked if he had warned the police department of the trap.

The involvement and duplicity of officials did not end with Bogart; even the prosecuting attorney of the grand jury investigation, Judge Kutch, was implicated. The testimony of several gamblers indicated they knew that if they came before Judge Kutch, charges against them would be dropped.[53] Kutch's exact role remained unclear, as Kutch himself conducted the questioning before the grand jury. His superficial and confusing inquiries foreshadowed what would become of any charges against him. The grand jury ignored what they heard. Their decision to do so could hardly have produced any surprise, for the outcome of the hearings could be anticipated from a resolution they passed after one Saturday morning of work. It stated: "A vote of thanks was extended to Judge Kutch for his efficient work and assistance to the Grand Jury, and for his cordial invitation to join him in a treat at the Elks Club Rooms. This being his last appearance before the Grand Jury as prosecuting attorney." [54]

The grand jury investigators returned no true bills and charged no Boise officials with misconduct. The end of the grand jury hearings assured that vice operations in Boise could continue uninterrupted. Specific, incriminating evidence against several public officials produced no legal response. Members of the grand jury chose not to endanger the status or reputations of colleagues in the community. The judgments of witnesses drawn from business and religious groups prevailed. Their early testimony largely supported the methods used by authorities to control the red-light district and gambling. Granted that officials might accept bribes, it mattered little as long as they kept social cancers away from those in society who found such topics distasteful. In return for this desired service to the community, why should other citizens challenge their actions? Members of shady professions complained, implicated, and testified, but to no avail. They rippled the bureaucratic surface only slightly as the community bestowed a free hand to public officers and looked the other way when in the performance of duty officials found ways to profit from those they supervised.

In Tombstone, Austin, Denver, and Boise, as well as in other frontier areas, public officials demonstrated a variety of twisted, dishonest relationships with prostitution. None of these communities promoted policies designed to ameliorate the conditions of prostitution; rather, they dumped both the responsibility and the authority for prostitution management into the hands of public officers. When personal greed and abuse of power dominated official conduct, no system of restraint existed to halt these practices.

Even in those instances when an individual officer rejected the opportunities for graft, the destructive nature of the interaction between prostitutes and law officers appeared. If an officer shunned malfeasance because of his own personal scruples, even if the very sight of prostitutes might be repugnant to him, the realities of frontier society and law enforcement clearly provided for, even demanded, the presence of prostitutes. Caught among these various forces, the law officer who found prostitution morally offensive faced a conflict between the exercise of his duties and his personal attitudes. Armed with broad powers, forced to tolerate prostitutes that repelled him, such an officer actively reinforced the marginal condition of prostitutes. The result enlarged the atmosphere of negative human relationships that marked the lives of prostitutes.

An episode in the career of Marshal Jim Clark of Telluride, Colorado, typified the sort of confrontation prostitutes experienced when they crossed paths with those who detested the profession. Clark, who had lived on both sides of the law, hardly possessed a saintly character, but his distaste for prostitutes never faltered. In the discharge of his other duties, according to his friend, U.S. Deputy Marshal Cyrus Shores, Clark handled himself with dignity.[55] The marshal made regular tours of "The Row," a slum area for the Telluride brothels, whose inhabitants he detested. In this district, Cyrus Shores witnessed an exchange that revealed the deep-seated hatred the town marshal harbored against prostitutes and the ugly explosions such feelings brought to encounters between the law and prostitutes. Shores recalled: ". . . as we were walking along the . . . slums, there was a great large heavy blonde woman, wearing a wrapper, who . . . was the boss of one house, came out. . . . She had her little old pug dog trotting along side . . . and she began to say to Mr. Clark, 'You see my dog is getting to be very old and worthless, and in the way. I wish you would take him out sometimes—out of town— and kill him for me.' Clark immediately jerked his six shooter out and . . . shot the dog . . . and then the old girl screamed. . . ."[56] Clark continued his tour of the district without breaking stride, and said only to Shores, "Damn them, I will not fool with them."[57] Whatever the cause, Clark's actions with the old dog suggested the marshal cared little for treating prostitutes civilly under any circumstances. Clark's scornful management of prostitutes conveyed their social status with the law in Telluride.[58]

Clark's friend, Cyrus Shores, on the other hand, may well have adopted a more flexible approach to prostitutes in his jurisdiction. As a law officer in Gunnison, Colorado, Shores dealt with many prostitutes.[59] Perhaps not all his dealings concerned law enforcement. Tucked among his marvelous papers, a letter fragment from a Denver prostitute hinted that Shores may have conducted some relationships on a friendly basis. Prostitute Mollie Foley wrote to Shores in 1884 to ask him for train fare to Chicago. Her letter, a blend of selfishness and pathos, played heavily on their past association. Among her florid passages, she included: "Now I don't want you to think that I am entirely composed of *Gall & Nerve* but . . . I know of no one . . . who would be more likely to help me than you. . . . I have been thinking of . . . writing. . . . Now don't think I only think of you when I want to ask a favor for I think of you always. . . . I know I must have appeared ungrateful . . . but I never felt that way *I am sure*. . . ."[60] Mingled with her endearments, Mollie prodded Shores to send the fare within two weeks and reminded him that she really did not care to travel to Chicago by second-class accommodations. She closed her appeal with love and the clearly printed address of her 16th Street brothel in Denver. Mollie Foley's mercenary pitch pointed out one final element in the negative relationships between prostitutes and law officers: some of those associations hinged upon the sexual services the women offered. The general pattern of prostitute/customer relations encouraged the continued subjugation of the women. Liaisons with officers of the law did not alter this situation but strengthened the social ostracism leveled against prostitutes in any community.

Folklore from the frontier often portrayed a lopsided relationship between law officers and prostitutes. In these tales, judges, sheriffs, and mayors, depicted as objective witnesses to the antics of frontier prostitutes, somehow remained detached from the sordid mechanics of the institution, yet frontier prostitutes survived by a vigorous, if debasing, interaction with those around them. Those most directly associated with prostitutes were public officials. The relationships that prostitutes had with law officers reinforced the low social condition of the women while expanding opportunities for personal gain, monetary rewards, or civic promotion for the officials. Communities showed themselves more than willing to grant officials unlimited power over vice groups in exchange for the luxury of indifference. Even when investigations confirmed the abuses of power, communities tried to look the other way and protect the reputations of public officials.

The circumstances surrounding the interaction of prostitutes with law officers reflected the experiences of individual lives, yet these personal stories served to set the stage for a larger issue, one concerned with the way the two groups aided the development of the frontier legal establishment. Prostitutes and public officials—partners in the evolution of the western judicial system.

Notes

1. James D. Hamlin, *The Flamboyant Judge: A Biography as Told to J. Evetts Haley and Wm. Curry Holden* (Canyon, Tex.: Palo Duro Press, 1972), p. 106.

2. Ibid.; for the summary of Ella Hill's experiences, see pp. 105–7.

3. The *Arizona Citizen* is particularly useful for demonstrating the vigorous business interests in Tombstone, as well as the sense of local boosterism. See issues for Sept. 5, 27, Nov. 15, 1879, July 24, 1880, and Feb. 27, 1881.

4. See Pat Ryan, "John P. Clum: Boss with the White Forehead," *Arizoniana* 5 (Fall 1964): 48–58, and "Trail Blazer of Civilization: John P. Clum's Tucson and Tombstone Years," *Journal of Arizona History* 6 (Summer 1965): 53–70; John Philip Clum, *It All Happened in Tombstone* (Flagstaff, Ariz.: Northland, 1965); *Tombstone Epitaph*, Jan. 4, 1881.

5. John P. Clum, *It All Happened in Tombstone*, p. 6.

6. Clum wrote prolific and strong editorials throughout his tenure as mayor; see *Tombstone Epitaph*, 1881.

7. Tombstone has attracted considerable attention because of its wildness. In truth, no different from other frontier mining towns, it probably would have faded into historical obscurity had it not been for the encounter between the Earps and the Clantons at the O. K. Corral. Some examples of the literature from Tombstone are Walter Burns, *Tombstone: An Iliad of the Southwest* (Garden City, N.Y.: Doubleday,

Page, 1927); William MacLeod Raine, *Famous Sheriffs and Western Outlaws* (Garden City, N.Y.: Garden City Publishers, 1929), pp. 100–113; C. L. Sonnichsen, *Billy King's Tombstone: The Private Life of an Arizona Boom Town* (Caldwell, Idaho: Caxton Publishers, 1942). Even in retrospect, Clum promoted a favorable image of the city; see John Clum, *It All Happened in Tombstone*.

8. *Arizona Citizen*, Mar. 6, 1881.

9. See Anne M. Butler, "The Fróntier Press and Prostitution" (Master's thesis, University of Maryland, 1975), pp. 45–60.

10. *Tombstone Epitaph*, Mar. 9, 1882.

11. Ibid.

12. Victoria F. Behan vs. John H. Behan, Complaint, Section Four, District Court, Yavapai County, Arizona Territory, May 22, 1875, John H. Behan File, AHS.

13. Ibid. Inexplicably, Victoria Behan requested support for only one child, Albert Price Behan, age four. The request for support of Henrietta Behan, age six, was stricken from the divorce petition. Whether Henrietta had been born in California before the marriage, in Arizona after the marriage, or had died during the court proceedings is unclear.

14. Reminiscences of Mrs. Ethel M. Macia of the Rose Tree Inn, Tombstone, Dec. 12, 1950, manuscript, AHS.

15. See Marshal Trimble, *Arizona* (N.Y.: Doubleday, 1977), pp. 273–78. Trimble says that when the Earps came to Tombstone they were known as the "Dodge City Gang," but in the Kansas cowtowns they had been called "The Fighting Pimps." In Tombstone, Wyatt Earp courted Josephine Marcus and married her, after he abandoned his second wife, prostitute Mattie Blaylock, who committed suicide in Pinal City, Arizona. As late as 1936 Josephine Marcus attempted to suppress some of these details about their Tombstone era. See Glenn Boyer, "Postscripts to Historical Fiction about Wyatt Earp in Tombstone," *Arizona and the West* 18 (Autumn 1976): 217–36.

16. *Arizona Republican*, Aug. 24, 1890. At least part of the editor's goal was to make Behan's superintendency a political issue. The summation of the article called for a rejection of the Democratic party in the coming elections. Political interests aside, the report on the internal conditions of the prison brought the dismissal of Behan.

17. Report, John Behan File, AHS.

18. *Arizona Republican*, Aug. 24, 1890; Manuscript, Yuma Territorial Prison; John Behan File, all AHS.

19. It should be noted that Behan served honorably in the Spanish-American War and returned to Arizona in 1901. When he died in 1912,

his funeral was conducted under the auspices of the Arizona Pioneers' Historical Society. The official eulogy declared, ". . . (he) held many positions of Public Trust, and in all was faithful, active, and honest." John H. Behan File, AHS.

20. For an excellent discussion of the manner in which nostalgia has produced our modern images of western personalities, see Robert V. Hine, "The Western Hero," in Hine, ed., *The American West: An Interpretive History* (Boston: Little, Brown, 1973), pp. 268–82.

21. For a full discussion of the relationship between frontier prostitutes and the public press see Anne M. Butler, "The Frontier Press and Prostitution."

22. An excellent example was the death of Eleanore "Madame Mustache" Dumont reported by the *Butte Miner*, Sept. 20, 1879.

23. San Antonio, Cheyenne, and Denver all engaged in these editorial campaigns from time to time. For example, see the *San Antonio Daily Express*, Mar. 1868; *Cheyenne Daily Sun*, June 1879; *Daily Rocky Mountain News*, May 1871, Nov. 1872.

24. The Denver papers were especially adept at this. For examples see the *Daily Rocky Mountain News*, Aug. 14, 1880, Apr. 11, June 18, 1882, Aug. 18, 1885, July 25, 1887; *Denver Republican*, Jan. 6, 1881, Apr. 12, 1882, July 15, 1889.

25. Austin Police Department, Record of Arrests, 1880, 1881, 1882, passim, ATCC.

26. *Austin Daily Democratic Statesman*, June 28, 1882.

27. *Daily Rocky Mountain News*, May 20, 21, 1871.

28. In 1870, St. Louis adopted a formal system of residence and medical control of prostitutes. The policy required all prostitutes to live within a prescribed section of the city and to submit to a regular medical examination by a physician. The program was largely a failure and was abandoned in less than five years. See John C. Burnham, "Medical Inspection of Prostitutes in America in the Nineteenth Century: The Saint Louis Experiment and its Sequel," *Bulletin of the History of Medicine* 45 (1973): 201–18. This program continued to be an issue in Denver, and for several years the editors and various Denver physicians urged the adoption of the St. Louis plan. See the *Daily Rocky Mountain News*, Oct. 26, 27, 1873, Mar. 7, 16, 19, Aug. 30, Sept. 2, 3, 1874, Apr. 20, 1875, and Mar. 18, 1877.

29. *Daily Rocky Mountain News*, Nov. 30, 1872.

30. *Weekly Central City Register*, Apr. 30, 1873.

31. *Daily Rocky Mountain News*, Apr. 10, 1874.

32. Ibid., Apr. 11, 1874.

33. Ibid., Aug. 12, 1874.

34. Ibid., Jan. 25, 1877, June 12, 1882, and Dec. 12, 1883.

35. Minutes of the Grand Jury empaneled Dec. 23, 1908, pp. 58–64, IHS.

36. Ibid., pp. 63–64.

37. Ibid., pp. 62–63.

38. Ibid., p. 62.

39. Ibid., p. 61.

40. Ibid., p. 59.

41. Ibid., p. 65.

42. Ibid.

43. Ibid.

44. Ibid., pp. 65–66.

45. Ibid., p. 67.

46. Ibid., pp. 88–89.

47. Ibid., p. 66.

48. Ibid., p. 82.

49. Ibid., p. 97.

50. Ibid., p. 98.

51. Ibid., pp. 86–87, 90–92.

52. Ibid., pp. 94–95.

53. Ibid., pp. 82–83.

54. Ibid., p. 83.

55. Manuscript, Cyrus W. Shores Papers, #85, pp. 15–16, WHC.

56. Ibid.

57. Ibid.

58. Ibid.

59. The Cyrus Shores papers represent an enormously rich collection and have already been cited in n. 55 above. These papers contain letters, telegrams, and miscellaneous items from Shores's law career, as well as a marvelous set of episodic memoirs from his varied life.

60. Manuscript, Cyrus W. Shores Papers, 1883, WHC.

5

Legal Entanglements

> Two of the Park Street girls had a battle with their tongues and
> used language that would make a bullwhacker blush. The girls
> plead guilty and said they were truly sorry and wouldn't do so
> any more if they could help it, and as evidence of their sincerity
> both promptly paid up and departed and the day closed in the
> Police Court with a handsome credit to the benefit of the city
> treasury.[1]

So reported the newspaper of Butte, Montana, in 1881. Hardly a stunning news bulletin, the contents related an all too familiar frontier scene. Once again a newspaper found room to jest about the easily identified local prostitutes hauled into court, charged with a misdemeanor, fined a municipal tax, and released to continue their profession. Witty and derisive, this short item, a duplicate of others in frontier newspapers everywhere, is surely of minor historical significance.[2]

Yet within this article, and others of the same genre, there lurk some nagging points. The images that spring from these abbreviated news stories are unsatisfactory. A feeling of incompleteness, of unanswered questions gives rise to suspicion that perhaps the frontier scenario of prostitutes, the courts, and law enforcement included more complexities than these simple newspaper articles suggest. In the grand sweep of frontier history, surely something has been overlooked in these repeated encounters between prostitutes and the law enforcement agencies of the early West. The relationship between frontier prostitutes and local legal systems in frontier communities was an important element in the lives of the women. Not exactly the halls of judicial eloquence, local courts, fraught with pettiness and parochialism, nonetheless provided the arena wherein prostitutes clashed with the law.

A definition of law must encompass several concepts. In its first form it means simply the code of rules assigned by any authority, society, or custom to give shape to an institution.[3] If codification could fully elucidate the meaning of law, then a process of cataloguing all the rules and regulations in society would end the need for further interpretation. For a definition of law to be significant, it is necessary to expand the meaning to include the very processes of society. In historical studies, law must encompass those elements that generated the code, the values that retained it, and the conditions that altered it.[4] Law studied outside the social context is a theoretical science.[5] Law viewed within the social structure promises to reveal something of our historical development. Moved apart from pure scientific analysis, law becomes one of the dynamics in the irrational but fascinating saga of man's attempts to bring order to his surroundings. Wythe Hold, professor of law at the University of Alabama, explained, " 'Law' has no meaning unless we are attempting to investigate why a statute was passed, what forces and factors influenced any given court decision . . . why members of the bench and bar play the rigid roles they play. Legal history is only social history, political history, educational history, urban history and labor history in a fashionable . . . disguise."[6]

In this chapter, law means the corpus of legislation in any frontier community, but the meaning also embraces the social, economic, and political structure wherein legislation existed. It is not only the letter of the law, but the forces that explain the uses of the law that command attention.

Fundamental to the American legal system are the lower courts. Here, ordinary citizens confront the basic machinery of the national legal system; the mundane business of the everyday world is thrashed out; the values, standards, and traditions of a community form the underpinnings of court conduct; the use of the law mirrors the spirit of local communities. Nowhere did the lower courts reflect these elements more than on the American frontier in the nineteenth century.[7]

Small towns haphazardly constructed in isolated regions hastened to strengthen social and political institutions as ballast for runaway economic bonanzas. Faced with both opportunity and chaos, community backers realized the great economic potential around them could only be harnessed in an atmosphere where some semblance of institutional stability emerged, yet substantial problems inhibited the opportunistic goals of urban clusters far removed from the traditional agencies of the social and political establishment. Frontier towns, populated by raucous workers suffering the hardships of economic and social dislocation, sought to impose order through the use of local offices. Within the legal system, the widespread and rapid appearance of justice of the peace jurisdictions served to meet this need.

The justice of the peace, an expedient employed widely throughout the United States, traced its antecedents to British law.[8] The American adaptation represented an effort to establish a local legal authority for the resolution of minor civil and criminal cases in a nation where population increases and community building out-paced needed advancements in government services. In the burgeoning nineteenth-century American society, this judicial office flourished devoid of the political heritage and the cultural traditions common to British law. The rapid-fire growth of American towns and the urgency of their legal needs militated against an order based on a slow-moving evolutionary process; rather, the American system absorbed the British justice of the peace office but pragmatically altered certain features to meet the needs of the moment.

Accordingly, American justices of the peace needed few qualifications to secure their positions. Neither knowledge of jurisprudence, practical legal training, nor family social status were conditions for employment. The absence of prerequisites for appointment guaranteed predictable results in local law enforcement. Obviously, the legal expertise of those administering the lower courts remained uneven. Although some justices of the peace strove for a measure of legal excellence, or at least exhibited a commitment to honesty and hard work, the system permitted and even encouraged the elevation to the bench of completely unqualified candidates. Frontier communities could always find willing persons to fill the office and to start the local legal machinery.

As the office took shape, other elements compounded the difficulties of a justice system grounded in the shallow sands of the present. Besides personnel problems, the system suffered from financial stresses. Funding for lower judicial offices came from local municipal or county budgets. Such treasuries, never solvent and with few sources of revenue, had little or no money to channel into the courts. A system of allocation based on agency use left the courts far behind other municipal services competing for public funds. Although the courts were permanent community agencies, their use varied from season to season. A diffuse population, dotted about the countryside, needed the courts in varying degrees. A spate of crime, a sudden economic fluctuation, a rash of deaths, or other unpredictable factors—any of these varied the work load of the justice court. The waxing and waning of court services made remuneration for court personnel burdensome to local government, so a fee schedule rather than a regular salary became the basis for compensation to justices. Other law officers, such as the sheriff or the county attorney, shared in the fee payment plan. Fee charges included taking the complaint, executing a search warrant, serving subpoenas, and conveying prisoners. Fees varied from town to town, but averaged about $10.25 per case. A defendant's inability to pay the fee resulted in a jail stay until the debt was worked off. One day in jail equaled seventy-five cents to $1 in credit.[9]

Local politics also governed the operation of the justice courts. Although the office originated as an appointed post, it quickly evolved into a short-term elected position. This did away with any lingering vestige of impartiality as frontier justices aligned themselves with political factions in an effort to win and retain office. Factionalism in the courts was reinforced by the failure to require the maintenance of a public record. With little or no documentation of court procedures, justices, freed from review or censure, could comfortably cast their lot with political allies. Inevitably, justice of the peace courts catered to local political groups and abused the fee schedule system at the expense of those before the court.

Almost as they formed, frontier justice of the peace courts emerged as special interest agencies staffed by officials notable for their lack of judicial training, unhampered by a sense of tradition and judicial protocol, influenced by political ties, and susceptible to financial shadiness. Scarred by so many negative qualities, valuable largely for their accessibility, frontier courts well deserved to be the objects of local scorn. Oddly enough, this was not the case. The citizens and the courts established a rapport that overrode the blatant corruption of those who administered their unevenhanded justice. What was it that this shaky legal order brought to the frontier community? How did the populace perceive the function of local authority? A partial answer can be drawn from the interaction of the justice courts with prostitution in any community.

The first responsibility of the courts centered on the practical management of crime. This involved two elements. The first hinged upon the local statutes that made prostitution a violation.[10] Despite mythical notions of frontier towns as wide-open, fun-loving communities where prostitutes were welcomed before respectability hit the West, all city councils passed laws prohibiting the presence of brothels and gambling dens. The umbrella of the law also covered the inmates of brothels, whether prostitute or client, those who rented housing to prostitutes, and those who managed the operation. Obviously, the presence of the law upon the books and the implementation of that law never meshed well. The statutes against prostitution became the instrument through which local authorities in all frontier areas could systematically tax vice as a source of local revenue. Taxation emerged as the first element in the management of crime.[11]

In Cheyenne, Wyoming, between June 13 and July 14, 1868, municipal taxation in one police docket register equaled $943 for fines specifically related to houses of prostitution.[12] In 1887, between March and December, the Cheyenne jail register showed a total of $1,028.50 collected from fines related to prostitutes.[13] Other towns followed similar patterns. For several years Laramie, Wyoming, charged brothel inmates a fine of $7. Between 1878 and 1880 the city added no less than $1,179.50 to its treasury from prostitution fines. In 1881 the fines increased but arrests decreased, and only $234.50 was recorded.[14]

Prostitutes ran the risk of facing several different misdemeanor charges besides that of "inmate." For example, prostitutes also collided with laws that prohibited drunkenness, disturbing the peace, cursing and swearing in public, indecent exposure, malicious mischief, and public fighting. The most common of these, vagrancy, did not mean loitering about the streets. Since prostitutes were commonly removed from inside a brothel and charged with vagrancy, this all-purpose violation covered all sorts of minor offenses. Any of these charges could be filed at the whim of the arresting officer, which meant that one prostitute often compiled an impressive array of charges in a town. Cherry Hardeman, a black prostitute in Austin, typified this in her three-year arrest record. Before she disappeared from the Austin police docket,

Cherry Hardeman's eleven convictions included vagrancy, drunk and disorderly, abusive language, offensive language, and assault.[15]

Charges against prostitutes were not always directly related to vice offenses. The misdemeanors of fighting or carrying a pistol sometimes spilled over into more serious areas. When lesser crimes changed into major felonies, prostitutes found themselves removed from the justice of the peace courts and referred to the district or county court system. Taxation as a management device gave way to punitive measures as the local police court yielded to a higher court. Despite the loss of some regular contributors, justice of the peace courts did not lack a continuing parade of prostitutes to be fined. Of 223 prostitutes arrested in Austin between 1876 and 1879, only one faced charges outside police court.[16]

The second duty of the authorities involved crime management. The courts, aided by the police, knew that the community expected local undesirables to be controlled. Rarely did citizens demand that "undesirables"—and prostitutes clearly came under that heading—be expelled from a city. Practical businessmen understood that a flourishing vice community attracted migrant workers, military personnel, and even legislators. The failure of serious attempts to eradicate vice in western towns persisted as a universal element in frontier town building. Communities centered their efforts on the restriction of vice areas and the curtailment of the most flamboyant behavior found in vice districts.[17]

Armed with the citizens' expectations, the legal establishment had the power to direct the physical and, in large measure, the psychological control of local undesirables. Equipped with an authority that operated free of restraints and staffed by a questionable crowd at best, the law possessed total latitude in decisions as to which persons would be arrested. In areas of vice control, this broad authority brought harassment to some, while others bought their way out of the arrest syndrome by the regular payment of protection money.[18]

For those without the means to pay, or of the wrong ethnic background, or whose alcoholism or drug addiction made them a public nuisance, the repeated arrests came with boring regularity. The experiences of Annie Hamilton and Nellie Davis of Laramie, Wyoming, reflected those of many of their colleagues in the West. Between August 8 and November 28, 1877, Hamilton and Davis were arrested at least five

times. On each occasion they pleaded guilty to the charge of being in a
bawdy house and paid the $7 fine. After this date their names did not
appear in the Laramie arrest record.[19] Perhaps they found the monthly
roundup not to their liking and moved on. If so, they did not have the
perseverance of their co-worker, Sophie Rickard, who between August 28, 1877, and May 28, 1883, was arrested no fewer than thirty-five
times. Convictions included both being an inmate and keeping a house
of prostitution. Despite the fact that Sophie Rickard identified herself as
a twenty-eight-year-old seamstress, Laramie police dockets marked her
as a working prostitute.[20] The frequency of her arrests and convictions
had to impress upon Mrs. Rickard, if she had any doubts, that although
she might try to align herself with the so-called respectable community,
the law said otherwise. As a convicted prostitute, Sophie Rickard, even if
she attempted to conduct a legitimate seamstress business, could expect that as long as she remained in Laramie her life would be circumscribed by the authority of the police and courts. Frequent arrests and
fines constituted the penalties imposed on her by the community in
return for allowing her to remain in her brothel shack by the railroad
tracks.

Some well known repeaters found ways to mitigate police control
and mold local restrictions to fit their lives. Bridget Gallager, a Cheyenne prostitute of the late 1880s, functioned for at least two years by
maintaining credit with the authorities. When arrested and jailed for
lack of the fine, she worked off three or four days of her sentence and
then won release on a promise to leave the city, which she never did.
Occasionally the authorities picked her up on back fines, but the resolution was the same. After serving about five days, Mrs. Gallager promised
to leave Cheyenne and was released from jail. Finally, in 1889, it occurred to someone that Bridget Gallager might not pay her fine or leave
town. The authorities then required Mrs. Gallager to pay $18 of a $41
fine and to serve the remainder in jail. After this incident, Bridget Gallager's name did not appear in the Cheyenne police register.[21]

Other towns also developed munificent, if unpredictable, policies in
an endeavor to curb the activities of prostitutes. In Canadian, Texas, the
court permitted prostitutes to pay a deposit on the fine and then return
to the streets to earn the rest of the money. This was not allowed to all
prostitutes before the court and may have been based on the woman's
record of dependability for paying off her outstanding debts. Also, court

favoritism appeared to influence some of these decisions. "Snuff Box Allie" English, a familiar face before the bench, could almost depend on special treatment. In ten appearances before Justice of the Peace C. W. Stump and State's Attorney B. M. Baker, Allie English secured dismissal three times. Of the seven convictions, at least once she was released to procure the fine, and one time the conviction was set aside by the justice of the peace and the state's attorney. In November 1888 the court returned a $10 fine to Allie English when she came to the justice with a doctor's note that stated she was ill and unable to pay her fine. "Snuff Box Allie" was not the only Canadian prostitute to receive special considerations in the justice of the peace court. From time to time the deputy sheriff, the constable, or the other two court officials pitched in part of a woman's fine. The court also accepted payment of fines for one prostitute by another who happened not to be charged that day.[22]

Although these may appear to be but amusing human interest tales and may indeed have indicated sympathy for the women from some local officials, such stories should not be dismissed. The little town of Canadian deftly employed the system of control. Here the authorities responded skillfully to the expectations of the community. Town officials raised revenues, paid their own salaries, kept a working group of prostitutes available for sexual service, and wielded subtle control with little kindnesses that helped the women misconstrue the actual purpose and intent of the law. The very act of allowing prostitutes to leave the court to earn the balance of a fine by the commission of the same crime for which they had been arrested demonstrated the real goals of the legal order. The judicial structure perpetuated and regulated institutionalized vice. Punishment and accommodation, censure and camaraderie, dispensed at the fancy of officials, kept prostitutes aware that the law decided the conditions of their residence and their freedom.

Both written legislation and capricious enforcement of the law made clear the criminal status of prostitutes. Prostitutes knew that their tenuous status could at any moment be altered by a change in the mood of the authorities. No matter how stable the truce with officials might appear, it was predicated upon everyone's realization that prostitution existed outside the law.

This statement is deceptively simple because prostitutes also lived inside the law. In addition to being known criminals, prostitutes participated in the community life as citizens with rights and duties. Society created a dual role for prostitutes—legal and illegal. Several instances showed that prostitutes enjoyed both the rights and responsibilities of citizenship, along with the burden of criminal stigmata.

First, county governments did not hesitate to tax prostitutes just like other citizens. Few prostitutes owned real estate subject to local property tax, but those who did could expect an assessment based on the size and condition of the holdings. Mary Brady, owner of a quarter section brothel ranch on the Big Laramie River, paid $62.72 in taxes in 1875. Her personal property evaluation totaled $33.72. Other fees included poll, poor, territorial, county, road and bridge, court, and school taxes, as well as the county bond.[23]

Taxes varied for women living in Laramie, but the basis of the assessment was not listed in the tax schedule. Amounts ranged from $13 to $68. The most indigent prostitutes were assessed only an annual poll tax of $2. Most of the poverty-stricken women ignored this tax from year to year.[24] Sallie Thixton, an alcoholic prostitute often arrested in Laramie as a bawdy house inmate, was one who never bothered to pay her poll tax. Evidently, the authorities never asked her for it. When she died from exposure and intemperance, Sallie Thixton, thirty years old and Laramie resident for at least seven years, left her taxes unpaid.[25]

Other towns, less benevolent about delinquent taxes, used them as but another weapon to hold over the heads of prostitutes. A delinquent tax bill might be excused for several years, but unexpectedly the authorities would press for collection. Dorothy Montoya of Santa Fe, a repeater on illegal gambling charges, suddenly found her delinquent tax bill added to her problems when she was charged with assault to murder.[26] In these circumstances, authorities could use any available charge to intensify controls on undesirables whose crime level escalated. Nonetheless, the expectation that prostitutes should pay their taxes gave these women a small entree into the circle of citizens with rights and privileges before the law.

Second, prostitutes, like other citizens, appeared in civil cases as either plaintiffs or defendants. This occurred even as they pursued their illegal profession within a community and where they were publicly recognized as prostitutes. These litigations added substantially to the identity of prostitutes as citizens.

In Colorado, prostitute Ida Martin's legal experience demonstrated the varieties of court appearances that the profession involved. In 1866

Ida Martin faced a lawsuit for a debt totaling $30. Ultimately the plaintiff withdrew these charges. The next court appearance brought charges of disturbing the peace when Ida Martin and another prostitute engaged in a public altercation. Next came a man who charged that Ida Martin held in her possession property that rightfully belonged to him. This type of charge appeared in many town dockets and usually implied that the plaintiff, a brothel customer, felt that he had been relieved of money or jewelry while he frolicked with an inmate. In this instance the charge had foundation, and Ida Martin surrendered the property when confronted by the constable.

More significant than these petty misdemeanor charges was the legal action that involved the mortgage on Ida Martin's brothel on Blake Street in Denver. With foreclosure threatening, she faced the loss of all goods, wares, and merchandise in her "business house," as well as two complete sets of bedroom furniture and assorted stable equipment. Martin succeeded in stalling this action until she secured a second mortgage of $1,000 on her house. Despite the publicly known illegality of Ida Martin's establishment, the mortgagee, S. A. Sprague, had sufficient confidence in the financial potential of the Blake Street resort to renegotiate the loan.[27]

Matters of real estate in the courts concerned a limited number of brothel workers. For most women, civil cases involved the payment of debts. In Laramie, Maude Terry, Annie Ponce, and Clara Jenkins, all police court regulars for brothel arrests, increased their problems when sued by Charles Wagner for various sums due him on the purchase of goods. Following this difficulty, Terry disappeared, but Ponce and Jenkins continued to be scooped up on prostitution charges.[28] Drifting off to the next town became a common resort of poor women who knew they could not secure the needed funds before their case came to court. Some, of course, chose to brazen it out, to see if they could beat the case, if they could get it dropped, or if they could possibly pay. One such was Laramie prostitute Bessie Summers, who bounced in and out of police court all through 1884. By September of that year, her rent overdue in the amount of $22.46 and beset with another debt for $30, Summers faced two court suits. The disposition of the latter case called for an agent of the Union Pacific Railroad to accept the contents of Miss Summers's house along with her piano, which was listed as a separate possession. Mrs. Mary Ash came forward, paid the bill for Bessie Summers, and the action was dismissed. In the interim the defendant managed to secure a continuation in the case of the unpaid rent. She remained in Laramie for the final months of 1884 and then left town before her January court date.[29] Even the most optimistic evaluation of her legal situation must have served to convince Bessie Summers that she had no chance in the rent case. Other prostitutes in Laramie had not fared well when delinquent to the same rental agent. When Laramie prostitute Susan Bannon failed to appear on rent charges, the court ordered her horse sold and the proceeds paid to the landlord.[30]

In civil matters, although the profession of prostitution was known to be outlawed, legal restrictions and conditions ruled business transactions. If prostitutes lapsed in the payment of their personal accounts, they could be sued and their property confiscated. Business establishments owned by prostitutes could be attached and their goods sold at public auction to satisfy overdue debts. At the same time, prostitutes could secure a mortgage on a saloon or brothel even though the financial community knew that illegal activities would constitute the normal business. Thus, prostitutes found another avenue whereby they entered the world of legitimate community members. They could own property through proper legal channels, they could generate credit, but, like other citizens, they were expected to pay their debts. If they did not, then the legal machinery for civil matters churned forward, and prostitutes were sued for their financial obligations independently of any criminal charges which might be lodged against them for prostitution.

Third, legal hearings heightened the citizen status of prostitutes. They lived under conditions that nurtured violence. Murder, suicide, and mysterious deaths were commonplace. When these occurred, the testimony of prostitutes provided the needed explanations to authorities. The law readily accepted the sworn statements of prostitutes to establish circumstances of death and to arrive at a legal judgment on culpability. Through their inquest testimony prostitutes added legitimacy to the development of the institutional order. Known to be habitual lawbreakers and their residences to be illegal establishments, prostitutes found it unnecessary to defend themselves on these points at inquests. Authorities chose not to introduce matters of background and profession in return for evidence which added to societal organization.

A dramatic shoot-out in 1879 in Cheyenne illustrated the ease with which prostitutes crossed to the side of the law when the occasion demanded that they be accepted as reliable witnesses and supporters of the legal system. Charles Boulter shot and killed Edward Malone after a scuffle in the room of prostitute Ida Snow. Several prostitutes, eyewitnesses to the fracas, presented substantial evidence in favor of Boulter.

At the investigation, Ida Snow recounted that Malone visited her at the brothel of Ida Hamilton. Snow and Malone quarreled, and he pulled a knife and threatened to cut her from her mouth to her stomach.[31] Ida Hamilton testified that, hearing screams for help from Miss Snow's room, she and Charles Boulter broke down the door and rushed in to find Ida Snow, blood pouring from her mouth, being savagely throttled by Malone. Boulter pulled Malone away, and the latter, in a frenzy of rage, rushed from the house and quickly returned with a pistol. The two men carried the argument to the street, where Boulter fired his gun and Malone fell, mortally wounded.[32]

Three other residents of the house, Florence Vaughn, Mary West, and Ida Moore, testified that Boulter ordered Malone to drop his gun, but Malone yelled that he would kill Boulter and pointed the pistol at him.[33] A prostitute from a brothel across the street agreed that Malone threatened Boulter and aimed as if to shoot.[34] The Cheyenne policeman who ran to the scene corroborated reports of the prostitutes by testifying that he saw Malone shot, found a cocked pistol under his body, and accepted the immediate and voluntary surrender of Boulter.[35]

The accumulated testimony created a strong impression that the attack on Ida Snow threatened her life, that Charles Boulter hurried to save her, and that the enraged Malone then intended to kill Boulter. Boulter acted in self-defense, but the legal resolution of that hinged upon the testimony provided by prostitutes. No questions were raised about their illegal participation in the events surrounding the shooting, nor was their credibility challenged as legitimate witnesses for a court of inquiry. The necessities of the moment allowed Ida Hamilton and the women of her brothel to be treated as citizens with a responsibility to the community and to another citizen. Both the rights of the deceased and of the accused rested on the testimony of the prostitutes.

Inquest testimony relevant to murders committed away from brothels also required the assistance of prostitutes. In the death of Private Roy Baker, whose body was found on the road to Fort Russell near Cheyenne, Wyoming, statements from his prostitute friend and her madam supplied information about the hours directly preceding his

death. Lack of certainty about the identity of the murderer led authorities to question the events of Baker's stay with Maudie Norton at
the house of Kate Welsh. Central elements in the inquiry concerned the
amount of money Baker carried, conversations or disagreements he
had with other soldiers, and the exact times that various soldiers entered and left the brothel. In all these matters Norton and Welsh proved
excellent witnesses.

Kate Welsh demonstrated that as madam of her own establishment
she missed no detail of events that occurred in her house. She knew that
Baker had $10 when he arrived. From this money he paid Maudie Nor-
ton $2 and contributed twenty-five cents for blackberry wine and $1 for
other drinks. Baker refused to exchange a five-dollar gold piece for Kate
Welsh's five silver dollars. His evening with Maudie Norton completed,
Baker left the house at exactly eleven o'clock in the company of Corpo-
ral Parkinson. After the departure of the two soldiers, Kate Welsh went
to the Chicago Saloon and purchased a pitcher of beer for some of her
customers and kept tabs on who went in and out of the house. According to Welsh, Parkinson returned to the house at 1:00 a.m. and demanded that Baker "jar loose" so that they could return to the post.
Three times Kate Welsh told the inebriated Parkinson, who jingled several coins while he talked, to go away and stop acting the fool. Besides
establishing that Parkinson had both opportunity and motive to kill Private Baker, Kate Welsh accounted for other soldiers at her house and
showed that their actions were either known or unexplained. Privates
Murray, Reed, and Reilley had visited the house, but beyond that Kate
Welsh could not speak for their activities. Privates Wise and Allen left the
brothel together at about 1:30 a.m. Private Miller had the best alibi because he and a prostitute named Rose visited the Chicago Saloon together at 9:30 p.m. At 10:00 p.m. Kate Welsh went to the bar, picked them
up, and they all returned to the house where Miller retired to Rose's
room. At 3:34 a.m. Welsh entered the room and roused the sleeping Miller so that he could get back to Fort Russell in time for reveille.[36]

In this case, the testimony of the prostitutes had nothing to do with a
murder committed in a brothel. The women had no knowledge of the
crime itself and did not know that Baker had been murdered for his
money as he returned to the post until they were informed the next day.
Here the law needed the observations of the prostitutes to help recon-
struct the events leading to the death of Private Baker. Evidence con-

cerning the flow of customers, the exchange of money, and the tone of conversations set a framework for police investigation. The mechanics of running a brothel operation produced a superior witness for detail in Madam Kate Welsh; she missed nothing in her house and could account for the whereabouts of her employees at every moment. From among the events of an evening, this keen observer sorted out names, events, and times. No suggestion appeared that the authorities would pounce upon all this verification of illegal activities for purposes of prosecution. In return for her wealth of information, the law willingly granted a brief immunity as Kate Welsh helped to sift through the events that led to the murder of one of her customers, although at the conclusion of the inquest no individual was charged with the crime.

Prostitutes also aided the law in connection with deaths that did not stem from murder or mayhem. Prostitutes sometimes happened upon a body quite by accident and later testified about the event. The death of Mrs. Annie St. Clair, alias Forbes, touched the life of illiterate prostitute Jennie Howard.[37] Inquest testimony revealed that Jennie Howard had never met the dead woman, a former inmate of the Colorado State Penitentiary, but had seen her about in the neighborhood. When the body was found, Howard was asked by an unidentified official to enter the house, examine the body, and check the residence for any valuables. After doing this, Miss Howard reported that neither the body nor the house showed signs of violence and that no personal valuables were found. The attending physician verified Miss Howard's nonprofessional evaluation of death and stated that the deceased suffered from a tumor on the neck which involved her heart and arteries. The coroner's inquest accepted the judgments of these two witnesses and rendered a decision that death occurred from natural causes.[38]

Occasionally prostitutes performed the task of testifying about the death of an associate whose body had been found. At the inquest into the death of Hattie Anderson, a black prostitute, several of her associates gave statements. Their information included her appearance on the day of her death, what they knew of her medical history, and the nature of the last conversations they had with her. When Hattie Anderson did not come out of her house to join several other prostitutes for dinner, they went to inquire and found her dead in her bed.[39] Prostitute Maud Brooks buried Hattie Anderson and listed "appoplectic [*sic*] fits" as the cause of death in the cemetery records.[40] The attending physician reported to the coroner's inquest that Hattie Anderson, aged thirty-five, died of constitutional syphilis.[41]

These dreary departures of the poor and the unknown would have remained unrecorded but for the bits and pieces of testimony offered by their colleagues in the grey world of prostitution. From these statements officials learned what, if any, legal action should be taken following an unattended death. Without that information the law, already a superficial agency at best, would have been further retarded and the development of formal legal procedures and record keeping stunted. As a secondary benefit to society, these documents tucked away in the permanent public record left some small word about the lives of the voiceless and forgotten.

Fourth, prostitutes as citizens received some protection from criminal attack under the law, although this remained one of the weakest areas of a prostitute's citizenship because prosecution of those who violated the rights of prostitutes never became forceful in any community. Crimes of this nature were viewed tolerantly, and prosecution of the guilty proceeded listlessly. Although enfeebled, the law did exist, and court dockets listed defendants charged with a variety of offenses against the persons of prostitute women.[42]

For example, at least mild disapproval greeted the murder of a prostitute, and in most cases the law attempted to arrest and try the guilty party. Seldom did community outrage accompany the episode, and so the outcome of the trial and the imposition of punishment could not be depended upon, even in cases where no question lingered about the identity of the killer. Three Denver prostitutes—one American, one French, one Japanese—all died by strangulation in the same year. Little doubt surrounded the name of the murderer, a local criminal, Richard DeMady. DeMady stood trial in two of these cases and won acquittal both times.[43] In cases where the prosecution managed to convict, the defendant could almost count on a reduced sentence after serving a portion of his time.[44]

The element of race added another dimension to cases involving murder and prostitution. When a black prostitute got mixed up in a murder, the full weight of the law descended upon her. Belle Warden, a black madam in Denver, and one of her employees, Mattie Lemmon, got entangled in a murder in Miss Warden's brothel, and both women faced ten-year sentences in the Colorado State Penitentiary.[45] Both were still incarcerated three years later when Mattie Lemmon died.[46]

Unfortunately, when the circumstances were reversed and a black prostitute was the murder victim, the law did not respond in kind. Mattison Hall shot and killed prostitute Georgie Cox in a brothel outside Fort Russell, but justice looked the other way. At Hall's trial, the judge instructed the jury to remember that the character of the deceased should not alter their regard for the severity of the crime. The jury chose not to follow the judge's advice and acquitted Hall. Hall confessed that he feared conviction on a charge of horse stealing far more than the murder charge, as the punishment for horse thievery exceeded that for murdering prostitutes.[47]

Prosecution of the guilty lessened even more when the crime involved the physical abuse and beating of a prostitute. Here the usual court decision imposed a misdemeanor fine for public fighting. Censure of these episodes often appeared in the newspaper accounts of the court proceedings, but small efforts were made to punish those who attacked and beat prostitutes.[48] In the genteel rationalization of the day, many people believed that prostitutes got only what they earned. Violent beatings, physical abuse, and hideous lives seemed the appropriate rewards of prostitution. These ideas extended to include the violence of rape. To the mind of society and, consequently, in the expression of the law, the rape of a prostitute was deemed impossible.[49] In a nineteenth-century mentality where rape was a sexual and not a violent act, the concept that a prostitute had a right to refuse an act of sex did not exist. Since her person had already been soiled by her own actions, a prostitute could not experience a personal violation from an involuntary sexual encounter. Despoiled in the eyes of all, her "virtue" lost, a prostitute had no honor to protect and therefore could not be raped. The almost complete absence of records of charges for the rape of prostitutes attests to the strength of this belief. Only two newspaper reports about raped prostitutes surfaced; they showed how ludicrous public sentiment thought rape of prostitutes to be.

In 1868 when two soldiers raped a camp follower in Texas, the press reported distress over the incident until the profession of the woman, Bridget Holland, came to light. Suddenly the press, the public, and the entire regiment of the two charged soldiers turned against Mrs. Holland

and demanded the release of the two defendants.[50] A similar episode in Cheyenne had a slightly different twist when a conviction was actually returned. Saner heads gained control though, and the *Cheyenne Daily Sun* reported: "Joseph Lucas, convicted . . . of committing rape upon Susie Bennett, a woman of ill repute, and sentenced to two and a half years imprisonment, has been pardoned by Governor Thayer. This action was taken on the recommendation of the warden of the penitentiary, the advice of the prosecuting attorney, the solicitation of the jury by whom Lucas was convicted, and the recommendation of a number of other citizens."[51] Everyone except Susie Bennett, it appeared, interceded on the part of the accused, yet the case was extraordinary in that it ever reached the point of conviction. Rape charges against those who violated prostitutes remained largely absent from the legal record.

The nature of the charges determined how much protection prostitutes received under the law. The quality of protection of rights and personal liberties for prostitutes remained superficial and reflected the general lack of concern that society felt for prostitutes. White prostitutes enjoyed slightly more protection than blacks, but in all cases protection of civil liberties depended on the benevolence of local officials. They dispensed just sufficient protection to keep prostitutes peripheral members of the community. In this negative manner prostitutes maintained their peculiar dual lives in frontier society.

The result was that prostitutes by their legal status as both citizen and criminal helped to heighten institutional awareness in a society where traditions hung by a thin thread. Prostitutes contributed to the legal order by their participation in the daily court routine. Through their appearances in civil cases, as well as through court and inquest testimony, prostitutes actively added to the weight of the public record. Their activity served to increase the legal corpus of the local authority and brought a greater awareness to the populace concerning the influence of law enforcement agencies. At the same time prostitutes, by virtue of their criminal role, intensified the importance of other social institutions and helped to give purpose and direction to new communities. Flamboyant and highly visible, prostitutes made the identification of crime groups easy and added merit to the virtuous presence of family, church, and school. These institutions gained a new self-importance as they perceived themselves surrounded by a lawless element that threatened the very moral fiber of youthful communities. The importance of home and church escalated as the representatives of society's mainstream sought to establish the requirements of a social order. Prostitutes provided a convenient target as the obvious representatives of the forces of social disorder. Success in restricting prostitutes and their associates convinced the population that through the legal system institutional order was triumphing.[52]

As for the prostitutes, their lives whirled about in various kinds of contributions to the legal order. They helped to build that order by their participation as both citizen and criminal, but it would be glib to assign them merely a passive role in the emergence of frontier law. A universal quality of prostitutes was an absolutely pragmatic understanding of their status in a community. Their survival depended in part upon an ability to comprehend the restrictions of society and then to exploit these restrictions to carve out an existence. In other words, prostitutes clearly knew the rules of the game.

Indeed, the legal establishment represented the one institution in society where prostitutes could feel comfortable. Rarely welcomed in church circles, never invited to the homes of the respectable, generally cut off from governmental welfare agencies, prostitutes knew their place and their role in the courts.[53] Here, among the police and court officials, prostitutes needed no introduction and gave no explanations. In the lowest courts, prostitutes, outcasts in every arena of life, found a tiny corner of society where they exercised power. In justice of the peace courts prostitutes felt at home, and here they brought their complaints and grievances about the police, about customers, about each other.

Prostitutes knew how to use the courts. In Cheyenne, prostitute Mollie Russell flounced out of court after making it clear that she had no intention of abiding by an arbitrary new ruling that she had to report her whereabouts before leaving town.[54] In San Antonio, a large group of prostitutes stormed into court to complain about a customer who had beaten a co-worker and left the brothel without paying.[55] In Tucson, Louisa Ochoa made seven court appearances in two years, five of which resulted from the charges of other prostitutes that she attacked and abused them.[56] In Clear Creek County, Colorado, Nellie Brown stole Bel Kay's green curtains. Both women appeared in court with attorneys, the defendant was dismissed, and the county paid the costs.[57]

Prostitutes saw that the legal establishment should do two things. First, the law should abide by the compromise rules that permitted prostitutes to sustain themselves in a community. Second, the law should provide an opportunity for prostitutes to exercise some rights as citizens in cases where their lives erupted into squabbles, thievery, or excessive abuse. For prostitutes the law emerged as the one frontier institution integral to the conduct of their battered lives.

Frontier authorities accepted with vigor the responsibility to regulate crime, but the sordid story of crime management cast the contributions of the frontier legal establishment into a negative framework. An impression emerges of a beleaguered frontier judiciary so preoccupied with the daily routine of vice that it could not really participate in the process of institution building. Locked into a legal holding pattern, frontier law seems divorced from major issues and precedents. Localism, factionalism, ineptness, and corruption appear to deny that the legal system nurtured the growth of institutions from within the western social order itself. Yet it is superficial to dismiss as unimportant the impact of local law upon the processes of enlarging social institutions in frontier communities. The frontier legal establishment was responsible for a greater contribution to the institutional development of the West than the mere management of crime.

Justice of the peace courts mirrored the values, standards, and expectations of frontier communities. Although flawed in the strictest judicial sense, the courts brought a variety of forces to frontier society. Communities charged justice of the peace courts with the responsibility for crime management. This the courts did by use of taxation and control. These practical chores did not constitute the only contribution of local courts to the development of the West. The relationship of the courts with frontier prostitutes showed how the legal order also made substantial contributions to institutional growth in the West, while denying the full expression of legal rights to prostitutes. The regulation of prostitutes, a highly visible crime group, added to the corpus of the public record and heightened the importance of social institutions in the community. The legal system assigned prostitutes a dual identity in society, and then enlarged the institutions of the social order by drawing on both the citizen and the criminal status of these women.

Prostitutes themselves did not respond in a passive manner to this treatment; rather, within the judicial system they found the only societal institution that welcomed them. From this vantage point prostitutes did not hesitate to use the law for assistance in the maintenance of their lives. In return for institutional exploitation, prostitutes expected the courts to honor the peculiar balance of criminal and citizen status that dominated their existence. Given the conditions of nineteenth-century society, prostitutes depended on this uneasy judicial relationship to guarantee themselves a marginal spot within the community framework. Without it, prostitutes, among the poorest and most abused of frontier people, would have been utterly powerless. The courts dispensed a fragmented and erratic justice to prostitutes, but these women clung to it as their single weapon in the dynamics of a society that systematically excluded them from the circles of social, economic, and political power.

The convergence of these many forces served to enlarge the legal system and to stabilize western social order. In no small measure frontier prostitutes assisted in this process. The mighty legal structure and the lowly frontier prostitute? Strange bedfellows indeed.

Notes

1. *Butte Miner*, Sept. 22, 1881.

2. For other examples, see The *San Antonio Daily Express*, Jan.–Apr. 1868; *Cheyenne Daily Sun*, Dec. 8, 1877, Feb. 6, 1878, Feb. 16, 1882, June 3, 1882; *Austin Daily Democratic Statesman*, Apr. 18, 1882; *Tombstone Daily Epitaph*, May 18, 1889; *Butte Miner*, Aug. 31, Sept. 2, 1880, Jan. 7, 1881.

3. William Morris, ed., *The American Heritage Dictionary of the English Language* (Boston: American Heritage Publishing and Houghton Mifflin, 1969), p. 741.

4. James S. Hurst stresses the importance of law as a social function in history. His work on nineteenth-century law emphasizes the evolution of the legal order as a barometer of the goals of the everyday world. Hurst argues that the legal order was viewed as an instrument of the community, and as such the American legal system supported the extension of individual and group power by policies which led to the concentration of capital. The development of American contract law provides the foundation for Hurst's thesis. See James W. Hurst, *Law and the Conditions of Freedom in the Nineteenth Century United States* (Madison: University of Wisconsin Press, 1967). Also see David Flaherty, "An Approach to American History: Willard Hurst as Legal Historian," *American Journal of Legal History* 14 (1970): 222–34; Wythe Holt, "Now and

Then: The Uncertain State of Nineteenth Century American Legal History," *Indiana Law Review* 7 (1974): 615–43; Jerome Michael and Mortimer Adler, *Crime, Law and Social Science* (Montclair, N.J.: Patterson Smith, 1971), pp. xxv–xxvii; Calvin Woodward, "History, Legal History and Legal Education," *Virginia Law Review* 53 (Jan. 1967): 89–121.

5. Hans Kelsen writes on this point, "The pure theory of law . . . seeks to discover the nature of law itself, to determine its structure and its typical forms independent of the changing content which it exhibits at different times and among different people. . . . As a theory its sole purpose is to know its subject. It answers the question of what law is, not what it ought to be." Kelsen maintains that the pure theory of law is science, while other legal questions really address politics. See his work "The Pure Theory of Law and Analytical Jurisprudence," *Harvard Law Review* 60 (Nov. 1941): 44–70.

6. Holt, "Now and Then: The Uncertain State of Nineteenth Century American Legal History," p. 615.

7. Several works point out the efforts of frontier communities to establish law and order. At the local level interest has centered on the frontier marshal or sheriff. Works that present the efforts of towns to bring law to the West include Wayne Gard, *Frontier Justice* (Norman: University of Oklahoma Press, 1949); W. Eugene Hollon, *Frontier Violence: Another Look* (New York: Oxford University Press, 1974); Walter Prescott Webb, *The Texas Rangers* (Boston: Houghton-Mifflin, 1935).

8. Information about the development, uses, and characteristics of American justice of the peace courts comes from James W. Hurst, *The Growth of American Law: The Law-makers* (Boston: Little, Brown, 1950), pp. 147–52.

9. See for examples Cheyenne Police Court Docket, Sept. 30, 1868– Feb. 8, 1869, WSAHD; Justice Docket, City of Denver, Mar. 21, 1864– Aug. 15, 1867, WHC; Criminal Docket, Hemphill County, Tex., July 25, 1887–Jan. 1, 1890, PPHM. Of course local variations can be found. In Phoenix, Ariz., as much as $2 a day might be credited for jail time. Maricopa County Justice Docket, Phoenix Precinct, Dec. 14, 1885– Dec. 30, 1886, ASA.

10. Calvin Woodward writes, "Every society has standards which render certain conduct and conditions intolerable. And each society endeavors by pressures exerted through its various institutions to abolish such conduct and conditions." "Reality and Social Reform: The Transition from Laissez-Faire to the Welfare State," *Yale Law Journal* 52 (Nov. 1962): 286. The presence of the statutes against prostitution represented the desire to give legal weight to the moral sanctions against this profes-

sion. A proliferation of such legislation has been found traditionally in Judaeo-Christian societies. For examples of frontier statutes see *The General Laws of New Mexico* (Albany, N.Y.: W. C. Little, 1882), p. 300; *San Antonio Ordinances: Standing Rules of City Government from 1837–1880* (San Antonio, Tex.: n.p., 1881), p. 39; *Abilene Chronicle*, May 12, 1870, Sept. 7, 1871; *Butte Miner*, Nov. 18, 1879; *Laramie Daily Sentinel*, May 28, 1870; *Tombstone Epitaph*, Mar. 9, 1882.

11. Important concepts in the processes of frontier town building can be found in Robert Dkystra's study *The Cattle Towns* (New York: Atheneum, 1976). His important contributions will lead to other analytical studies about the forces and devices of the urban frontier. For example, see Dorothea Muller, "Church Building and Community Making on the Frontier, A Case Study: Josiah Strong, Home Missionary in Cheyenne, 1871–1873," *Western Historical Quarterly* 10 (Apr. 1979): 191–216.

12. Cheyenne Police Court Docket, June 15, 1868–Aug. 3, 1868, WSAHD.

13. City of Cheyenne Jail Register, Mar. 2, 1887–Jan. 1, 1890, WSAHD.

14. Justice of the Peace Docket, Albany County, City of Laramie, Aug. 2, 1877–Aug. 2, 1886, ACCH.

15. Records of Arrest for the City of Austin, Jan. 1, 1876–Jan. 1, 1879, ATCC.

16. Ibid. Arrest records for Canadian, Cheyenne, Denver, Laramie, and Phoenix followed the same pattern. For citation of these records see nn. 9 and 14 above.

17. Reform efforts were sporadic and short-lived. Cheyenne, for example, attempted one in 1873 and again in 1878; the second was a campaign to drive black prostitutes from the city. Both attempts were miserable failures. An 1868 reform movement in San Antonio literally drove prostitutes beyond the city limits. The resulting horror of women without food or shelter, exposed to the elements and battered by a terrible storm, caused the authorities to capitulate. See Dorothea Muller, "Church Building and Community Making on the Frontier," and Anne M. Butler, "The Frontier Press and Prostitution" (Master's thesis, University of Maryland, 1975), pp. 25–31, 80–83.

18. Minutes of the Grand Jury, Boise, Idaho, empaneled Dec. 23, 1908, pp. 51–53, 55–56, 65–68, 88–97, IHS. This grand jury investigation looked into a twenty-year period of prostitution in Boise. Testimony concerned brothel and gambling operations in Boise and the involvement of officials in the regular receipt of bribes. No action was taken at the conclusion of the investigation.

19. Justice of the Peace Docket, Albany County, City of Laramie, Aug. 2, 1877–Aug. 2, 1886, ACCH.

20. Ibid. Wyoming Census for 1880, City of Laramie, WSAHD.

21. City of Cheyenne Jail Register, Mar. 2, 1887–Jan. 1, 1890, WSAHD.

22. Criminal Docket, Hemphill County, Tex., July 25, 1887–Jan. 1, 1890, passim, PPHM. For Allie English see July 25, Aug. 23, Sept. 23, Oct. 22, Nov. 25, Dec. 26, 1887, and June 7, Aug. 2, Oct. 3, and Nov. 24, 1888. No arrest was reported for Allie English in 1889, and an 1890 note in the docket indicated that after being confined in the jail, Allie English left town.

23. Albany County Tax List, 1875, ACCH.

24. Ibid. Remarks about status of taxes for previous years listed next to delinquent accounts.

25. Ibid. Justice Docket, Albany County, City of Laramie, Aug. 2, 1877–Aug. 2, 1886, see May 28 and Sept. 6, 1878, ACCH; Wyoming Census for 1880, City of Laramie, WSAHD; Inquest, July 21, 1881, ACCH.

26. Criminal Docket for Santa Fe County, Feb. Term 1871–July Term 1876; see Feb. 1874, July 1874, and Feb. 1875, NMSRA.

27. Justice of the Peace Dockets, Civil and Criminal Cases for Apache County, Colo., Aug. 1866–Dec. 1869; see Oct. 29, 1866, May 13, 1867, July 19, 1867, and Oct. 30, 1869, CSA.

28. Justice of the Peace Dockets, Albany County, City of Laramie, Aug. 2, 1877–Aug. 2, 1887, passim for the years 1884–86; Justice Docket, Albany County, City of Laramie, Jan. 3, 1884–May 22, 1886, see Oct. 1, 1885, ACCH.

29. Justice Docket, Albany County, City of Laramie, Jan. 3, 1883–May 22, 1886; see Sept. 4, 10, 21, 27, 1884. Summers's last recorded arrest was Nov. 14, 1884; see Justice of the Peace Dockets, Aug. 2, 1877–Aug. 2, 1887, ACCH.

30. Justice Docket, Albany County, City of Laramie, Jan. 3, 1884–May 22, 1886; see Mar. 6, 1885 and an earlier case of delinquent rent, Sept. 2, 1884, ACCH.

31. Coroner's Inquest, Nov. 1, 1879, Cheyenne, Wyo., p. 1, WSAHD.

32. Ibid., pp. 2–4.

33. Ibid., pp. 5–11.

34. Ibid., pp. 26–28.

35. Ibid., pp. 18–20.

36. Coroner's Inquest, Oct. 3, 1890, Cheyenne, pp. 26–33, WSAHD.

37. Coroner's Inquest, Mar. 10, 1888, Cheyenne, WSAHD. Unable to write her name, Jennie Howard only marked a crude "x" at the end of her testimony.

38. Testimony in this case was very brief. The only other witness besides Jennie Howard and the physician was a minister who had known the deceased when she was confined to the women's ward of the Colorado penitentiary.

39. Coroner's Inquest, June 23, 1882, Cheyenne, pp. 1–3, WSAHD.

40. Register of Burials, Cheyenne Cemetery, 1875–1932, June 25, 1882, WSAHD.

41. Coroner's Inquest, June 23, 1882, Cheyenne, p. 6, WSAHD.

42. For example, see the Justice Docket for Clear Creek, Colo., Aug. 1867–June 24, 1871, WHC. On Apr. 3, 1868, Clay Forbush was fined $50.10 for assault and battery on a prostitute. But in January 1869 when Mary Hayes tried to bring intent to kill charges against Michael O'Hare, the court dismissed O'Hare and committed Hayes.

43. Description Record, City and County of Denver 1863–1921; the *Murder Book* by Detective Sam Howe of the Denver Police Department, CHS. See the cases of Marie Contassiot, Kika Oyasana, and Lena Tapper. (This is a personal scrapbook and has neither pagination nor order by date.)

44. Ibid.; see cases of Mable Brown murdered by Harry Chablis, Effie Moore murdered by Charles Henry, Vina Moore murdered by Agnes Mellon, Bonnie Wilson murdered by Callie McPherson, and Lizzie Wright murdered by Charles W. Spurrier.

45. Ibid., see cases of Belle Warden, Mattie Lemmon, Charles Smith, and Benny Gates.

46. Biennial Report of the Commissioners, Warden, Chaplain, and Physician of the Colorado State Penitentiary to the Governor; Immigration and Penitentiary Papers, 1865–1877, Report of Dr. E. C. Grey, CSA.

47. *Cheyenne Daily Sun*, Feb. 3, June 6, 1882.

48. *Black Hills Daily Times*, Sept. 5, 1877; *Butte Miner*, May 23, 1880, July 23, 1881, Dec. 11, 1881; *Laramie Daily Sentinel*, May 11, 1871; *San Antonio Daily Express*, Jan. 12, 1867.

49. Although the literature on the topic of rape has increased greatly, the content usually deals with twentieth-century legal concerns. Thus

an excellent work like that of Barbara A. Babcock, Anne Freedman, Eleanor Holmes Norton, and Susan Ross, *Sex Discrimination and the Law: Causes and Remedies* (Boston: Little, Brown, 1975) is grounded too much in the present to help a historian grapple with the nineteenth-century setting of the law, the prostitute, and rape. Of great help in establishing a historical perspective for this topic is the work of Sally Gold and Martha Wyatt, "The Rape System: Old Roles and New Times," *Catholic University Law Review* 27 (Summer 1978), reprint edition. Their skillful legal summary shows how American law evolved to include two elements necessary for the prosecution of rape: force and lack of consent, both of which the victim must prove. With the burden of proof placed upon the victim, prostitutes have always found courts unwilling to believe "lack of consent."

50. *San Antonio Daily Express*, Mar. 20, 1872, pp. 24–27.

51. *Cheyenne Daily Sun*, Feb. 7, 1877.

52. The *Laramie Daily Sentinel* reported on Oct. 24, 1872, ". . . our thoughts would constantly wander back three or four years ago when our city was in its swaddling clothes, when we were struggling for an existence against anarchy and crime, and when it was a matter of serious doubt whether the virtuous or the vicious were to rule, which part would be obliged to leave. And in those early days when we were without law and without social, religious or political organizations, when everything had to run itself, Mrs. Ivinson was first and foremost in every good word and work." This tribute from the paper was offered on the occasion of the thirty-third birthday of Mrs. Edward Ivinson, Laramie pioneer, who had worked tirelessly for the church, schools, poor, and sick.

53. "Respectable women" in communities seldom demonstrated a friendly attitude toward prostitutes. In Cheyenne a woman complained: "Shall we go to their abodes and urge them to repentence. . . . Shall we invite them to our homes, to our social circles, private dances. . . ." *Wyoming Tribune*, Apr. 23, 1870. In Tombstone a mother wrote to the *Tombstone Epitaph* on Mar. 10, 1882, and protested the "incursions of the vilest elements of the community," when the city council lifted a housing ban on brothel locations.

54. *Cheyenne Daily Sun*, June 25, 1879.

55. *San Antonio Daily Express*, Apr. 11, 1868.

56. Justice of the Peace Records of Charles H. Meyers, Pima County, Ariz., Jan. 1, 1871–July 25, 1872; see Aug. 12, Nov. 20, 1871, Feb. 22, May 14, Oct. 14, Dec. 9, 1872, and July 24, 1873, AHS.

57. Justice Dockets, Clear Creek County, Colo., Aug., 1867–June 24, 1871; see Feb. 15, 1871, WHC.

6

The Military Game

On the 8th July 1863, while my boat was under charter by U.S.
. . . these prostitutes were put on board . . . by a detachment of
soldiers . . . ordered to do so by Lt. Col. Spauldings . . . and
Capt. Stubbs . . . who were acting under orders of Gen. Morgan.
I protested against their putting these women on my boat. . . . I
told them it would forever ruin her reputation as a passenger
boat. . . . It was done so she is now & since known as the float-
ing wh_re house.[1]

In 1865 steamboat Captain John Newcomb filed the above complaint,
part of a suit against the U.S. Army. The suit stemmed from Newcomb's
financial losses during the Civil War when 111 Nashville prostitutes were
herded onto his boat, the *Idahoe*, for deportation to any city along the
Ohio River that would accept them. This military order, designed to
control the spread of venereal disease among army personnel in Nashville, launched Newcomb on a month-long odyssey marked by black humor and military ineptness.

At Louisville, Kentucky, the officer in charge of transportation, Captain
J. H. Ferry, received the migrants less than enthusiastically and immediately ordered Captain Newcomb to take his unsavory cargo on to Cincinnati. Captain Ferry conceded that the task of prohibiting prospective
clients from swimming to the vessel and boarding illegally exceeded
the limits of both Newcomb's responsibility and the crew's physical
prowess, and assigned a twelve-man guard for the duration of the trip.
Reinforced with a military escort that mingled freely with the prostitutes
and took its meals at the public table (at Newcomb's expense), the har-

ried captain continued to Cincinnati where the nonplussed and per-plexed commanding officer, Captain Schmidt, uncertain of the correct procedure, ordered the women held on board the *Idahoe*. The steamer remained at anchor for several days during which time the civil authorities, for reasons unexplained in the military documents, removed twelve or fourteen of the women. Whether this prodded Schmidt is unknown, but he finally ordered Newcomb to return the vessel to Louisville. This Newcomb did, but Colonel Mundy, the commanding officer at that city, wasted not a moment in sending the steamer back to Nashville, its original point of departure.

When he filed his suit two years later, Newcomb maintained that he had suffered not only from social disgrace to his boat but, more particularly, from monetary losses because ". . . the stateroom furniture is very much soiled the glasses in the saloon were broken the chairs were cut and the tables were broken from frequent fights of the women."[2] During the actual voyage, the army had refused to provide Newcomb with any rations, and he had been forced to purchase food, medicines, and ice for the women, many of whom were sick and destitute. Those few with funds argued that the trip, forced on them by the army, remained the obligation of the military, and they would not contribute to their own support in any way.

After he returned to Nashville, Newcomb demanded that some military personnel inspect the steamer to make an appraisal of its condition. The inspecting officer confirmed Newcomb's own claim and declared that "I would recommend that he be paid one thousand dollars for damages to the boat."

Armed with detailed depositions from his crew and this inspection report, Newcomb filed his claim repeatedly, only to be ignored. Finally, in 1865, despairing of any action from lower level officials, Newcomb submitted his claim to the office of the secretary of war. Within two months Captain Newcomb received payment of $1,000 for transportation and damages and $4,316.04 for subsistence and medical supplies.[3]

This entire episode might so easily be added to those amusing bits of social trivia about prostitutes, humorous for its scene of Newcomb, a nineteenth-century Flying Dutchman, haplessly navigating up and down the Tennessee and Ohio Rivers, his vessel overrun with a flamboyant and volatile crew of "painted ladies." The ludicrous picture is made more so by the image of Newcomb desperately swatting and batting at the amorous swimmers trying to board while the bawdy passengers raucously cheered them on. Beyond this sordid joke lies a social puzzle of intriguing interest. This concerns the institutional relationship—official or quasi-official—between the U.S. Army and prostitution. It is usual to assume that there was no authorized official bond between the two, no recognition by military authorities of prostitution beyond diligent but futile attempts to control it, and no direct official encouragement, since these women invaded camp areas uninvited by authorities who despised the traffic.

The documents in the bizarre case of the *Idahoe* contradict these assumptions. They offer two clues to support the existence of a well-established bond. The first was an absence of any tone of the unusual in the correspondence. The Washington office merely wished to verify the expenses and decide upon the correct military office for disbursement. There were no questions raised about the appropriateness of several military officers, clearly identified, meddling in civil affairs of this nature. General Morgan's original order of banishment was actually defended. The second clue, more subtle, was found in the statement of payment to Newcomb. Here, below a printed certification that the disbursement paid was for public services, the agent wrote in his own hand, "These women being all effected with venereal disease were giving the disease to the U.S. soldiers serving in the army of Tenn, and it became necessary and for the good of the service to have them removed from Nashville."[4] Presumably disease constituted the reason for removal, and not an official rejection of the profession itself. If disease equaled removal, then the opposite end of this logic indicated that lack of disease made the prostitutes' presence acceptable. This suggested that while the occupation remained unacceptable within society at large, it was not only an expected, but perhaps an encouraged accoutrement at military sites, and caused neither surprise nor control as long as the social and physical excesses did not become too visible. Should either get out of hand, officials exercised certain restraining measures—medical inspection, quarantine, or banishment—but authorities seldom sought to eliminate this extralegal recreation.

From this rather blurred administrative behavior there emerges a sense of vague military policy that exceeded simple tolerance of prostitution and moved into the area of official endorsement. Such a policy almost defied definition. A clear program for the promotion of institutionalized vice for the gratification of enlisted personnel was not to be extracted from the bulk of military law. Vain would be a search of army regulations for a body of orders about transport, supply, and protection of prostitutes per se, but the ambiguous phrasing of some regulations, coupled with a variety of odd episodes, blended together into a complex structure indicative of a de faço policy for the accommodation of prostitutes at military sites.

The notion, transferred to the milieu of the trans-Mississippi West, offered new dimensions to the investigation of prostitution on the frontier. Military fortifications in the Far West greatly increased in the immediate post–Civil War years. As the nation turned its attention from the strife of the East to the economic promise of the West, demands for an enlarged army multiplied. The insistence of entrepreneurs for a governmental agency of order and protection in a territory largely devoid of stable institutions and inhabited by an unfriendly native population prompted the construction of more than eighty-five garrisons between 1865 and 1890. In addition, forts that predated the Civil War were renovated and strengthened. With this massive construction program came the manpower for building and staffing the garrisons. Although the number fluctuated constantly, the approximately 8,400 men stationed at trans-Mississippi posts in the 1850s had almost doubled by the 1890s.[5]

Frontier garrisons represented unique communities. Perhaps more than any other cluster of people in the American West, the military population epitomized the meaning of the frontier experience. Garrison communities, assigned to the most remote, inhospitable regions of the West, attempted to transplant intact the structure of the military life and protocol as they knew it in the East. This proved an impossible task. Caught between the forces of environmental menace and rigid traditions, military personnel and their associates responded vigorously. The most immediate attempt was to intensify the military code to preserve the standards of military conduct as officials understood them. The move was futile. The frontier overpowered the traditions they sought to preserve and produced garrison communities where social conduct often defied traditional patterns. Officials superficially struggled to maintain the image that life at the forts did not deviate from fixed military customs. In truth, all levels of persons at frontier garrisons acted outside the so-called military code of conduct. Officers, their wives and families, enlisted personnel, civilian employees, and attached citizens felt the isolation and insecurities of frontier living.

All persons close to the forts contributed to the dynamics of human sexuality certain to be explosive among communities of isolated men and women. Prostitution within and around garrisons represented the visible acknowledgment of that sexuality. The response of officials to these powerful human forces never assumed a consistent or honest stance. The result produced a frontier military establishment that dealt with prostitution in an ambivalent and deceitful manner that largely ignored the sordid behavior prevalent among army personnel. Ultimately, the official response of the military, despite the endeavors of some individuals, added to the maintenance of prostitution as a frontier phenomenon and encouraged the military to suppress evidence of its participation in the promotion of institutionalized vice.

Although frontier garrisons formed a chain of bachelor communities strung out across the West, some women resided at even the most distant posts. These women played a crucial role in the structure of military life. They contributed to the continuation of the firm divisions between officers and enlisted men so integral to military society. Some of these women, the wives and family members of officers, secured for themselves a favorable place in history, for they appeared to fit with such ease into a "heroic pioneer wife and mother" role.

Indeed, this analysis is not entirely erroneous. Colonel Percy M. Ashburn, of the U.S. Medical Corps, championed the army wives of the 1870s as a special breed of women, worthy of the highest praise and respect. Their travel conditions were often rough and hazardous, their living quarters shabby and unattractive, their opportunities for comfort and luxury few. Ashburn found particularly admirable the manner in which they introduced social refinement, family life, and gracious hospitality to a frontier world that often lacked all three.[6] Ashburn's somewhat romantic view of these wives, seemingly ever cheerful, sweet, and loving in the face of deprivation and adversity, provided a comforting if one-dimensional dash of gentle femininity to the image of the military outpost. It was perhaps a favorite American vision of woman as ameliorator.

The crux of that vision, the assumption that ladies were entitled to fashionable clothing, lovely homes, and kindly treatment, and that those who did without these to follow a spouse proved especially noble, received no little boost from the wives themselves. Perhaps no more famous cheerleader for the frontier wives existed than Elizabeth Bacon Custer, wife of George Armstrong Custer. Her descriptions of camp life painted rich detail of domestic ritual, and she warmly applauded her own patience and cleverness. In her efforts to lavish praise upon her husband's exploits, she managed to spare no plaudits for herself and other officers' wives. Cheerful martyrdom permeated her accounts, as when she wrote, ". . . we women occupied ourselves mostly in finding amusement for the men, who looked to us for diversion in their leisure hours . . . our lives were occupied with reading and domestic detail . . . to fill up the time and make it go faster . . . we tried to vary the monotony of the table with all the ingenuity we were capable of. . . ."[7] This particular passage omitted the information that Mrs. Custer had two black servants to do all her chores and cooking.

Nonetheless, interwoven among her stories of sewing parties and Custer's grandness, she tucked some informative observations about the usual camp attitudes toward married women. Throughout the chronicle appeared numerous references to the wild conduct of neighboring towns and the ease with which the soldiers slipped past the guard to avail themselves of the inviting debauchery. When no town was within access to the fort, sexual tensions in the military camp heightened. Even the intensely proper Mrs. Custer conceded this when she wrote about the stress created for a married officer when his turn came for twenty-four-hour guard duty. "It was pretty solemn business when the detail came to either of the two officers whose wives were with them; but when they obtained permission to bring their wives to the regiment, it was with the understanding that their presence should not interfere with any duty . . . we three women made as little trouble as possible. With a whole camp of faithful soldiers who, no matter what they did outside, would never harm their own, the wives . . . were perfectly safe. . . ."[8]

Her comments demonstrated a clear recognition of the potential sexual explosion that exists in an isolated society where the men far outnumber the women. Mrs. Custer couched this admission in rather bland terms. As she intended her publications to depict the most favorable presentation of military life, she may have consciously omitted any instances when the underlying sexual tensions spilled out into assault, as was recorded at Fort Davis, Texas, in 1873. ". . . on the night of the 20th about 2 o'clock AM Corpl Taliafero "J" Co 9th Cvry attempted a forcible entrance into the sleeping apartment of Mrs. S— Kendall—whose husband was absent at the time on duty. Mrs. Kendall warned the man from the window but he persisted in his efforts. Driven to distraction Mrs. Kendall seized a revolver and just as the scoundrel had succeeded in getting his head through the window she fired, sending a bullet through his brain and killing him instantly."[9]

The reality of human sexuality threatened to strip away any code of honor imposed upon men and women. Its demands surfaced above any notions of good manners or proper conduct. It intimidated the female unguarded for even a moment. In response, officers and their wives intensified an already rigid nineteenth-century standard of moral conduct to convey an aura of "untouchable" to the surrounding masculine society. Committed to this highly idealized notion of their own sexual sanctity, these military residents could not tolerate the open violation of that standard by any of their own set of females as it would weaken the barrier of protection for the group at large. Any crack in the veneer from within the officers' society rattled the entire framework of military conduct and demanded immediate response—either corrective or suppressive. It was imperative that the notion of "code" be maintained. These concepts seem to have been involved in an episode at Fort Union, New Mexico, in 1877.

In November of that year Lieutenant Colonel N. A. M. Dudley, the commanding officer at Fort Union, faced a court-martial on charges that he mismanaged the fort. The heart of the case appeared to be rooted in an angry dispute between Dudley and the quartermaster of the post, A. S. Kimball, over the operation of the quartermaster's depot. The testimony documented extensive fraud perpetrated by Kimball, but he had won the favor of the commander of the district, General Edward Hatch. These two joined forces to oppose Dudley and effect his conviction. To supplement their charges of disobedience of a superior officer's lawful commands and disrespect toward a commanding officer, they threw in "conduct to the prejudice of good order and military discipline." At the outset the apparent thinness of the indictment prompted Dudley's accusors to include the blatantly trumped-up charges of drunkenness while on duty and involvement in a titillating sexual scandal. The several hundred pages of testimony read like a silly squabble among officers and left the impression that quartermaster Kimball and not Colonel Dudley should have been tried. Of greater importance, the tale revealed more about military sexual attitudes than any of the participants probably realized.

Much of the court-martial testimony centered upon Colonel Dudley's attempt to intervene in the private affairs of a Doctor Tipton, a young physician who resided in nearby Tiptonville. It was brought to Dudley's attention by other officers at the post that Miss Lizzie Simpson, daughter of the post chaplain, accused Doctor Tipton of seducing her on an occasion when the two were out riding in his carriage. She offered as proof an affadavit swearing to the events and three innocuous letters from Tipton. These letters supposedly proved that Tipton tried repeatedly to lure Miss Simpson to a private meeting and then tried to make excuses for not seeing her. This lack of clarity and the harmless nature of the letters (which were entered as evidence) were not touched upon in the trial.

According to the testimony, during the afternoon drinking session in the officers' room at the post trader's store, Dudley and three other officers discussed this scandal and the hardship it brought to the chaplain, a fellow officer. They decided to use any influence they had on Tipton to correct the situation immediately. So resolved, and fortified with about four drinks, Dudley and three other officers took a military ambulance to Tiptonville to find the doctor. Dudley told Tipton that he would have to return to the fort with the officers and be married forthwith to Miss Simpson. Dudley assured Tipton that following the marriage Reverend Simpson promised the entire Simpson family, including Lizzie, would move from the area within four days. Although the officers never mentioned it, apparently Miss Simpson found herself pregnant, and in casting about for a father to supply the name for the infant, she settled on Doctor Tipton. As a civilian, he could be conveniently left behind when Simpson moved the family, and he would not have the opportunities to gossip among service people when Simpson went to another post.

Doctor Tipton angrily rejected the plan for a hasty marriage and denied he was guilty of seduction, for he maintained, "I have proof that the girl has been on it before, that she has made solicitations of the soldiers at the garrison."[10] Tipton did not return to the fort that evening, and, ultimately, filed civil suits against the four officers.

Tipton's testimony became a focal point for the attack of the judge advocate. It became the prosecutor's goal in the trial to establish that Miss Simpson enjoyed a notorious reputation at the fort long before the Tipton affair. Evidently he was correct. Over and over, witnesses agreed that Miss Simpson was rumored to be promiscuous and to have been intimate with more than a few of the males at the post. One officer, perhaps as a nod to the status of her father, maintained that the reports were only speculative, and had he believed them, he would not have received Miss Simpson in his home. Other witnesses indicated there was little question about the veracity of the stories, which were discussed freely at the sutler's store. These officers agreed that Miss Simpson overstepped the propriety of the fort by "flirting" with enlisted men. It was this flagrant disregard for the taboo on fraternization with enlisted personnel that first prompted Reverend Simpson to discuss his wayward daughter with other officers. By this time, Miss Simpson's reputation was well established at Fort Union. Thus, the judge advocate argued that Colonel Dudley's visit to Tiptonville could not have been inspired by the admirable desire to protect the name of a brother officer, because Dudley knew long before, from events at the fort, that "the character of the lady whose reputation he assumed so zealously to protect was bad." [11]

If Miss Simpson had reputation problems at the start of this court-martial, by its conclusion she was clearly branded. Tipton's charge that the young woman "made solicitations of the soldiers" elevated her activities from amateur promiscuity to those of professional peddler. Whatever his daughter's proclivities, Reverend Simpson faced an awesome problem if he tried to keep her at his parsonage.

For Colonel Dudley and his companions, the important point was the protection of the reputation of a brother officer whose daughter acted scandalously. This need to act only crystallized after it became known that the woman was cavorting with enlisted men, for her intrigues with officers had been common knowledge for some time. This sexual activity could be tolerated when confined to Miss Simpson's own social set where the favors could be enjoyed and the situation regarded in a jocular way—presumably as long as Reverend Simpson was not present! Once she crossed the line to the enlisted personnel, Miss Simpson struck at the "untouchable" quality that respectable women strove to maintain where numbers and force clearly outweighed their guardian spouses.

Mrs. Jane Elizabeth Ryan and her daughters, Julia Helen Wallace, Mona and Annie Ryan. Mrs. Ryan ran saloons in several Colorado mining towns before settling her family business in Denver. (Courtesy Amon Carter Museum, Fort Worth, Texas)

Exterior view of the Wallace Saloon at 1937 Market Street, Denver. (Courtesy Amon Carter Museum, Fort Worth, Texas)

Annie Ryan and Fiddler John enjoy a light moment at one of the family's Denver establishments. (Courtesy Amon Carter Museum, Fort Worth, Texas)

Interior of the Wallace Saloon. (Courtesy Amon Carter Museum, Fort Worth, Texas)

This is the interior of the Monte Carlo Saloon in the popular Market Street prostitution district. (Courtesy Amon Carter Museum, Fort Worth, Texas)

This was the Gunnell Hill district of Central City, Colorado, where prostitutes operated in the 1890s. (Courtesy Amon Carter Museum, Fort Worth, Texas)

Lou Bunch, a madam from the Gunnell Hill district of Central City, Colorado. (Courtesy Amon Carter Museum, Fort Worth, Texas)

Sadie Orchard by 1901 looked like a movie version of a madam.
(Photo by Jacob Pasevich; courtesy Museum of New Mexico)

Mrs. Sadie Orchard stands outside the Ocean Grove Hotel in Hillsboro, New
Mexico, with two unidentified companions, one black. (Photo by George T. Miller; courtesy Museum of New Mexico)

This Dodge City photograph of a prostitute known only as "Timberline" suggests some of the hardship and sorrow that these women endured. (Kansas State Historical Society)

The Miss Simpsons of a frontier post endangered the sexual purity and physical safety of the officers' ladies.

That Miss Simpson represented an embarrassing problem for her family could not be denied, but among the pages of testimony there appeared almost as much insight about the conduct of her officer associates. Their references to intrigues with Miss Simpson suggested that they were not strangers to the allure of sexual escapades outside the bounds of morality. In a larger view, officers seemed less aloof to the professional prostitute than the military establishment cared to admit.

A variety of other episodes revealed that among the officers on the frontier a wide range of situations defined their relationships with prostitutes. Those that generated the most military response involved the officer who brought public scandal to his regiment. Such an infraction produced demands from commanders and district superintendents that the offending officer be punished, transferred, or dismissed from the military.

Between October 1866 and March 1867, a Lieutenant Speed, attached to New Mexico's Fort Union, became an object of concern to his commanding officer. Speed's offenses apparently stemmed from a severe case of alcoholism, for he suffered from repeated attacks of delirium tremens and failed to report for duty because of his drunken condition. Described as a totally dissipated man, Speed bordered on violent insanity.[12] Other officers at the post complained of his bad conduct, his antagonism, and his refusal to pay his accounts. In a final explosion of debauchery, Speed returned in a nearly nude condition from the brothel district of Loma Parda, an off limits zone for all Fort Union personnel.[13] Speed represented an extreme case, a man whose alcoholism had escalated to such a degree that he was probably unaware of his behavior in front of the enlisted personnel at Loma Parda. When the military dismissed Speed, he headed for the little brothel town. His superiors must have wished that they could point to Speed as the unfortunate exception among the officers. Such was not the case.

Within a year Captain G. O. McMullin of Fort Bascom, New Mexico, faced almost identical charges. The post traders filed charges of a three-year delinquent account, and McMullin's records showed that he was known as a thief, liar, and swindler among his fellow officers. Even the intercession of his father and his wife, both of whom appealed to military authorities in the East for a reprieve, could not save McMullin from dismissal when the testimony indicated that ". . . he publicly promenaded the streets with two mexican women known as common prostitutes, creating disturbance by ringing a bell, offering to be on a prize fight in the presence of citizens, soldiers, and prostitutes, being very much under the influence of liquor, promenading with common prostitutes, riding a horse in and out of a store and failing to pay for 5 gallons of oil. . . ." [14]

His unsavory record did not stand alone. Similar episodes erupted at other garrisons. The charges were repeated in the same language, with the same descriptions. Only the forts, the dates, and the names of the officers changed. Always the official complaint remained the same: the conduct of the officer had become disgraceful because the gambling, drinking, and whoring were committed in the presence of the enlisted personnel.

In the case of Lieutenant John Conline of New Mexico, his wretched conduct became known both in the nearby town and at the post. While in an intoxicated state he ordered soldiers to burn down the houses of private citizens. While this was being done, Conline himself acted in a scandalous manner throughout the town. At the post he continued his bizarre actions by breaking into the quarters of laundress Kate Holland, who lived in the home of another lieutenant at the post. Conline's district superior indicated the problem in the case grew out of the interest the local press developed in Lieutenant Conline. [15] The newspaper, cognizant of Conline's offensive treatment of private citizens, stood prepared to continue the flamboyant stories about the recalcitrant officer. This interest by the press could only serve to bring further scandal down upon the regiment, according to this officer, who recommended that the lieutenant be allowed to resign quietly.

These episodes captured the attention of the public because the antics spilled over into the private sector. These offenses happened to number among the more excessive, but the officers' conduct was hardly singular. Sometimes the military enjoyed greater success at keeping debauchery confined to the garrison areas. At the 1879 court-martial of Marcus Reno, the *Butte Miner* noted that the testimony showed that gambling, drinking, and other vices filled the officers' quarters at Fort Meade in the Dakota Territory. The paper added, ". . . investigation . . . brought out . . . young officers . . . are weakening their bodies, ruining their morals and destroying their intellects by midnight carouses, excessive drinking and indulgence in a dozen other forms of enervating dissipation."[16] These events transpired at Fanshane's Saloon, a private club situated on the highway leading into the military reservation. Easily accessible to both civilian and military persons, the saloon was the scene of a drunken brawl in which Reno threw a chair through a window. On the witness stand one officer testified that he had seen much worse happen at the saloon. This prompted an inquiry about whether these things he had seen had been done by officers, and, if so, what had the actions been. At this moment the court intervened and prevented the accounts.[17]

This proved to be a common military scenario. Officers got involved in drunken brawls in which prostitutes lurked about the edges in the official documents. If the episodes could be confined to sutler stores, removed from the general civilian population, army officials had no great dilemma. In these situations, raucous conduct and contacts with prostitutes who had easy access to the traders' stores could be ignored. For military superiors the difficulty arose when an officer lost control, left the area of the military reservation, and became a public spectacle among private citizens. When this occurred wayward officers usually headed for those brothel towns adjacent to the reservation, forcing officials to act. These little vice districts were almost always listed as off limits to all enlisted personnel. In view of that, superiors could not tolerate the presence there of garrison officers who caroused with enlisted personnel in a drunken and offensive manner. Officials desired to convey the impression that officers did not become drunk and consort with prostitutes.

When the contacts of officers with prostitutes could be more constrained, the military often looked the other way. Officials discouraged the documentation of such events. The officer who attempted to report moral abuses found his path blocked. Captain Nicholas Nodt of Fort Wingate, New Mexico, encountered obstacles for four years while he tried to inform his superiors about an episode he witnessed in 1861. Finally, in 1865, Nodt filed a report about an experience of the Navajo Indians at Fort Fauntleroy in New Mexico.[18] In his letter, Nodt explained that the Navajo and the government had been enjoying an era of particularly good relations during the early 1860s. According to Nodt, Indians by the hundreds visited inside the fort every day. During this period officers at the post indulged in horse racing with the Indians. This developed into a huge sport with high stakes gambled on both sides. One day the contestants placed especially large bets on a prize horse. A dispute broke out when the Indians complained that the officers had cheated in the race. In the chaos that followed, a shooting spree erupted in which the soldiers indiscriminately slaughtered Indian men, women, and children. Nodt reported that the surviving Indians fled throughout the valley, attacked the post herds, and caused general destruction everywhere. His report continued: "After the massacre there were no more Indians to be seen about the post with the exception of a few squaws, favorites of the officers. The commanding officer endeavored to make peace by sending some of the favorite squaws to talk with the chiefs, but the only satisfaction the squaws received was a good flogging."[19] With Navajo and army relations in a shambles, the appalled Nodt found he could not get official communications out of Fort Fauntleroy, and private letters were intercepted and opened at the town post office. Not only did the episode portray a disastrous moment in Indianmilitary affairs, but it also demonstrated some long-range Indian problems. Obviously among the officers at that post, "keeping squaws" had become a common fort practice. Further, the commanding officer had full knowledge of this custom and did not hesitate to play upon the situation when he needed emissaries to the Indians. The callousness of sending this truce delegation of Indian women to the Navajo after a massacre reflected the general military mentality that failed to grasp the indignity that native prostitution brought to Indians.

Officers did not establish liaisons only with the Indian prostitutes. Other women lived at military establishments as the courtesans of officers. In 1875 the post surgeon at Fort Randall, Dakota Territory, reported the death of a prostitute who collapsed at his hospital while trying to make her way from Fort Sully in the territory to Missouri. This woman, "Ella Emmerson, a destitute colored woman, about 30 years of age," arrived at Fort Randall in a debilitated condition.[20] Unable to proceed on her journey, the woman had to be admitted to the post hospital, where she failed rapidly. Although the surgeon listed scrofula, a tubercular affliction, as the cause of death, the graphic medical report of Ella Emmerson's final days sounded very much like another youthful victim of constitutional syphilis. Before she slipped into a final coma, Ella Emmerson told the surgeon she had been living with the quartermaster at Fort Sully for several months. When her health declined, she decided to return to Missouri. The surgeon expressed no surprise at her living arrangements at Fort Sully, nor at the fact that the quartermaster allowed her to set off sick and penniless into the frontier.[21]

Ella Emmerson died the characteristic death of the prostitute, but more than that, her attempted journey marked one more detail about the relations the army maintained with prostitutes. Although the record did not clearly indicate with whom Ella Emmerson traveled, clearly some prostitutes had to have made their way about the frontier with military escort. References to this practice, cloaked with a thick veil in the military documents, nevertheless made their way into military orders. Repeatedly, orders to move troop locations included the warning that only authorized laundresses should accompany the troops. Orders warned against the inclusion of unauthorized female personnel and also noted that food rations should be dispensed only to those women legally attached to the service.[22] The necessity of these directives came from military commanders who understood the frequency with which women attached themselves to moving troops.

On rare occasions an officer acknowledged directly that prostitutes traveled with military expeditions. John Bourke, military critic of ranch/brothels, wrote a diary account of a trip of eight or ten men whose military entourage included prostitute Mollie Shepherd. This woman traveled as the companion of the chief clerk of the captain of the expedition. Evidently Bourke found her presence worthy of comment because she was wounded in an Indian attack and shortly after died.[23] Again, the report of her presence on the expedition brought no comment of surprise or disapproval from Bourke, whose diary often demonstrated displeasure with free-wheeling social situations he encountered. Mollie Shepherd only rated an observation because she was killed; beyond that she elicited no comment from Bourke or the captain in charge of the trip.

The usual military response to such situations was simply to ignore them. While this was difficult to do when the extraordinary happened, an incident like the death of Mollie Shepherd could be covered over and necessitated little official comment. The thorny problem for officials concerned any indication that women drifted in and out of military reservations. These rumors the military hierarchy attempted to discredit, for the presence of prostitutes on garrison grounds violated military policy. While prostitutes lived in their miserable hog ranches beyond the boundaries of the fort, or while they traveled with moving troops, the officials could exonerate the army from any complicity in the maintenance of prostitution. Glibly, army spokesmen denied that the military encouraged the presence of prostitutes and asserted that the women victimized the soldiers by a parasitic pursuit that the men could not escape.[24] Military officials found themselves trapped in an awkward spot when the facts showed that prostitutes easily slipped on and off the garrison grounds.

Such cases often did not lend themselves to any simple solution, as the commanding officer of Fort Union, New Mexico, learned in 1867. Offended by the unsightly condition of a group of buildings known as the "Old Post," the commander ordered the quartermaster to make a thorough inspection of the shacks to ascertain who lived in them.[25] The ordered inspection revealed the huts were inhabited by a collection of gamblers and prostitutes. The women lived with civilian employees of the garrison and a clerk from the sutler's store. At night they entertained the enlisted personnel, who did not even have to ride over to Loma Parda for their amusements. The quartermaster recommended that the women be driven from the reservation and the buildings destroyed so that the undesirables could not reconvene on military grounds. His report included the information that an earlier commanding officer at Fort Union had wanted to destroy the buildings but had been forbidden to do so by the verbal order of General Carleton, the district commander. The quartermaster ignored this by requesting that the new commanding officer grant permission to destroy the building.[26] Two weeks later no action had been taken to demolish the dwellings, possibly because the officers found Carleton's orders protecting the prostitutes' shacks had not changed.[27] The connection of General Carleton to those brothel shacks remained one of the unanswered intrigues in Fort Union's long involvement with prostitution, but in 1878, long after his departure, male and female squatters remained on that reservation.[28]

Other avenues also brought prostitution directly onto the grounds of Fort Union. Military officials permitted native residents to enter the compound and set up a Mexican market each day. By 1870 the owner of the post restaurant began to complain about the Mexicans' market. Not only did they steal his chickens and vegetables, but, complained the trader, the Mexicans brought a daily contingent of gamblers and prostitutes to service the enlisted men. His allegations gained support from a statement of the post surgeon, who complained about the filth and the contamination from the Mexican prostitutes.[29] In reply, the post commander did not end the practice of the daily Mexican market but ordered a closer watch be kept on its activities.[30] The ineffective nature of this directive guaranteed that gambling and prostitution could continue within the garrison. The women arrived each day to hawk their sexual wares on the property of the fort. They joined the Navajo women of Fort Fauntleroy and the Sioux women of Fort Randall, who, with full knowledge of garrison officers, also had daily access to the men of the post.[31]

These episodes demonstrated that regardless of the remoteness of a fort's location, a native population lived nearby and supplied prostitutes. Moreover, although troops often entered these frontier zones to control hostiles, they quickly established ambivalent relations with native populations. During times of peace, regulations relaxed and native people moved freely inside the forts. They established various social and business relations with post soldiers. Among these contacts, some local women bartered sexual favors for commodities and goods from the soldiers. When hostilities erupted, the natives moved out from the garrison for a brief period, but the prostitute women often stayed in or close to the fort and continued their assignations. The sudden reversal in post/native relations exposed native prostitutes to castigation from their people. Having participated as their culture encouraged to secure goods and monies for families, these women suddenly found themselves traitors when political and social situations over which they had no control altered. These difficulties did not terminate the custom of allowing native women daily access to post grounds for sexual service to enlisted personnel; they merely influenced the ease with which the practice continued.

Where these native women were not present, other avenues permitted enlisted personnel to find sexual release through commercial contacts on military garrisons. One agency of the garrison designed to play a crucial role in this matter of recreation for the men was the sutler's store. This institution functioned under a strange dual identity. The store, run by a civilian, had to be licensed by the commander and accordingly was subject to his regulations. The army maintained complete control over the sutler's operation. Often that control fell into a lax state, but the military felt free to impose it at any time. One sutler received a sharp letter from General Carleton when he learned that the trader had made some alterations on the store building.[32] The sutler needed the permission of the commander before he could build. The location could be anywhere within the limits of the post or just beyond the line of defenses, but the building remained a government-controlled operation licensed at the benevolence of the commanding officers.[33]

These sutler stores, often the target of special orders and memos, proved difficult to control because of their semi-civilian status.[34] In addition, often constructed along the public highway leading into the post, the stores were open to any passing travelers. The general history of the stores was one of corruption and the extension of special privileges from friendly commanders. Accordingly, they became centers of drinking, gambling, and brawling.

The sutlers themselves often became powerful local figures and wielded considerable financial clout over the garrison staff. As the only supplier of non-military goods, the sutler monopolized the sale of numerous items such as coffee, sugar, soda, bacon, calico, and tobacco. Under the district command of General Carleton, the Fort Union sutler exercised so much power that he ordered the general to send him the soldiers' pay envelopes each month. The sutler extracted the amount due to him, and then turned over the balance of the pay to the soldier.[35]

In such an atmosphere sutlers had little trouble keeping prostitutes available. If questioned about the unattached females, traders readily identified the women as domestic servants working in the store. Periodically, commanders would complain about unauthorized females around the sutler's store and order them from the post. These directives appeared with such regularity that they were automatically ignored.

If a scandalous situation arose, the military orders took on a stronger tone for a few days, and then returned to their usual ineffective level. In 1866 the murder of an enlisted man by an officer at a sutler's store prompted an order that every women should leave the post except the legally authorized laundresses. Further, the sutler was ordered to stop the sale of intoxicating liquors.[36] This always proved a silly order, for officers' clubs and enlisted men's rooms were intended to provide all the customary social diversions.

Although the sutler's store could be an annoyance to a commander, most officers were satisfied to file regular orders about whiskey and women but avoid enforcing them. In this manner the sutlers and the commanding officers each understood the law and each quietly ignored its violation. The matter shifted if the sutler ran afoul of the commanding officer.

Such a difficulty arose in 1868 at Fort Selden, New Mexico, when the trader and the commander fell into a bitter argument. The officer expelled several men from the post. Almost immediately the district commander received information from these citizens that the commanding officer permitted the residence of a prostitute at the sutler's store. The commanding officer, Captain J. G. Tilford, in an angry reply, did not deny that women resided at the sutler's; he simply said he did not know if they were prostitutes. They worked, he thought, as servants. One woman did live there with a soldier, Tilford admitted, and drew rations as the soldier's laundress wife, although Tilford did not seem sure that she was married to the man. Tilford's final argument to his superiors stated that even if such things did go on at this post, of what business was it to whiskey dealers and stage drivers?[37] Apparently his commanding officer agreed, for no reply came from Santa Fe on this matter. This item fell into that category of events best ignored.

Despite Tilford's haughty letter, it seemed clear that he knew that prostitutes lived at the sutler's store but had not found it appropriate to interfere in this illegal arrangement. The post trader's store represented a licensed governmental agency; the toleration of prostitutes in these quarters represented an official endorsement by military commanders of these women at military garrisons.

These conditions existed because officials, although they spoke against vice and prostitution, recognized male sexual desires, the tensions at frontier posts, and the need to protect those respectable women who followed officer husbands to distant outposts. The officials thought that ways had to be provided to accommodate male sexual needs. The presence of prostitutes in sutlers' stores did not represent the only provision for masculine sexual release. Although both military documents and private accounts tended to draw a most respectable picture of the laundresses at frontier garrisons, these women also contributed to the sexual activity of soldiers.

The earliest military laws passed to make "more effectual provision for the protection of the frontiers of the United States," allowed that matrons in the hospital should receive a compensation of $8 per month.[38] Over the years these provisions were adjusted along with other military rules so that by 1816 the regulations for daily rations referred to "camp women, matrons, and nurses." The law defined the duties and pay of hospital nurses and then stated, "Women infected by the venereal disease shall in no case, nor on any pretense, be allowed to remain with the army, nor draw rations."[39] How this law would be enforced under stark frontier conditions, where its implementation would be inhumane, was but one instance of official fogginess when dealing with prostitution. The next section of this law stated that "more than four women shall not be allowed to a company when organized. . . . Nor shall any be allowed to accompany recruiting parties which shall be fewer than seventeen men. . . . No contractor or commissary shall be justified in issuing rations to women, who are followers of the army, beyond the number allowed."[40] By 1869 the general orders had been revised to read, "Laundresses will be allowed to each company or detachment of twelve or more enlisted men . . . to do the washing for the company or detachment."[41]

The multiplicity of terms used was not a minor point. Overlapping terminology—"matrons," "nurses," "female attendants," "camp women," "followers of the army," and "laundresses"—has served to keep identification of female roles confused and permitted officials to avoid any direct acknowledgment of prostitution on military grounds. Some order can be drawn from the medical histories of both Fort Davis, Texas, and Fort Union, New Mexico, where employees at the hospitals were consistently listed as "Matron (Laundress)." A clearer use of the terms and the roles came from Elizabeth Custer in a story she related about a fort quartermaster.

Mrs. Custer once encountered a quartermaster whose wife was the envy of the garrison because her home was by far the nicest at the fort. The quartermaster, with access to all the supplies, saw to it that all the paint and improvements went into his own quarters, while others lived in shabby dwellings. He was most unpopular with the post ladies, and Mrs. Custer and her friends laughed delightedly when he was roused from his sleep one Christmas dawn. ". . . he went barefoot through his hall, while his heart was beating with alarm for fear of disaster or fire, as he answered the bell. . . . On opening the door a dishevelled tipsy Jezebel of a camp-woman, bracing herself against the wood-work as best she could, said to him, 'It's cold, and my nose bleeds,' and with this information she departed."[42] Her terminology cannot be overlooked.

"Jezebel," drawn from common usage, required no further explanation by Mrs. Custer. She expressed no surprise at all at the presence of this camp woman. Beyond that, she had no word of concern for this woman, drunk and wandering about in the cold dawn with a bloody nose, perhaps received in some holiday altercation among the troops. Her callousness was in keeping with much of the nineteenth-century response to prostitutes. For women who had turned away from the standards of proper sexual conduct, society seldom appeared bothered by their condition of physical and economic deprivation.

At Fort Union some ambiguity over terms was removed by the physician's lengthy report about a local smallpox epidemic in 1877. Doctor Carvallo, who figured prominently in the court-martial of Lieutenant Colonel Dudley that same month, gave a full accounting of his futile efforts to control the spread of the disease. Part of his failure he attributed to the contact soldiers had at Loma Parda. Carvallo believed that the main contagion had been brought into the post by Sylvia Francisco, a servant of Dudley and a former post laundress.[43] Speculation about Sylvia Francisco must remain that, for there was no stated evidence that she engaged in prostitution, but it cannot be overlooked that she served as a post matron/laundress, was relieved of that duty to become a servant to Dudley, and trafficked back and forth to notorious, off limits Loma Parda. The evidence showed yet another official acknowledgment of a connection between post employees and the most disorderly brothel area near Fort Union.

Further in his report, Doctor Carvallo included a list of all persons vaccinated during the epidemic. After his list of all military personnel, he recorded the following: "20 Qr. Mr. employees, 21 women, 4 children & 13 men, officers; servants and camp followers were revaccinated."[44] If laundresses were included among employees of the quartermaster (although they do not appear in quartermaster pay records, nor in the monthly personnel returns for Fort Union), or if they were included among the twenty-one women of the fort, that still leaves the term "camp followers" undefined at the end of Doctor Carvallo's list. The military laundresses may be placed in any of Carvallo's four categories that include women, and the universal meaning of "camp follower" still stands as unarguable. If "camp follower" represented a separate group of women, they had connections with the saloon at the post trader's. Doctor Carvallo's single notation about vaccinating camp followers marked an official acknowledgment of a direct military attachment to prostitutes gathered at and about frontier posts.

Other elements in the circumstances of the frontier laundresses seemed questionable. One concerned the identity of the laundresses. At Fort Union several Mexican women were employed: Paulita and Clementi Gutierez, Guadalupe Garcia, and the ubiquitous Sylvia Francisco.[45] At Fort Davis where the same matrons/laundresses were hired and fired repeatedly over a period of a year, the women were either black or Mexican.[46] It may be that their rapid sequence of employment and unemployment resulted from a post surgeon who complied with the 1816 regulations forbidding diseased women on the post. If so, he was the exception, for in 1875 General Tasker Bliss had said of post surgeons "that they had nothing to do but to confine laundresses and treat the clap."[47] Although laundresses were depicted as women of "good character," all too often the post commanders identified them as disruptive, "immoral" persons.

At Fort Phil Kearny, Wyoming, "Colored Susan" caused a stir by selling "ardent spirits" and fruit pies made courtesy of government supplies. She organized other activities of a strange nature, perhaps designed to populate her own post brothel. Susan rated a warning but not dismissal in a special order of November 1866. ". . . the same woman is disorderly, breeding mischief in the garrison by inciting officers' servants to abandon their situations, and as an inducement setting forth the large sums of money she realizes and accumulates by the methods above referred to. This woman, profane, abusive and of bad repute before her arrival must observe better behavior or she will not be tolerated in the garrison."[48] "Colored Susan's" entrepreneurial spirit may single her out as one frontier prostitute who realized a profit, and if so, she was unusual. Since the laundresses' ranks attracted those indigent women whose ethnic status—black, Mexican, and Irish—relegated them to social and economic inferiority within the mainstream of society, they were excellent candidates for prostitution with the military. Females from these minority groups certainly staffed the civilian brothels in surrounding urban areas and seldom counted high monetary rewards from their work.

Identification of laundresses as a prostitute group did not disregard those instances where laundresses legitimately married enlisted men, but it challenged any premise that might dismiss laundresses as possible prostitutes by a convenient assertion that the residents of "Sudsville" were all married to soldiers. Both the 1870 publication *Report on Barracks and Hospitals* and the 1875 volume *Report on the Hygiene of the United States Army* referred repeatedly to quarters for "married soldiers or laundresses." The division of the two was even clearer in the 1870 report from Austin, Texas, which stated, "Each married soldier has a wall tent for quarters and a common tent for kitchen. The laundresses who are not soldiers' wives, are similarly quartered."[49]

The 1870 Fort Russell, Wyoming, census report gave a good example of the divisions between married and unmarried laundresses. Nineteen laundresses lived at the post without soldier husbands; no more than five resided with husbands. Of the single laundresses seventeen had children. The ages of these unmarried laundress mothers ranged between seventeen and forty-four. Two laundresses, ages sixteen and twenty-three, had no children. Two additional single women, ages twenty-three and twenty-eight, appeared in the census under the euphemistic heading, "keeping house."[50] Clearly, substantial single female populations with sexual experience lived at military garrisons. Most in their twenties had given birth to as many as three children, each born in a different frontier location. The sexual liaisons between these women and enlisted personnel, evident from the birth rate, brought added supplies and goods to washerwomen who lived under pitiful conditions at the posts.

The inferior quality of laundresses' quarters and their usual location on the post raised further questions about the status of these women. In a military atmosphere where Mrs. Custer noted the civility and respect shown to officers' wives, it is poignant to note the sites selected for the laundresses' shacks and tents. Maps for the western forts show laundresses' quarters directly behind the soldiers' barracks, or just off the post grounds, along the road to town or by a creek. All too frequently when they were on the post, their shacks and tents were those closest to the outdoor privies and stables within close range of dreadful accompanying odors. Most posts reported that their quarters were tents, shacks, sod buildings, dugouts, log huts, or dilapidated frame houses.[51] Even allowing for the deprivations experienced by all persons at a military outpost, it is apparent that the laundresses lived in the most hideous circumstances of all. In a nineteenth-century motif that allowed for "good" women who were revered and pampered and "bad" women who were degraded and abused, the circulars of 1870 and 1875 unrelentingly demonstrated that the physical environs of the laundresses placed them in the latter category.

Even though some of the marriages in "Sudsville" were certainly valid ones, with wives and children following the soldier from camp to camp, it should not be assumed that all of these marriages were legitimate. Don Rickey's book, *Forty Miles a Day on Beans and Hay*, recounts the startling tale of a company laundress identified as "Mrs. Nash." For ten years, between 1868 and 1878, this person lived at Fort Meade, Dakota Territory, "married" to a string of soldiers. When one was transferred or discharged she simply "married" another. In 1878 while the current spouse was in the field "Mrs. Nash" died. During the preparations for the burial it was discovered that "Mrs. Nash" was a male.[52] Aside from the interesting implications about homosexuality in the military, the story raised questions about the "marriages" between bona fide females and enlisted men. Apparently over this ten-year period no official of the garrison questioned "Mrs. Nash's" practice of remaining at Fort Meade while "husband" after "husband" departed. It certainly suggests that no inquiry was made because this was a usual practice and these marriages of convenience avoided any necessity for an official recognition of the sexual services laundresses provided for the garrison at large. This notion gained some support from an entry in the Fort Union medical history for January 1877 that reported: "Quarantined: Mrs. Maria Straw, wife of Patrick Straw, Band 9th Cavalry with Chancroid Quar. to prevent contagion among the troops. Still under treatment."[53]

It can hardly be dismissed as simply a domestic crisis for the Straw household, an unfortunate infection brought home by Patrick Straw from some extramarital affair.[54] The move to prevent contagion among the troops eliminated that simple explanation. The quarantine reflected the medical decision of a physician who recognized that Mrs. Straw was an available sexual partner for the men at Fort Union. Again, it must be noted that there was no indication of the unusual in the report, and the post surgeon, Doctor Carvallo, felt it unnecessary to elaborate or explain the surrounding circumstances.

Laundresses lived in hovels without a single amenity. Their provisions minimal, their treatment grotesque, it seemed incomprehensible that anyone would willingly pursue the life of a military laundress. The answer to that could be found in the economic realities of these women's lives. For all its horrors, the military offered one ration a day, a place to live, and medical assistance. Additional benefits could be extracted through the goods and supplies enlisted men contributed for sexual favors. In the prostitution industry, where unlimited competition hindered the career opportunities of most women, military laundresses worked in a setting where the men dramatically outnumbered the women. That the women garnered so few profits from this situation only reinforced the basic flaw in prostitution: it did not prove a profitable life for the majority of workers regardless of the circumstances. The degrading lives of the military laundresses added only misery to the general picture of prostitution on the frontier.

Within frontier military garrisons, officials tried to convey the image of a well-controlled and ordered society. In the area of sexual conduct the image was warped. It was evident that prostitution flourished in and around garrisons with the full knowledge and often the active support of military officials. Officers themselves did not avoid sexual contact with prostitutes, especially with those from the native populations. Military decorum frowned not on the liaison but on the public spectacles officers sometimes created.

For enlisted personnel several opportunities, known to their superiors, permitted the soldiers to secure sexual contacts. One means relied on the numbers of native women who had daily access to posts and engaged in prostitution in exchange for government goods. Other women lived in shacks scattered about the military reservation. Often these women lived under the protection of civilian employees of the post, or the greater protection of a ranking officer. Some prostitutes lived in brothel towns just beyond the borders of the military reservation, so soldiers only commuted a short distance to find vice districts. An additional opportunity for contact with prostitutes came from the agency known as the sutler's store. Here, with separate lounge rooms set aside for officers and enlisted men, sutlers found it an easy matter to keep prostitutes within the garrison and claim the women as servants. Finally, the contingent of military laundresses provided an additional opportunity for prostitution to exist within the forts. Poor women who lived under the most disastrous conditions at the forts were eager to supplement their small wages. Often unmarried and burdened with several young children, these women needed to secure the income soldiers brought in the way of supplies and goods.

The military establishment routinely insisted that it did not permit prostitution at frontier garrisons and that it did not encourage prostitution in surrounding towns. On the contrary, it was evident that every level of officer knew fully about the transport, presence, and residence of prostitutes in and around military reservations. Ultimately, the military created a de facto policy in support of prostitution. The frontier army, on the one hand, cultivated the entrenchment of institutionalized vice while, on the other hand, officials denounced and deplored its existence. The power with which they assisted prostitution far outweighed their shallow utterances. The military game? Duplicity and deceit.

Notes

An earlier version of this chapter appeared in *Prologue* (Winter 1981).

1. John N. Newcomb to Secretary of War Edwin Stanton, Aug. 16, 1865, Accounts and Claims, RG 217, NA.

2. Ibid.

3. Ibid. Documents, letters, statement of account, and the statement of payment are all contained in one box of the report of the third auditor.

4. Ibid. Statement of payment to John M. Newcomb, Aug. 4, 1863. Newcomb did not actually receive this money until after Oct. 19, 1865.

5. A full discussion of these figures, as well as excellent detail about all of the forts west of the Mississippi River can be found in Robert W. Frazer, *Forts of the West* (Norman: University of Oklahoma Press, 1965).

6. Percy M. Ashburn, *A History of the Medical Department of the United States Army* (Boston: Houghton Mifflin, 1929), pp. 110–11.

7. Elizabeth B. Custer, *Following the Guidon* (Norman: University of Oklahoma Press, 1966), p. 226.

8. Ibid., p. 156.

9. Medical History of the Posts, Fort Davis, Tex., 1873, RG 94, NA.

10. Testimony of Dr. Carvallo, General Court-Martial Proceedings of Lt. Col. N. A. M. Dudley, 1877, RG 153, NA.

11. Ibid. Remarks in summation, Judge Advocate, Court-Martial of Lt. Col. N. A. M. Dudley.

12. Col. E. G. Marshall to Maj. C. DeForrest, Oct. 5, 1866, AC.

13. Col. E. G. Marshall to Assistant Adjutant General, Mar. 5, 1867, AC.

14. General Court-Martial of Capt. G. O. McMullin, Feb. 8, 1868 at Fort Bascom, N. Mex., RG 153, NA.

15. Santa Fe District Headquarters to Maj. James F. Wade, Aug. 6, 1877, AC.

16. *Butte Miner*, Dec. 6, 1879.

17. General Court-Martial of Marcus Reno, Oct. 25, 1879, p. 85, RG 153, NA.

18. Capt. Nicholas Nodt to Maj. Ben Cutler, Sept. 7, 1865, printed in the *Condition of the Indian Tribes*, pp. 313–14, AC.

19. Ibid., p. 314.

20. Medical History of Fort Randall, Dakota Territory, Aug. 12, 1875, p. 229, RG 94, NA.

21. Ibid.

22. For examples see Circular Letter #658, Aug. 2, 1865; Circular Letter #714, Aug. 9, 1865; Gen. J. H. Carleton to Maj. DeForrest, May 18, 1866; Special Order #17, Apr. 13, 1867; A. P. Caraher to Post Adjutant, Jan. 11, 1871; Headquarters at Santa Fe to Lt. B. S. Humphrey, Apr. 30, 1877; Headquarters at Santa Fe to Lt. Charles Bradley, May 26, 1879; Lt. Col. N. A. M. Dudley to Assistant Adjutant General for the Dept. of Mo., Feb. 8, 1880, all in AC.

23. John G. Bourke Diary, volume 3, pp. 114–15, UNML.

24. Although the military often maintained a discreet silence on this topic, after 1905 a series of medical advances altered official interest in prostitution and venereal disease. The official statement did not appear until 1913, but probably summed up long range military attitudes. "Syphilis is never acquired in the Army. The individuals with whom the soldier comes in contact that infect him with syphilis are civilians, and the civil communities surrounding Army posts are responsible for permitting this traffic. The Army is, therefore, in no way responsible to the civil community for the syphilis that is acquired by the soldier." U.S. Department of War, Office of the Surgeon General, *The Prevalence of Syphilis in the Army*, by Edward Vedder, Bulletin no. 8 (Washington, D.C.: GPO, 1915), p. 79.

25. Lt. Col. William B. Lane to Lt. Granville Lewis, Mar. 21, 1867, AC.

26. Lt. Granville Lewis to Lt. Col. William B. Lane, Mar. 22, 23, 1867, AC.

27. Lt. Col. William B. Lane to depot Quartermaster, Apr. 4, 1867, AC.

28. Dept. of N. Mex. Letter Book, vol. 52, pp. 279–80, RG 98, NA, as cited in AC.

29. A. Adolph Griesinger to commanding Gen. Gregg, June 19, 1870, with endorsement enclosed from Dr. D. C. Peters, AC.

30. Fort Union, N. Mex., Order #33, June 20, 1870, AC; also Fort Union, N. Mex. Orders, vol. 44, p. 188, RG 93, NA, as cited in AC.

31. See n. 18 above, and nn. 36 and 37, in Chapter 1.

32. Gen. J. H. Carleton to sutler Shoemaker, Dept. of N. Mex. Letter Book, Volume 16, p. 506, RG 98, NA, as cited in AC.

33. John D. Drum to James Arrott, Mar. 5, 1951, p. 2, June 26, 1951, AC; Thomas Lahey and Edward McDonald to Col. J. Gregg, Nov. 1, 1872, Fort Union, N. Mex., Letter Books, Letters Received, vol. 2, p. 247, RG 98, NA; Gen. J. H. Carleton to commanding officer of Fort Bascom, N. Mex., July 13, 1865, AC.

34. General Orders #20, Fort Union, N. Mex., May 11, 1865; Circular, Fort Union, N. Mex., Dec. 8, 1866; W. B. Lane to Maj. Cyrus DeForrest, June 5, 1867; W. B. Lane to Messrs. Moore and Co., July 4, 1867, all in AC; Fort Randall, Dakota Territory, Medical History, vol. 2, Jan. 10, 1874, p. 154, RG 94; Orders issued at Fort Sisseton, Dakota Territory, 1880–89, Apr. 1, Oct. 7, 1880, RG 393; Special Orders issued at Fort Hale, Dakota Territory, Order #18, Mar. 28, 1882, RG 393, all in NA.

35. "Fort Union's Sutler Store," as related in *The Second William Penn* (Kansas City, Mo.: Frank T. Riley, 1913), Chapter 20, p. 1, AC.

36. Santa Fe Headquarters to Capt. William F. French, Fort McRae, N. Mex., June 1, 1866, AC.

37. Capt. J. G. Tilford to Lt. Edward Hunter, Mar. 26, 1868, AC; see also Dept. of N. Mex., Fort Selden Letters Sent, vol. 7A, pp. 269–70, RG 98, NA, as cited in AC.

38. John Callan, *The Military Laws of the United States Relating to the Army Volunteer Militia and to Bounty Lands and Pensions from the Foundation of the Government to 3 Mar. 1863*, 2nd ed. (Philadelphia: George W. Childs, 1863), pp. 92–3.

39. *Military Laws and Rules and Regulations for the Army of the United States* (n.p.: E. de Kraft, 1816), p. 140.

40. Ibid., p. 30.

41. General Order #72, *Index of General Orders*, Office of the Adjutant General (Washington: GPO, 1869).

42. Custer, *Following the Guidon*, pp. 228–29.

43. Medical History of the Posts, Fort Union, N. Mex., May, 1877, RG 94, NA.

44. Ibid.

45. Ibid., passim.

46. Medical History of the Posts, Fort Davis, Tex., 1869, passim, RG 94, NA.

47. Ashburn, *A History of the Medical Department of the U. S. Army*, p. 112.

48. Special Order Number 75, Fort Philip Kearny, Wyo. Territory, Nov. 24, 1866, RG 98, NA, cited in Robert A. Murray, *Military Posts in the Powder River County of Wyoming, 1865–1894* (Lincoln: University of Nebraska Press, 1968), p. 57.

49. John S. Billings, *Circular No. 4: Report on Barracks and Hospitals*, Office of the Surgeon General (Washington: The War Department, 1870; reprint ed., New York: Sol Lewis, 1974), p. 179.

50. U.S. Bureau of Census from the Ninth Census (1870), Fort Russell, Wyo., Roll 1748, RG 29, NA.

51. John S. Billings, *Circular No. 4: Report on Barracks and Hospitals*, and John S. Billings, *Circular No. 8: Report on the Hygiene of the United States Army with Descriptions of Military Posts*, Office of the Surgeon General (Washington: The War Department, 1875; reprint ed., New York: Sol Lewis, 1974), passim. Their housing fit their income. An 1870 order at Fort Union set prices for laundry as follows: officers, single or married, $5 per month, each additional family member, $3 per month; officers casually at the post, $1.25 per dozen; enlisted men, $1, trousers and overcoats, twenty-five cents, white shirts, ten cents; Fort Union, N. Mex. Orders, #149, vol. 44, p. 256, RG 93, NA, as cited in AC.

52. Don Rickey, Jr., *Forty Miles a Day on Beans and Hay: The Enlisted Soldier Fighting the Indian Wars* (Norman: University of Oklahoma Press, 1963), pp. 170–71.

53. Medical History of the Post, Fort Union, N. Mex., Jan., 1877. RG 94, NA.

54. Percy M. Ashburn, *The Elements of Military Hygiene: Especially Arranged for Officers and Men of the Line*, 3rd ed. (Boston: Houghton Mifflin, 1920), p. 347. Chancroid, a localized, highly infectious form of venereal disease begins as a small ulcer on the penis. Col. Ashburn of the Medical Corps reported that the incubation period "probably depends on . . . the degree of infection in the woman . . . and the violence, length, and frequency of the infective intercourse."

Conclusion

Between 1865 and 1890 the United States forged permanent settlements out of frontier land in the trans-Mississippi West. The excitement and chaos of that era could not last forever. Possession of the land, pioneer settlement, improved communications, and reservation confinement for Indians ended the wilderness aura that permeated the frontier years. Bonanza industries stabilized and moved into more balanced endeavors. Americans turned their attention to new concerns in a modern world filled with technology and progress. The West entered the twentieth century and, except for a few vestiges, left the frontier world behind.

Nevertheless, Americans retain a strong affection for the western experience. The frontier compels a fascination that appears never to diminish, as scholars and nonscholars alike try to delineate the importance of this era within the national experience. That no single explanation satisfies is but one aspect of the frontier mystique. Recognition that a panorama of events and forces swirled through the West forces historians to examine the frontier montage piece by piece. Surely knowledge of even so tawdry a group as the prostitutes elucidates some of the patterns of frontier society.

Prostitutes actively participated in this western era so cherished by Americans, but that participation has been defined largely by notions of morality and mockery. Seen through a lens less clouded by these traditional attitudes, prostitution sharpens into a more meaningful element in the development of western society. This study has included the following generalizations about frontier prostitution that are intended to help place the subject within the western framework.

Prostitutes came from among the poorest groups of women on the

150

frontier. They were the daughters of cultures where servitude had taken a toll. Such women turned to prostitution at an early age and entered the profession with few skills and only rudimentary education. They brought little that would help them alter lives marked by ignorance and impoverishment. A few exceptions aside, prostitutes, whether in urban or rural frontier settings, came from the ranks of the young and the poor.

Prostitutes did not live as single, isolated beings; the image of the dance hall girl alone in the world has not been entirely accurate. Prostitutes established personal relationships that included husbands and children. In marriage prostitutes often fared badly, and the men they selected often succeeded only in adding to the disorder of the women's lives. Their husbands, usually unskilled laborers or criminals, frequently encouraged the wives to participate in prostitution. In these family situations the children of prostitutes suffered both economic and social deprivations. The prospects for the children of prostitutes were bleak, and daughters frequently followed their mothers into the profession. These domestic arrangements weakened the notion that frontier prostitutes, who lived in a region where women were scarce, could marry well and move away from the profession into respectable lives of anonymity. On the American frontier where personal disorder reigned among the most stable, prostitutes and their families lived in a setting of intense chaos.

Prostitutes also had limited ability to establish friendships with others in the profession. Although the women lived intimately with each other, the general contact between prostitutes was fraught with suspicion and distrust. Petty events triggered angry responses and hindered the development of deep-seated, constructive friendships. As with all people, death temporarily washed away differences and a gush of affection surged among prostitutes. These occasions, often charged with emotion, disguised the more typical hostile exchanges that characterized day-to-day encounters.

In an arena of unchecked competition, the economic rewards proved marginal. Most prostitutes did not earn substantial sums, mainly because they drew their clientele from among other workers with little money. When prostitutes did secure a windfall, they seldom demonstrated that they had the stability to handle their finances soundly; money filtered through their fingers. Even if they tried to be cautious, the overhead expenses of prostitution served to keep profits slim. Prostitutes found it difficult to establish financial independence because of the monies they had to pay to pimps, officials, and madams. A complex system of expenses levied against prostitutes also helped to solidify their marginal status in the community. They seldom had money for court expenses, lived poorly, and had little personal property.

Their poverty might have been expected to incite some community assistance, but on the frontier where such institutions were weak, systematic help simply did not materialize. Without secular agencies to assist prostitutes, it might be thought that churches, motivated by some understanding and compassion, would pick up the banner of aid. Such did not prove to be the case. The churches, guided by traditional interpretations of morality and geared to provide for the spiritual well-being of the mainstream of society, could not find practical ways to assist prostitutes. Even when they attempted to help, their efforts appeared unattractive to prostitutes. Only through a program that brought the complete removal of prostitutes from society was there a chance for success. This approach, used by one order of Catholic nuns, the Sisters of the Good Shepherd, proved effective for some prostitutes, yet this solution had limited appeal; few prostitutes had contact with the Sisters, and, although efficacious, the program did not provide a way to resume life within society.

If prostitutes did not live fully in society, they still lived at its edges. In communities, the daily existence of the prostitutes hinged upon the parasitic relationships they developed with various agencies. Of these the frontier press, confronted with a unique chance to alter public thinking, failed to respond to the challenge. Hampered by ambivalent attitudes about prostitution, the frontier press allowed itself to settle for a general theme of humor and scorn when dealing with prostitution. Articles often cloaked in moral indignation or outrage became little more than lewd advertisements for local prostitutes. The responsibility and the status of the frontier press was admittedly unofficial, but journalists and editors did little to enlarge serious concerns about prostitution.

On the other hand, society charged its public officials with the authority to manage the vice population; officials, in turn, tended to abuse that public trust and twist it to their own benefit. With almost no system of checks and balances, the public authority used extortion to force prostitutes to skim off monies to them. Prostitutes knew this was the price for remaining active in the profession. The result of this relationship between prostitutes and public officials was to provide the underpinning for the larger institutional implications that arose out of the prostitution in the West.

The experiences of prostitutes on the American frontier showed that the women, through a dual status of criminal and citizen, contributed to the development of western institutions. In a society where social structure was sketchy, but where communities struggled to impose order, the prostitutes provided an invaluable assist. More than slightly visible, but politically and economically crippled, prostitutes became one stepping-stone for the building of social institutions.

The process of this development at the expense of the prostitutes was best demonstrated through the rise of the western legal order. Through justice of the peace courts and local jurisdictions, the legal establishment found its ballast. The rise of the institutional order needed the presence of malleable people to help enlarge the power and activity of the legal system. Prostitutes contributed to this process, although their own civil liberties were systematically curtailed by society. The experiences of frontier prostitutes with a fledgling legal structure indicated that the rise of powerful institutions in part hinged upon the ability of society to build upon the rights and lives of the politically weak. The good offices of the community, grudgingly extended to social undesirables as a means to further enhance community stability, became the hallmark of prostitutes' legal experiences on the frontier. Prostitutes of the American West exemplified the contribution made by the seemingly insignificant to the rise of the institutional order in America.

The legal establishment did not act alone in these endeavors. Other institutions of society encouraged the presence of prostitutes for their own purposes. Among these, the frontier army cultivated an attitude of blindness about prostitution. While actively supporting and encouraging prostitution, military officials often insisted that they had nothing to do with the institution. In addition to the maintenance of prostitution as a frontier phenomenon, these actions by the military reinforced the civil actions found in the court system. The agencies of society employed prostitutes but granted censure and ostracism in return; the result was that the powerful forces of society formed a front difficult to surmount. Society dispensed enough compromises to permit prostitutes to exist but restricted them through community agencies—the law, the military, the press, the churches. Given just the thinnest of institutional protection, prostitutes had few weapons against this community arsenal, and so they accepted and maneuvered the regulations imposed upon them to their own advantage where possible.

Prostitutes were not passive in these events and showed themselves to be pragmatic about the conditions of their lives. They seldom complained about society but spent their efforts on ways to capitalize on their own role in the community. Thus, prostitutes expended their energies on adjusting to the society at hand and seldom showed an inclination to extricate themselves from these many societal constraints. They manipulated the agencies of society for their own purposes where they could, but they generally revealed little or no political or economic astuteness. Their conduct in general showed that, with other groups in society, prostitutes accepted themselves as lesser people in the community. The acceptance of this notion robbed them of the vigor they needed to direct their attention to ways to improve their lives. Instead, many prostitutes lived with the harsh judgment of society, intensified by their own intellectual and physical inertia. Preoccupation with the concerns of the moment hampered attempts to remove themselves from the degrading aspects of prostitution that rained down violence and disorder from a variety of sources. Prostitutes suffered at the hands of customers who inflicted assault and mayhem, both deliberately and accidently. They suffered at the hands of each other through beatings and thieveries. They suffered at their own hands from alcoholism, drug addiction, and suicide. This violence dominated the lives of the prostitutes.

Faced with these apparent hardships in prostitution, observers have always wanted to know what precisely motivated women to enter or continue in the profession. Interest ranges from the most prurient fascination with graphic sexual details to more sober questions about the women's perceptions of society and themselves. One would like to delineate the concepts of femininity that prostitutes held, to understand their joys and their fears better. It is tempting, given the volume of unattractive evidence from the frontier era, to speculate more fully about prostitutes' inner feelings. The danger is that one stereotypical image will be exchanged for another: the dance hall girl with the heart of gold will give way to the desperate downtrodden victim or the professional who chose her job after carefully crafting her career plans. It is probable that all these types and several variations of them can be counted among the prostitutes of the American West. Unfortunately, the prostitutes in this study reflect the characteristic of most frontier groups: their collection of personal written records is fragmented, scattered, or non-existent. The available evidence reveals much about the physical environment and the structure of society, but the internal responses of prostitutes themselves remain shrouded.

It is regrettable that for such a long time society regarded members of this profession only as "fallen women." Such glib labels limited the examination of the role of the prostitutes as workers on the American frontier. Indeed, prostitutes' lives reflected much more than amusing sexual glitter. The lives and experiences of these women meshed with the emergence of frontier institutions. Prostitutes made contributions to the emergence of that western society; that their contributions appear less "good" or "noble" does not make them less important. Unfortunately, as the West passed from its nineteenth-century formative days, the prostitutes faded into the American memory as only the tarnished decorations of the frontier world.

Bibliographical Note

In the past ten years publications in a variety of disciplines have added to our knowledge about prostitution. Among those attracted to research in prostitution have been a number of sociologists. From an impressive array of publications, Charles Winick and Paul Kinsie's *The Lively Commerce* (1971), Barbara Heyl's *The Madam as Entrepreneur* (1979), and Robert Prus and Styllianoss Irini's *Hookers, Rounders, and Desk Clerks* (1980) are indicative of both the personal insights and overarching structure of prostitution that can be gleaned from the sociologists' research. Although most of these studies center on modern-day prostitution, they aid the historian to understand better the process of personal relationships.

For historians the general studies of Vern Bullough, *The History of Prostitution* (1964), and Fernando Henriques, *Prostitution and Society* (1966), served as the basic guides to the subject. In 1981 Richard Symanski's *The Immoral Landscape: Female Prostitution in Western Societies* added a wealth of historical information from the intriguing perspective of a geographer. These far-reaching surveys serve as springboards for historians who wish to explore specific aspects of prostitution.

Two such contributions investigated prostitution in Victorian England. Frances Finnegan in *Poverty and Prostitution* (1979) presented a convincing study of the manner in which the pervasive and destructive nature of poverty limited all dimensions of prostitutes' physical and mental well-being. Judith Walkowitz in *Prostitution and Victorian Society* (1980) used nineteenth-century English reform legislation as the framework for her analysis of prostitution in Victorian society. Walkowitz's observation that the control prostitutes exerted over their own subculture was always subordinate to larger societal restrictions is central to understanding the ways in which prostitutes everywhere developed mechanisms for survival.

Historical analysis of prostitution in the United States is of relatively recent origin. In 1974 the publication of Al Rose's *Storyville: New Orleans* demonstrated that the United States, with its diverse regions and cultures, was hiding a piebald assortment of prostitution materials. The appearance in the same year of the Hallers's book *The Physician and Sexuality in Victorian America* underscored the message for scholars.

The richest publications about American prostitution come from the hand of Ruth Rosen. Her editing of the *Maimie Papers* (1977) offered rare insights into prostitution through letters written by one of the employees. Only those who have researched in the topic and dealt with the frustrations of fraudulent memoirs piously written by non-prostitutes can appreciate the breadth and scope of this fine collection. Rosen's second work, *The Lost Sisterhood* (1982), painted a compelling picture of the life of American prostitutes during the early years of the twentieth century.

1. *Manuscript Collections*

Albany County Courthouse, Laramie, Wyoming.
 Albany County Inquests, 1874–81.
 Albany County Tax List, 1875.
 Criminal Appearance Dockets, 1869–74.
 Criminal Files, 1869–83.
 Justice of the Peace Groesbeck Docket, 1884–70.
 Justice of the Peace Pease Docket, 1874–76.
 Justice of the Peace Roberts Docket, Civil Cases, 1881–90.
 Laramie Justice Docket, Civil Cases, 1884–86.
 Laramie Justice of the Peace Dockets, 1877–86.
 Probate Register, 1872, Books A and B.
Arizona Historical Society, Tucson, Arizona.
 John Behan Papers.
 Cochise County Court Records, 1881.
 Cochise County Criminal Cases, 1885–1905.
 Cochise County Docket, 1883–89.
 Cochise County Records, 1880–1912, Box #1.
 Cochise County Sheriff's Records, 1884–85.
 Graham County Justice of the Peace Records, 1881–83.
 Justice Court Records, 1881–86.
 Justice of the Peace William Long Papers.

Pima County Criminal Register and Fee Books, 1882–92.
Pima County Justice of the Peace Records, 1871–73.
Reminiscences of Arizona Pioneers: (not precisely cataloged, but see notations, passim).
Yuma Territorial Prison File.
Arizona Department of Library, Archives, and Public Record, Tucson, Arizona.
Gila County Criminal Actions, 1882.
Index to Apache County Criminal Cases: Territorial Records, 1882–90.
Index of Gila County Criminal Cases: Territorial Records, 1881–1912.
Maricopa County Justice Dockets, 1885–86.
Pima County Justice Dockets, 1881–90.
Pima County Sheriff's Register of Actions, 1881–90.
Austin Public Library, Austin-Travis County Collection, Austin, Texas.
Austin City Directories, 1872, 1881–89.
Jail Registers, 1884–86, 1888–92.
Justice of the Peace Docket Books, 1876–79.
Police Calls Register, 1879–81, 1883–84.
Records of Arrests, 1878–91.
Colorado Historical Society, Denver, Colorado.
Francis Byrne Papers.
Major Henry Foote Papers.
Detective Sam Howe Murder Scrapbook, Record of the City and County of Denver, 1863–1913.
Diary of Rose Bell.
Diary of James Curran.
Colorado State Archives, Denver, Colorado.
Arapahoe County Civil and Criminal Docket, 1866–69.
Arapahoe County Civil Docket, 1869–70.
Arapahoe County Court Docket, 1864–66, 1871–73.
Arapahoe County Justice of the Peace Docket, 1871–72.
Central City Miscellaneous Records of Law Enforcement, 1880–83.
Central City Police Docket, 1884–96.
Colorado Penitentiary Papers, 1865–77.
Gilpin County Police Docket, 1867–69.
Denver Public Library, Western History Collection, Denver, Colorado.
Caroline Bancroft Papers.
Henry Boyer's Mortician's Register.
Frances Boyle Papers.

City of Denver Justice Docket, 1864–67.

Clear Creek County Docket, 1867–71.

Regin Constant Journal.

H. C. Cornwall Papers.

M. Dunagan Scrapbook Collection.

Reminiscences of Dr. John Elsner.

Fairmount Cemetery Register of Burials, June 1, 1876–March 3, 1891.

Eli Glover Diary.

Lawton Scrapbook Collection.

Welch Nossaman, Life Story.

J. P. C. Poulton Papers and Lecture Book.

Cyrus Shores Papers.

P. A. Spengler, Letter.

George Watrous Scrapbook.

Weld County Docket Book, 1871–76.

Fort Union, New Mexico.

Fact and Personnel File.

Kansas State Historical Society, Topeka, Kansas.

Abilene Minute Book, 1870–76.

Abilene Ordinance Book, 1869–74.

Dodge City Police Dockets, 1886–89.

Sedgwick County Grand Jury Investigation, 1887–88.

National Archives, Washington, D.C.

Records of Accounts and Claims, Record Group 217.

Special File #8124/65.

Records of the Adjutant General's Office, Record Group 94.

Returns from U.S. Military Posts, 1800–1916; Medical Histories of the Forts, 1869–80; Letters Received by the Adjutant General's Office, 1861–70; Files of Sutlers and Traders.

Records of the Bureau of the Census, Record Group 29.

Census Returns for the Ninth Census (1870).

Census Returns for the Tenth Census (1880).

Records of the Bureau of Indian Affairs, Record Group 75.

Letters Received by the Office of Indian Affairs, 1824–81.

Arizona Superintendency, 1863–80.

Records of the Judge Advocate General, Record Group 153.

General Courts-Martial of the U.S. Army.

Records of the U.S. Army Continental Command, Record Group 393.

Orders Issued and Orders Received at the Posts,
not available for every post.
Records of the U.S. Quartermaster, Record Group 92.
Miscellaneous correspondence and records of accounts and
payments to civilian employees at the forts.
New Mexico Highlands University, Rogers Library, Las Vegas, New
Mexico.
Arrott Collection: a collection of public and private papers relating
to the history of Fort Union, New Mexico. This collection also
has numerous items dealing with other forts of the Southwest; its
material numbers more than 50,000 papers preserved on micro-
cards. All the items are kept in chronological order with private
journals and letters filed at the end of the collection.
New Mexico State Archives, Santa Fe, New Mexico.
Bernalillo County District Court Records, 1865–72.
First Judicial District Court, 1883–90.
Grant County Criminal Docket, 1874–81.
Justice of the Peace Records, 1851–89.
Santa Fe County Criminal Docket, 1871–76.
Texas Tech University, Southwest Collection, Lubbock, Texas.
J. W. Moar Papers.
C. C. Rister Papers.
Oral Interview Files.
University of New Mexico, Special Collections, Albuquerque, New
Mexico.
Field Notes, General and Personal, of John E. Bourke, U.S. Army,
November 18, 1872–June 8, 1896.
University of Wyoming, Western History Collection, Laramie, Wyoming.
Dr. Pinfrock Papers.
C. C. Whittenburg Collection.
Manuscript Folders:
Fort Sanders.
Freighting.
Laramie:
crime.
court cases.
hospital.
hotels.
lawmen and law.
penitentiary.

Wyoming History;
badmen and bad women.
state prisons.
West Texas State University, Panhandle-Plains Historical Museum, Canyon, Texas.
Hemphill County Criminal Docket, 1887–89.
Interview Files: WPA manuscript interviews with Texas pioneers.
Wyoming State Archives and Historical Department, Cheyenne, Wyoming.
Cheyenne Jail Register, 1887–90.
Cheyenne Police Court Docket, 1868–69.
Cheyenne Police Register, 1888.
Cheyenne Trial Docket, 1884–87.
Coutant Collection.
Evanston Criminal Docket, 1880–90.
Laramie County Inquests and Coroner's Reports, 1870–90.
Record of Convicts at the State Penitentiary, 1876–92.
Register of Burials for Cheyenne Cemetery, 1875–1932.
Sheriff's Record Book, 1881–90.
Sweetwater Sheriff's Jail Record, 1876–91.
U.S. Penitentiary Books for Descriptions of Convicts, 1873–78.
Vinta County Justice Court Docket, 1888–1901.
Dr. W. A. Wyman Visiting Lists, 1882–1920.

2. *U.S. Government Publications*

Annual Report of the Commisioner of Indian Affairs to the Secretary of the Interior, 1887, 1888, 1889, 1891. Washington: Government Printing Office.
Billings, John S. Office of the Surgeon General. *Circular No. 4. A Report on Barracks and Hospitals with Descriptions of Military Posts.* Washington, D.C., 1870; reprint ed., New York: Sol Lewis, 1974.
———. Office of the Surgeon General. *Circular No. 8. A Report on the Hygiene of the United States Army, with Descriptions of Military Posts.* Washington, D.C., 1875; reprint ed., New York: Sol Lewis, 1974.
Callan, John L. *The Military Laws of the United States: Relating to the Army, Volunteers' Militia, and to Bounty Lands and Pensions from the Foundation of the Government to 3 March 1863.* 2nd ed. Philadelphia: George W. Childs, 1863.
Index of General Orders, Adjutant General's Office. Washington, D.C., 1869, 1877, 1878.

Military Laws and Rules and Regulations for the Army of the United States. Adjutant and Inspector General's Office. n.p.: E. deKraft, 1816.

U.S. Congress. House. *Report of the Secretary of War*, vol. 1, ex. doc. 1, 44th Cong., lst sess., 1875.

U.S. Congress. House. *Report of the Secretary of War*, vol. 1, ex. doc. 1, 46th Cong., 2nd sess., 1879–80.

U.S. Department of War. Office of the Surgeon General. *The Prevalence of Syphilis in the Army*, by Edward Vedder. Bulletin no. 8. Washington, D.C.: Government Printing Office, 1915.

U.S. Department of War. Office of the Surgeon General. *Studies of Syphilis*, by Charles Craig and Henry Nichols. Bulletin no. 3. Washington, D.C.: Government Printing Office, 1913.

3. Newspapers

Abilene Chronicle (Kan.)
Alamo Express (Ariz.)
Arizona Daily Star (Tucson)
Arizona Democrat (Tombstone)
Arizona Enterprise (Tucson)
Black Hills Daily Times (Deadwood, S. Dakota)
Butte Miner (Mont.)
Caldwell Post (Kan.)
Central City Daily Register (Colo.)
Cheyenne Daily Leader (Wyo.)
Cheyenne Daily News
Cheyenne Daily Sun
Cheyenne Weekly Sun
Colorado Miner (Georgetown)
Daily Democratic Statesman (Austin, Tex.)
Daily Rocky Mountain News (Denver, Colo.)
Deadwood Times (S. Dak.)
Denver Daily Times (Colo.)
Denver Daily Republican
Denver Tribune Republican
Dodge City Times (Kan.)
Ford County Globe (Kan.)
Georgetown Courier (Colo.)
Junction City Union (Kan.)
Laramie Daily Sentinel (Wyo.)
Las Vegas Daily Optic (N. Mex.)
Leadville Daily Chronicle (Colo.)
San Antonio Daily Express (Tex.)
San Antonio Ledger
San Antonio News
Semi-Weekly News (San Antonio, Tex.)
Solid Muldoon (Ouray, Colo.)
Tombstone Epitaph (Ariz.)
Tri-Weekly Alamo Express (Ariz.)
Tucson Arizona Citizen
Wichita Daily Eagle (Kan.)
Wyoming Tribune (Cheyenne)

4. Journals and Memoirs

Butler, Josephine. *Reminiscences of a Great Crusade*. London: O. Horace Marshall and Son, 1910.

Clark, T. D., ed. *Off At Sunrise: The Overland Journal of Charles Glass Gray*. San Marino: Henry E. Huntington, 1976.

Clum, John. *It All Happened in Tombstone*. Flagstaff: Northland Press, 1965.

Cook, Joseph. *Diary and Letters*. Laramie, Wyo.: Laramie Republican Co., 1919.

Cox, John E. *Five Years in the United States Army*. Owensville, Ind.: n.p., 1892; reprint ed., New York: Sol Lewis, 1973.

Custer, Elizabeth. *Boots and Saddles or Life in Dakota with General Custer*. New York: Harper and Row, 1885.

————. *Following the Guidon*. Norman: University of Oklahoma, new ed., 1966.

Dimsdale, Thomas J. *The Vigilantes of Montana or Popular Justice in the Rocky Mountains*. Virginia City, Montana Territory: Montana Post Press, 1866; reprint ed., Ann Arbor: University Microfilms, 1966.

Griffin, John S. *A Doctor Comes to California, The Diary of John S. Griffin Assistant Surgeon with Kearny's Dragoons, 1846–47*. Introduction and notes by George Walcott Ames. Ann Arbor: University Microfilm, 1976.

King, Richard C., ed. *Victorian Lady on the Texas Frontier: The Journal of Ann Raney Coleman*. Norman: University of Oklahoma Press, 1971.

Owens-Adair, B. A. *Gleanings from a Pioneer Woman Physician's Life*. Portland, Oregon: Mann and Beach, n.d.

Parker, Dr. George. [George Parker Stoker, pseud.] *Oil Field Medico*. Dallas: Banks, Upshaw, 1948.

Rehwinkel, Alfred. *Dr. Bessie: The Life Story and Romance of a Pioneer Lady Doctor*. St. Louis: Concordia Publishing House, 1963.

Rosen, Ruth, and Sue Davidson, eds. *The Maimie Papers*. Old Westbury, N.Y.: Feminist Press, 1977.

5. *Unpublished Theses*

Butler, Anne M. "The Press and Prostitution: A Study of San Antonio, Tombstone, and Cheyenne, 1865–1890." Master's thesis, University of Maryland, 1975.

Forliti, Reverend John E. "The First Thirty Years of the House of the Good Shepherd: St. Paul, Minnesota." Master's thesis, St. Paul Seminary, 1962.

Schubert, Frank. "Fort Robinson, Nebraska: The History of a Military

Community, 1874–1916." Ph.D. Dissertation, University of Toledo, 1967.

6. *Articles and Pamphlets*

Appler, Jules. *Street Avenue and Alley Guide of San Antonio, Texas*. n.p.: n.p., 1892.

Bakken, Gordon M. "Judicial Review in the Rocky Mountain Territorial Courts." *Journal of Legal History* 25 (Jan. 1971): 56–65.

Bancroft, Caroline. *Six Racy Madams of Colorado*. Boulder, Colo.: Johnson Co., 1965.

Best, Joel. "Careers in Brothel Prostitution: St. Paul, 1865–1883." *Journal of Interdisciplinary History* 12, 4 (Spring 1982):597–619.

Bigelow, Jacob. *Discourse on Self-Limited Diseases*. Boston: Nathan Hale, 1835.

Bloomfield, Maxwell. "Lawyers and Public Criticism: Challenge and Response in the Nineteenth Century." *American Journal of Legal History* 25 (Oct. 1971): 269–77.

Boyer, Glenn. "Postscripts to Historical Fiction about Wyatt Earp in Tombstone." *Arizona and the West* 18 (Autumn 1976): 217–36.

Burnham, John. "Medical Inspection of Prostitutes in America in the Nineteenth Century: The St. Louis Experiment and Its Sequel." *Bulletin of the History of Medicine* 45 (May/June 1971): 203–18.

Flaherty, David. "An Approach to American History: Willard Hurst as Legal Historian." *American Journal of Legal History* 14 (1970): 222–34.

Hammack, David. "Problems of Power in the Historical Study of Cities, 1800–1960." *American Historical Review* 83 (Apr. 1978): 323–49.

Hirata, Lucy Cheng. "Free, Enslaved, and Indentured Workers in Nineteenth Century Chinese Prostitution." *Signs* 5 (Fall 1979): 3–29.

Howe, Mark DeWolfe. "Juries as Judges of Criminal Law." *Harvard Law Review* 52 (1939): 582–616.

Humphrey, David C. "Prostitution and Public Policy in Austin, Texas, 1870–1915." *Southwestern Historical Quarterly* 86 (Apr. 1983): 473–516.

Ichioka, Yuji. "Ameyuki-san: Japanese Prostitutes in Nineteenth Century America." *Amerasia Journal* 4 (1977): 1–21.

Johnson, Claudia. "That Guilty Third Tier: Prostitution in the Nineteenth Century American Theatres." *American Quarterly* 27 (Dec. 1975): 575–84.

Kelsen, Hans. "The Pure Theory of Law and Analytical Jurisprudence." *Harvard Law Review* 55 (Nov. 1941): 44–70.

Leonard, Carol, and Isidor Wallimann. "Prostitution and Changing Morality in the Frontier Cattle Towns of Kansas." *Kansas History* 2 (Spring 1979): 34–53.

Luebke, Frederick. "Ethnic Group Settlement on the Great Plains." *Western Historical Quarterly* 8 (Oct. 1977): 405–30.

Petrik, Paula. "Capitalists with Rooms: Prostitution in Helena, Montana, 1865–1900." *Montana, the Magazine of Western History* 31 (Apr. 1981): 28–41.

Riley, Glenda. "Images of the Frontierswoman: Iowa as a Case Study." *Western Historical Quarterly* 8 (Apr. 1977): 189–202.

Ryan, Pat. "John P. Clum: Boss With the White Forehead." *Arizoniana* 5 (Fall 1974): 48–58.

———. "Trail-Blazer of Civilization: John P. Clum's Tucson and Tombstone Years." *Journal of Arizona History* 6 (Summer 1965): 53–70.

West, Elliott. "Scarlet West: The Oldest Profession in the Trans-Mississippi West." *Montana, the Magazine of Western History* 31 (Apr. 1981): 16–27.

Williams, Jean. *The Lynching of Elizabeth Taylor.* Santa Fe: Press of the Territorian, 1967.

Woodward, Calvin. "Reality and Social Reform: The Transition from Laissez-Faire to the Welfare State." *Yale Law Journal* 52 (Nov. 1962): 286–328.

———. "History, Legal History and Legal Education." *Virginia Law Review* 53 (Jan. 1967): 89–121.

7. *Books*

Abbott, Edith. *Women in Industry: A Study in American Economic History.* New York: D. Appleton and Co., 1910.

Acton, William. *Prostitution Considered in Its Moral, Social and Sanitary Aspects in London and other Garrison Towns.* London: John Churchill and Sons, 1870.

Appel, John J., ed. *The New Immigration.* New York: Piman, 1971.

Ashburn, Percy M. *The Elements of Military Hygiene: Especially Arranged for Officers and Men of the Line.* 3rd ed., rev. Boston: Houghton Mifflin, 1920.

————. *A History of the Medical Department of the United States Army.* Boston: Houghton Mifflin, 1929.

————. *The Ranks of Death: A Medical History of the Conquest of America.* New York: Coward-McCann, 1947.

Babcock, Barbara, Ann Freedman, Eleanor Holmes Norton, and Susan Ross. *Sex Discrimination and the Law: Causes and Remedies.* Boston: Little, Brown, 1975.

Barth, Gunther. *Bitter Strength: A History of the Chinese in the United States, 1850–1870.* Cambridge, Mass.: Harvard University Press, 1964.

Benjamin, Harry, and R. E. L. Masters. *Prostitution and Morality.* New York: Julian Press, 1959.

Best, Hillyer. *Julia Bulette and Other Red Light Ladies.* Sparks, Nev.: Western Printing, 1959.

Billington, Ray Allen. *America's Frontier Heritage.* New York: Holt, Rinehart and Winston, 1966.

Brodsky, Annette M. *The Female Offender.* Beverly Hills: Sage, 1975.

Brown, Thomas. *Irish-American Nationalism: 1870–1890.* Philadelphia: J. P. Lippincott, 1966.

Bullough, Vern. *The History of Prostitution.* New York: University Books, 1964.

————, and Bonnie Bullough. *An Illustrated Social History: Prostitution.* New York: Crown, 1978.

Burgess, William. *The World's Social Evil: A Historical Review and Study of the Problems Relating to the Subject.* Chicago: Saul Brothers, 1914.

Burns, Walter. *Tombstone: An Iliad of the Southwest.* Garden City, N.Y.: Doubleday, Page, 1927.

Campbell, Helen. *Women Wage Earners: Their Past, Their Present, and Their Future.* Boston: Roberts Brothers, 1893.

Connelly, Mark Thomas. *The Response to Prostitution in the Progressive Era.* Chapel Hill: University of North Carolina Press, 1980.

Day, James, et al. *Women of Texas.* Waco: Texan Press, 1972.

Dkystra, Robert. *The Cattle Towns.* New York: Atheneum, 1973.

Duchatelet, Parent. *Prostitution in Paris Considered Morally, Politically and Medically.* . . . Boston: Charles H. Brainard, 1845.

Edholm, Charlton. *Traffic in Girls and Florence Crittenton Missions.* Chicago: Women's Temperance Public Association, 1893.

Edis, Arthur. *Diseases of Women: A Manual for Students and Practitioners.* Philadelphia: Henry C. Lea's Son, 1882.

Finnegan, Frances. *Poverty and Prostitution: A Study of Victorian Prostitutes in York.* Cambridge: Cambridge University Press, 1979.

Fitch, Charles. *Diseases of Women: Their Cause, Prevention and Cure.* Bridgeport, Conn.: City Steam Publishing, 1890.

Flexner, Abraham. *Prostitution in Europe.* New York: Century, 1920.

Frazer, Robert W. *Forts of the West.* Norman: University of Oklahoma Press, 1965.

Friedman, Lawrence. *A History of American Law.* New York: Simon and Schuster, 1973.

Funk, H. John Clarence. *Vice and Health: Problems—Solutions.* Philadelphia: J. P. Lippincott, 1921.

Gard, Wayne. *The Chisholm Trail.* Norman: University of Oklahoma Press, 1954.

———. *Frontier Violence.* Norman: University of Oklahoma Press, 1948.

Gilman, Charlotte Perkins. *The Home: Its Work and Influences.* Reprint of 1903 edition. Urbana: University of Illinois Press, 1972.

Gluech, Sheldon, and Eleanor Gluech. *Five Hundred Delinquent Women.* New York: Alfred A. Knopf, 1934.

Goldman, Marion S. *Gold Diggers and Silver Miners: Prostitution and Social Life on the Comstock Lode.* Ann Arbor: University of Michigan Press, 1981.

Gould, Lewis. *Wyoming: A Political History. 1868–1896.* New Haven: Yale University Press, 1968.

Gray, James H. *Red Lights on the Prairies.* New York: Signet, New American Library, 1971.

Griffin, William D. *The Irish in America 550-1972: A Chronology and Fact Book.* New York: Oceana Publications, 1973.

Groppner, Max. *New and Natural Method of Hygenic Treatment for the Permanent Cure of all Diseases of Women.* Berlin: Max Groppner, 1891.

Haley, J. Evetts. *Jeff Milton: A Good Man With a Gun.* Norman: University of Oklahoma Press, 1948.

———, and William C. Holden. *The Flamboyant Judge: James D. Hamlin.* Canyon, Texas: Palo Duro Press, 1972.

Haller, John, and Robin Haller. *The Physician and Sexuality in Victorian America.* New York: W. W. Norton, 1974.

Henriques, Fernando. *Prostitution and Society.* New York: Grove Press, 1962.

Hibbert, Christopher. *The Roots of Evil: A Social History of Crime and Punishment.* Boston: Little Brown, 1968.

Hine, Robert V. *The American West: An Interpretive History.* Boston: Little Brown, 1973.

Hinton, Richard J. *The Hand-book of Arizona: Its Resources, History, Towns, Mines, Ruins, and Scenery*. First publication 1878, reprint ed., Glorieta, New Mexico: Rio Grande Press, 1970.

Holt, Wythe. *Essays in Nineteenth Century American Legal History*. Westport, Conn.: Greenwood Press, 1976.

Hooton, Earnest A. *The American Criminal: An Anthropological Study*. New York: Greenwood Press, 1939; reprint, 1969.

Horan, James. *Desperate Women*. New York: G. P. Putnam's Sons, 1952.

Hunt, Inez, and Wanetta W. Draper. *To Colorado's Restless Ghosts*. Denver: Sage Books, 1960.

Hurst, James W. *The Growth of American Law: The Law-makers*. Boston: Little Brown, 1950.

———. *Law and the Conditions of Freedom in the Nineteenth Century United States*. Madison: University of Wisconsin Press, 1967.

Janney, O. Edward. *The White Slave Traffic in America*. New York: National Vigilance Committee, 1911.

Kanowitz, Leo. *Women and the Law: The Unfinished Revolution*. Albuquerque: University of New Mexico Press, 1969.

Kessler-Harris, Alice. *Out to Work: A History of Wage-Earning Women in the United States*. New York: Oxford University Press, 1982.

Lamar, Howard R., ed. *The Reader's Encyclopedia of the American West*. New York: Thomas Y. Crowell, 1977.

Law, Norine. *The Shame of a Great Nation: The Story of the "White Slave Trade."* Harrisburg, Pa.: United Evangelical Publishing House, 1909.

Leckie, William H. *The Buffalo Soldiers: A Narrative of the Negro Cavalry in the West*. Norman: University of Oklahoma Press, 1967.

Lee, Rose Hun. *The Chinese in the United States of America*. Hong Kong: Cathay Press, 1960.

McCarthy, John L. *Maverick Town: The Story of Old Tascosa*. Norman: University of Oklahoma Press, 1946.

Michael, Jerome, and Mortimer Adler. *Crime, Law and Social Science*. Montclair, N.J.: Patterson Smith, 1971.

Miller, Max, and Fred Mazzulla. *Holladay Street*. New York: Ballantine Books, 1962.

Miller, Stuart Creighton. *The Unwelcome Immigrant: The American Image of the Chinese, 1784–1882*. Berkeley, California: University of California Press, 1969.

Miner, Maude. *Slavery of Prostitution: A Plea for Emancipation*. New York: Macmillan, 1916.

Nash, Gary B. *Red, White, and Black: The Peoples of Early America*. History of the American People Series, Leon Litwack, ed. Englewood Cliffs, N.J.: Prentice Hall, 1974.

O'Grady, Joseph. *How the Irish Became Americans*. New York: Twayne, 1973.

Pivar, David. *Purity Crusade, Sexual Morality and Social Control, 1868–1900*. Westport, Conn.: Greenwood Press, 1973.

Pollak, Otto. *The Criminality of Women*. New York: A.S. Barnes, 1950.

Powell, Aaron. *State Regulation of Vice*. New York: Wood and Holbrook, 1878.

Powell, John Wesley. *Report on the Lands of the Arid Region of the United States*. Edited by Wallace Stegner. Cambridge, Mass.: Belknap Press of Harvard University, 1962.

Prostitution in the Victorian Age: Debates on the Isssue from 19th Century Critical Journals. Introduction by Keith Nield. Westmead, England: Gregg International, 1973.

Raine, William MacLeod. *Famous Sheriffs and Western Outlaws*. Garden City, N.Y.: Garden City Publishing, 1929.

Red, George Plunkett. *The Medicine Man in Texas*. Houston: Standard Printing & Lithographing, 1930.

Richey, Elinor. *Eminent Women of the West*. Berkeley: Howell-North Books, 1975.

Rickey, Don. *Forty Miles a Day on Beans and Hay*. Norman: University of Oklahoma Press, 1963.

Riemoeller, Adolph F. *Sexual Slavery in America*. New York: Punurge Press, 1935.

Roger, C. E. *Secret Sins of Society*. Minneapolis: Union Publishing, 1881.

Rose, Al. *Storyville: New Orleans*. University: University of Alabama Press, 1974.

Rosen, Ruth. *The Lost Sisterhood: Prostitution in America, 1900–1918*. Baltimore: Johns Hopkins University Press, 1982.

Ryan, Michael. *Prostitution in London with a Comparative View of that of Paris and New York*. London: H. Bailliere, 1839.

Sanger, W. W. *History of Prostitution: Its Extent, Causes and Effects Throughout the World*. New York: Medical, 1897.

Seward, George. *Chinese Immigration: Its Social and Economic Aspects*. New York: Charles Scribners Sons, 1881, reprinted, New York: Arno Press, 1970.

Shannon, William. *The American Irish*. New York: Macmillan, 1963.

Sigler, Jay. *Double Jeopardy: The Development of a Legal and Social Policy*. Ithaca, N.Y.: Cornell University Press, 1969.

Smith, Duane A. *Rocky Mountain Mining Camps: The Urban Frontier*. Bloomington: Indiana University Press, 1967.

Smith, Henry Nash. *The Virgin Land: The American West as Symbol and Myth*. Cambridge, Mass.: Harvard University Press, 1950.

Smith, William. *The Conquest of Arid America*. New York: Macmillan, 1905.

Stallard, Patricia. *Glittering Misery: Dependants of the Indian Fighting Army*. San Rafael, Calif.: Presidio Press, and Fort Collins, Colo.: Old Army Press, 1978.

Symanski, Richard. *The Immoral Landscape: Female Prostitution in Western Societies*. Toronto: Butterworth, 1981.

Trimble, Marshall. *Arizona*. New York: Doubleday, 1977.

Utley, Robert. *Frontier Regulars: The United States Army and the Indian, 1866–1891*. New York: Macmillan, 1973.

Walkowitz, Judith R. *Prostitution and Victorian Society: Women, Class, and the State*. Cambridge: Cambridge University Press, 1980.

Walsh, James B., comp. *The Irish: America's Political Class*. New York: Arno Press, 1976.

Webb, Walter Prescott. *The Great Plains*. Boston: Ginn, 1931.

———, ed. *The Handbook of Texas*. Austin: The Texas State Historical Association, 1952.

West, Elliott. *The Saloon on the Rocky Mountain Mining Frontier*. Lincoln: University of Nebraska Press, 1979.

Whiteley, C. H., and Winifred Whiteley. *Sex and Morals*. New York: Basic Books, 1967.

Winick, Charles, and Paul M. Kinsie. *The Lively Commerce: Prostitution in the United States*. Chicago: Quadrangle Books, 1971.

Woolston, Howard B. *Prostitution in the United States*. 2 vols. New York: Century, 1921.

Wright, B. F. *The Growth of American Constitutional Law*. Boston: Houghton Mifflin for Reynal and Hitchcock, 1942.

Wulfen, Erich. *Woman as a Sexual Criminal*. New York: American Ethnological Press, 1934.

Index

A Note on the Author

Anne M. Butler received her M.A. degree from the University of Maryland in 1975 and her Ph.D. from the same university in 1979. She is currently a member of the history and geography faculty at Gallaudet College in Washington, D.C.

DATE DUE